DISCARDED

Inventing North America

HC
95
P64
2001

Inventing North America

Canada, Mexico, and the United States

Guy Poitras

LAMAR UNIVERSITY LIBRARY

LYNNE
RIENNER
PUBLISHERS

BOULDER
LONDON

Published in the United States of America in 2001 by
Lynne Rienner Publishers, Inc.
1800 30th Street, Boulder, Colorado 80301
www.rienner.com

and in the United Kingdom by
Lynne Rienner Publishers, Inc.
3 Henrietta Street, Covent Garden, London WC2E 8LU

© 2001 by Lynne Rienner Publishers, Inc. All rights reserved

Library of Congress Cataloging-in-Publication Data
Poitras, Guy E., 1942–
Inventing North America : Canada, Mexico, and the United States / Guy Poitras.
p. cm.
Includes bibliographical references and index.
ISBN 1-55587-964-0 (alk. paper)
1. North America—Economic integration. 2. North America—Economic conditions. 3. North America—Foreign economic relations. I. Title.
HC95.P64 2001
337.7—dc21 2001018070

British Cataloguing in Publication Data
A Cataloguing in Publication record for this book is available from the British Library.

Printed and bound in the United States of America

♾ The paper used in this publication meets the requirements of the American National Standard for Permanence of Paper for Printed Library Materials Z39.48-1984.

5 4 3 2 1

Contents

1

The World in North America/ North America in the World

The second millennium left many legacies for the next one. What challenged or excited the world in the waning twentieth century is still around for those of us who will make our way in the twenty-first. Trends and transformations in world politics transcend any mere turn of the century.

It is commonplace to comment on the fast-changing world we live in. But change and continuity are bonded together in the new century just as they were in the old. This is still a world of states, but it is also a world of telecommunications, globalized production chains, portfolio managers, ethnonationalist leaders, and other nonstate actors. This is still a world of war and military power, but it is also a world of expanding transborder cooperation based upon economic and other imperatives. This is a world of the powerful and the weak, the rich and the poor, as it has always been. But neither the rich nor the poor can take for granted that what they have always done will be what they will do in the future. The world of greatly enhanced interchange and competition means that the powerful and the weak, despite their obvious differences, are in some sense in the same boat. This is a world of integration as well as fragmentation. Economic and technological forces drive states and people closer together, but gaps in wealth, cultural identities, and political differences can lead to the clustering of peoples, states, and regions of states. The result is a world with an increasing number of states or countries engaged in a system that makes it impossible for states or countries to act economically or politically without concern for what happens elsewhere.

To make some sense of this world, we must continue to ask basic questions about why things occur. What we are trying to fathom is just as compelling in this century as it was in the last: Why do states do what they do? Even more difficult to grasp is why they do something they have not done before. Of course, states do not have the world to themselves. The way they act is linked to what other actors want or do.

Toward the end of the twentieth century, the world witnessed an outburst of startling developments and dynamic trends. A great power threw in the towel, leaving a lone superpower at the head of the pack of great powers. The United States is still trying to sort out for itself what it should do in a world without a single adversary. In a half century or so of U.S. leadership, this is a new predicament. The United States is not alone. Many states are going through a reappraisal. Former adversaries have become rivals and to some extent partners. Cultural challenges and economic competition have driven many states to reorient how they act domestically and internationally. Old orthodoxies have been questioned as never before. Although capitalism and democracy in some form have become more widely acceptable, neither has yet proven that it can govern or even manage the world effectively.

North America has not remained unaffected by these tectonic shifts. The three states of North America may not be a microcosm of the world, but they can be a window through which to view the world better. Trying to understand more fully what happened in North America toward the end of the twentieth century and what that might mean for the early twenty-first century is one way to see why some states do what they do and why they decided to do something differently than they had done before. In North America the most significant trend at the end of the previous century was that the states came closer together as a region. Inventing North America as a region may remain the most intriguing prospect for the United States, Canada, and Mexico well into this century.

This North American odyssey is not just about three states in one corner of the world. It is also about the world itself. Examining how the world has intruded on the three North American states is important; it allows us to see more clearly how global forces or imperatives make North America a part of the world rather than a region unto itself. It is as well a starting point for discovering how the United States, Canada, and Mexico have responded in a somewhat similar fashion to global trends.

Seven global trends are fundamental to world politics. They also affect the invention of North America as a region. These trends are driving world dynamics, and they reflect critical transformations. No state or other major actor is untouched. These trends are (1) the evolving balance of power, (2) the shifting role of the state, (3) globalization and its impact, (4) multilateralism in the world economy, (5) relative gains and growing gaps in wealth and power, (6) the global North-South divide, and (7) the resurgence of ethnonationalism and ethnic politics within states. To a greater or lesser extent, all of these shape North America.

Balance of Power

Very little stays the same in world politics. Great powers rise and fall (Kennedy 1987; Gilpin 1987). Sometimes this happens with a bang; in the late twentieth century it happened with a whimper. In the past global wars were the harbingers of basic power shifts. Some states would surge to the head of the list of great powers and others ebb as great powers. This was certainly what happened in 1945. But the balance of power among the leading states may be resilient, too. It may last decades and then may be dissolved or change only slowly. Unipolar or multipolar, the world at the century's dawn is not shockingly different from the later stages of bipolarity at the end of the twentieth century.

If states still matter, then the balance of power among great powers also matters. Since 1945 the balance of power in the world has remained fairly stable, but it has not been static. The Cold War (1947–1989) was an anomaly. Two great powers had never before vied for strategic leadership like the Soviet Union and the United States did. A bipolar world reinforced by ideological and nuclear foundations was witness to a harsh but mainly peaceful competition between these two. This balance could perhaps not endure. As other states recovered from World War II and as new states appeared on the scene with decolonization, the strategic balance was modified. A loose bipolarity testified to a messier, more complex world during the last third of the twentieth century. Allies could be rivals as well as partners. Adversaries could sometimes be partners as well as rivals.

The end of the Cold War left one superpower standing. The aftermath of the Soviet implosion meant that only the United States had both the military and economic power to claim world leadership. For the first time since its active role as world leader in the 1940s, the United States had no single great-power adversary. For some, this unipolar moment in the balance is ephemeral. For others, it may represent a more enduring period of U.S. domination. The United States may stand head and shoulders above other states, but it is also clear that it does not run the world.

This contradiction was present even before the collapse of the Soviet Union. The exact nature of U.S. power in the world has always been open to interpretation. For decades, U.S. leadership could be challenged only from Moscow. Otherwise, the United States was a power so overwhelming as to deserve the appellation "hegemon." A hegemon is a state that so dominates others that it can use its relatively overwhelming capabilities to call the shots and define the rules by which others engage in international exchange. From 1944, with the Bretton Woods system, and for the decades to follow, the United States led the way in creating a liberal world order. It sponsored and led like-minded states into a liberal economic order even as it afforded them assurances against possible Soviet designs. U.S. strength was a global myth to some; U.S. hegemony in the post–World War II world was perhaps overstated (Nye 1990). And so, too, has its decline been exaggerated (Nye 1990; Strange 1996).

The economic ascent and eventual decline of others had a mixed impact on U.S. power. The spread of technologies and power centers in the world made the United States less preeminent, especially in economic power. The United States has the largest economy, but it does not lead by as much as it once did. Europe and Asia look to the United States for economic leadership, but they are less likely than ever to heed every wish and whim of U.S. policy. Strangely, the eclipse of its great adversary in the late twentieth century left the United States with little or no euphoria. Rather, it turned to new challenges. On the one hand, it enjoys the "trappings of primacy" (Posen and Ross 1996–1997: 50). No single great power (except possibly China) can or wants to challenge U.S. primacy in the world. On the other hand, the traditional balance of power is less relevant than it once was. The global strategic balance is less pertinent to the task of managing global problems in a world in which even not-so-great powers must be taken seriously. Although the United States may have "won" the Cold War in some narrow sense, it is unclear what this really means for the United States, not to mention for the world as a whole.

The post–Cold War world did not point in one direction. Some, like Canada and Mexico, may jump on the U.S. bandwagon, whereas others, like Asian and even European states, may be less eager. The post–Cold War world may be harder to manage from the hegemonic center. What is more, the United States must deal with more complex and quarrelsome realities than it did during the Cold War. This has forced it to use its power to protect its own national interests, sometimes unilaterally, rather than play the role of benevolent global hegemon the way it once did. It is not a global balance of power that is so important anymore; rather, it is a world of regions that have come to the fore in economic and security matters with the waning power of great powers and their conflicts (Lake and Morgan 1997: 5). The world, the balance of power, and U.S. leadership have all changed, at least to some extent.

The State of the State

The state itself is changing as well. No state, large or small, is above this trend. This sea change is the latest installment in the state's evolving role in the world.

States remain the building blocks of the 1648 Westphalian system in Europe. But what is a state? A state or country is a politically organized territorial unit with a permanent population and legal sovereignty to make its own decisions independent of any external authority. Depending on how the marginal cases are counted, there may be as many 200 or so states in the world. Challenged domestically and internationally, most states, even the big ones, have great trouble living up to this increasingly antiquated ideal.

Some states come closer to the ideal than do others. Not all states are equally adept at governing themselves or even making their way in the world. States are complex; they are institutions, processes, and groups with their own ways of interacting. Social, ethnic, and cultural groups as well as business firms, private institutions, and labor groups are nonstate actors. They are indispensable for making the state work even as they challenge the state.

The fate of the state is not entirely clear, but the state does appear to be in retreat. It is hard-pressed to hold onto many of its traditional prerogatives (Strange 1996). States are less important and central to the world system than they once were. There is more to this than merely the collapse of the Soviet state. Even in Asia the state is retreating from a highly visible and determined role in the management of the economy at the national and international levels. The state no longer has the legitimacy to remain an extremely intrusive actor in the economy. Public policy, economic management, conflict resolution, and matters of welfare are shared among many centers. The "imbedded liberalism" of the twentieth century, in which the state supported capitalism but made up for market flaws with social programs, is being severely challenged.

The quality of state authority has eroded. This is particularly apparent in the areas of law and order, defense, monetary stability, and rules about exchange of property (Strange 1996: xii). Two very important economic activities are finance and production; they lie beyond the regulatory reach of the state in many countries. The state theoretically remains responsible for the prosperity of its national economy. In fact, the domestic and international challenges to the state make it hard for it to do what it is supposed to do. Under siege, the state nevertheless refuses to put itself out of business as an independent sovereign actor by creating a supranational governmental body to replace it.

The state is in flux. But, to borrow a remark from Mark Twain, the rumor of its death is greatly exaggerated. In the late twentieth century, the state lost some of its prominence, but this has hardly made it irrelevant. The global tilt toward markets has no doubt weakened it. International trade agreements, investment rules, and the rapid movement of portfolio capital throughout the world all reflect this. But the state cannot be counted out, even in North America, with its emerging consensus that the state should do less and do it more efficiently.

Globalization

Globalization is one of the most touted trends in the world political economy. The retreat of the state and the advance of globalization seem to occur simultaneously. But there is far more to it than this.

Globalization is regarded as either the inevitable salvation for the world economy or the scourge of the world's states and peoples. Some see it as free market capitalism and others as something quite different. A debate rages over the benefits and costs of globalization for all involved—who gets how much in the world political economy. Opposition to globalization has come from those who believe that without a robust state to moderate its impact, globalization is a license to plunder. Proponents think of globalization as material progress on a global scale; critics fear that it will make things worse for the majority while benefiting very few.

At its most basic, globalization is a process, and not a particularly recent one at that. Essentially, it is the intensification of all relations across borders, especially by nonstates. Above all economic and technological, this process nevertheless has profound implications for states and their ability to control their own economies. Globalization is most often associated with the growing integration of financial markets, the internationalization of corporate strategies, the diffusion of technology (such as the Internet), transformation of cultural baggage into consumer markets, coordination of national regulatory capabilities, and a diminished role for the national governments in global governance (Petrella 1996: 64). Globalization can also be seen as McWorld, a consumer's world of homogenized, even Americanized, tastes (Barber 1995). Fast food, fast computers, and fast music pulse through this network. At its most grandiose, globalization is an economic, cultural, technological, and ultimately political transformation of the world.

But globalization exists in the eye of the beholder. The most liberal view is that globalization is an inevitable triumph of markets on a global scale without any important role for the state. Markets are the ultimate guarantor of world prosperity. Classic barriers to trade and economics are facing extinction, and well they should. In this "borderless" world, globalization would mean the virtual end of state sovereignty, nationalism, social regulation, and cultural autonomy. Only global markets would really matter. National economies would be subsumed under a globalized economy; they would not have any degree of independence in setting macroeconomic policy. Economic sovereignty would all but end at the national level. In this view, globalization ironically preempts Marxism: Both envision the withering away of the state.

Another view is more in keeping with twentieth-century practice. In this view intensification of relations takes place but not without the state. Governments are the "midwives" of globalization (Brodie 1996: 386). Instead of a neoliberal world of markets and firms regulating the world economy, states would still be involved. State intervention would be more limited than in the welfare state or even in the embedded liberalism of the past. In other words, states would exercise modest power to protect their own economies from the larger global one. Defending local interests against global ones would remain a state function. Globalization limits but does not emasculate state power. It complicates the traditional tasks of governing, such as implementing social policies, but it does not mean the end of such policies (Burtless et al. 1998: 117). States are needed to correct market failures or at least diminish their draconian impact (Boyer and Drache 1996: 108).

National economies would not be obliterated. They would remain differentiated, if not always clearly, from other national economies as well as from the global one. Economic competition among states would coexist along with competition among firms. Markets hold sway, but the state does not go away.

Designing the Global Economy

The modern world economy has evolved. And to some extent it has also been designed. Since 1944 many countries have negotiated a generalized system of economic relations in several stages, or "rounds." Led by the United States and other developed countries, this designing of the global economy remains an important facet of the world's political economy at the dawn of the new century.

Multilateralism has been the blueprint for designing the world economy at least since the mid-twentieth century. Its institutional base is the General Agreement on Tariffs and Trade (GATT), since 1995 called the World Trade Organization (WTO). The purpose of the WTO is to create a truly universal set of economic practices by reconciling national differences on key economic issues.

Multilateralism enshrines key liberal principles for the world economy. These include the most-favored-nation principle, nondiscrimination, the free exchange of goods and services, and other ideas based upon classic economic theory. To boost the cause of a more efficient and integrated world economy, committed multilateralists sought to maximize global welfare through reducing barriers to world trade. The wider the net cast, the larger the gains for everyone. In other words, GATT would promote global economic integration without creating a supranational political structure. Multilateralism would stop short of actually harmonizing domestic policy as the European Union (EU) seeks to do, but clearly it would be a prime mover in the integration of the world economy (Lawrence 1996: 29).

It is, and remains, an arduous and even frustrating exercise. The movement toward greater multilateralism severely tested the patience of many members of GATT. During the eight years of the Uruguay Round, quarrels erupted over several important issues. For example, the United States attacked subsidies as an unwise state protection and a violation of free trade. For their part, European and Japanese members objected to U.S. "fair trading" provisions of its domestic trade laws, such as antidumping (AD) and countervailing duties (CVDs) for below-market pricing. It seems everyone had something to complain about, but no one was willing to abandon the enterprise.

Multilateralism remains a dynamic force in the world. But it has had to make some adjustments to political and economic realities. States do not want to put all their eggs in the GATT basket. For example, regionalism is an acceptable practice within multilateralism. It has become so important that much of what is often seen as multilateralism and globalization is really a regional variant of both. Most of the economic relations of the world take place within three regions: Europe, North America, and Asia. For some, this means that a globalizing economy with a multilateral commitment is in fact a triad. By way of illustration, 92 percent of interfirm strategic cooperation agreements were made by businesspeople from the three economic poles of Europe, Japan (Asia), and North America (Petrella 1996: 77).

Is multilateralism safe in a world in which most of the economic activity takes place within three regions? Some see multilateralism and regionalism as irreconcilable; others see them as complementary. No one has the ultimate answer as to whether regional economic blocs are stumbling blocks or building blocks for designing a genuinely multilateral, global economy. The rise of regionalism is a threat to some (Bhagwati and Panagariya 1996: xiii). The creation of free trade agreements (FTAs) under the GATT raises the issue of whether such regional integration agreements (RIAs) like the European Union and the North American Free Trade Agreement (NAFTA) really advance the cause of multilateralism. Critics argue that these are preferential and discriminatory against nonmembers rather than free trade agreements in the spirit of multilateralism.

These objections to regionalism, however, have not yet carried the day. Regional integration agreements or free trade agreements like NAFTA blossomed in the late twentieth century. Only Asia as a whole has shied away from official regionalism along the lines of Europe and North America. These two regions are sentinels of multilateralism, but each in its own way has also embraced regionalism. The EU and NAFTA rest on the premise that states can and should band together in order to advance the free trade and other market practices within regions and therefore treat nonmembers differently. For them, extending multilateralism does not mean shrinking regionalism.

Gains and Gaps

Who gets what and how much is a never-ending source of controversy and conflict. Hopes and fears swirl around the gains and gaps that emerge from the everyday workings of the world's political economies. States are under the gun to provide a prosperous economy for their peoples. If they do not fare as well as they should or slip in their relative standings in the world, then there may be consequences. The rise of the Asian exporting economies during the last quarter of the twentieth century and their decline during the 1990s roiled the waters of the world's political economy. The rise and decline of Arab oil exporters during the same time period were similarly important.

Gains are important; so are gaps. Absolute gains are promised in the long term by liberal proponents of globalization. They cite the liberal credo that globalized capitalism leads to productivity gains, benefiting everyone sooner or later to some extent. Put another way, all boats rise together. But some boats are bigger than others and better prepared to stand up to rough seas. Important though absolute gains may be, then, so, too, are relative gains. If some states, economies, or economically active peoples do better than others, especially over the long haul, then this has potentially important impacts on the world.

Take North America, for example. In the first part of the twentieth century, the United States, Canada, and Mexico prospered, even factoring in the Great Depression. This helped all three to be important in their own bailiwicks: The United States had a huge economy fueling its world leadership, Canada had an economy granting it a special place among the world's most affluent, and Mexico vaulted to the head of the global South as a major success. All three did better than most. But the relative gains began to shift toward the end of the century. Other countries began to do relatively better, cutting the lead that the three had previously earned. For one thing, North America was facing a dynamic Asia and an integrating Europe. Their emergence after World War II narrowed the gap. Other regions proved to be even less fortunate. Eastern Europe, Russia, south Asia, and sub-Saharan Africa fell behind. Relative gains shifted power and created new gaps.

Gains and gaps go beyond regions and states at the international level. They also affect the domestic well-being of states. What the globalization of the world may mean for the lives and prospects of people and groups within states is far from clear, but world economic changes can affect workers and others within national economies. Some are better prepared to face a free market world with reduced barriers than are others. High-tech, highly capitalized multinational firms with high mobility in capital and investment are well situated to drive and reap advantages from globalization. Small business, labor, and less-educated groups may find the going very tough. In other words, global trends could worsen rather than improve the incomes of many even in wealthier countries, at least in relative terms (Boyer and Drache 1996: 16; Goldsmith 1996: 176).

North and South

Relative gains and growing gaps are trends in the world as well as within the states of the world. A trend that outlasted and even transcended the Cold War is the enduring cleavage between the global North and the global South. The North is the wealthy three dozen or so states generally located in Europe, North America, and the Asia Pacific. The South is the vast underclass of poverty-ridden states mostly in Asia, Latin America, and Africa. The divide between the North and South and how to bridge it is the most serious challenge for a stable, prosperous world order.

North and South are about gains and gaps. There is more to it than that, however. The global North and global South are the result of historical and economic factors with overwhelming consequences for the world as a whole. It is a trend unto itself. The rich North enjoys affluence, democracy, peace, and technology; the poor South is plagued with "zones of turmoil" fomented by poverty, ethnic conflict, disease, and overwhelming economic and social problems. On spaceship Earth a few ride in opulent splendor while the vast majority languish marginally in steerage.

The differences go far beyond the gains and gaps as normally understood within countries like the United States or Canada. Rather, this is a massive schism between 20 percent of the population that controls 80 percent of the world's wealth and the great mass of people who have very little. A mere 1 percent of the world's wealth goes to the poorest fifth of the population (Kegley and Wittkopf 1999: 118). Even within North America, the wealth gap is impressive. The U.S. gross national product (GNP) per capita is 6.6 times greater than Mexico's. Compared to India, the world's largest democracy and soon to become the world's most populous country, Mexico seems relatively well-off: Per capita income is eighty times greater in the United States than in India (Kegley and Wittkopf 1999: 113).

The gap between the extremes is growing. The poorest of the poor are falling behind because of a decline in real income. It is also because of the relatively greater gains in the North after the economic trauma of the South in the 1980s. That the rich are getting richer and the poor are getting poorer is a shibboleth with more than a bit of truth to it. Of course, it is more complicated than that. Some states of the South are making both absolute and relative gains. The fast-growing, high-exporting states of Asia; the resource-rich states of the Middle East; and the larger "emerging markets" of Mexico, Brazil, Turkey, and China, among others, suggest that it is possible for some to escape the fate that awaits many in the global South.

There is an adage: The rich do what they want and the poor do what they must. Where does this leave the global South? During the 1990s the only real option was to jump on the North's liberal bandwagon. The global South could not viably seal itself off from the international economy as Myanmar once did, nor could it practice revolution like Cuba once did. For many, the only game in town was to abandon these traditional Southern strategies and to become more like the North in policy and in inclinations.

Those state leaders in the South with some hope of integrating more closely with the global economy implemented domestic reforms and made the most of international adjustments. The task was to attract Northern investment and technology and to secure access to its markets by becoming more open and liberal. Although the jury is still out, some have done better than others in making this transformation. Mexico, Chile, Argentina, and even to some extent Brazil have adopted the liberal economic mantra emanating from the United States. Yet much of Africa remains out in the cold. The Asian South made some movements toward liberal economic policies, but it generally still clings to a unique brand of heavy state involvement in the economy.

Nations and Ethnonational Politics

Historically, nations came before states. With the end of the Cold War, some have flexed their muscles against states. Others have sought to negotiate the terms of coexistence within states in which two or more nations live. At the dawn of the century, the sometimes uneasy coexistence of nations, nationalism, and states has renewed importance in the world.

A nation is a relatively large group of people usually living in a defined area, sharing common traits, and thinking of themselves as a distinct or even special group. A nation forms a self-identifying community

(Nietschmann 1994: 226). Nations or peoples rely on a sense of belonging or attachment. They rally around certain traits, or "idols," such as language, history, religion, race, and nationality (Isaacs 1989).

The vast majority of states have more than one nation. With approximately 200 states in the world, there are about 4,000 nations. The true nation-state, with one nation in one state, is a rare creature indeed. The more common multinational state often has a difficult task. Such a country may seek accommodation among its nations, but there is also a marked trend toward ethnonationalist antagonism and even separatism in some states. Ethnopolitical conflict tends to revolve around one nation's attempt to break away from another to form its own state. But it may be less extreme: It may simply be a struggle to ensure the minority rights of an ethnopolitical group within a state dominated by another nation (Gurr and Harff 1994: 15–26).

The siren call of self-determination remains an important force. The idea of "one nation, one state" may promise more conflict, however. Nations seeking independence from colonial rule led to the emergence of new states during much of the twentieth century; ethnonationalism was reenergized toward the end of the century as nations broke up into fragile and artificial states. The Soviet Union, Czechoslovakia, Yugoslavia, India (and Pakistan), Ethiopia, and others could not withstand the forces of ethnonationalism within their own territories. The changes in the Soviet bloc in the early 1990s and the end of the Cold War as a state priority were particularly significant for unleashing pent-up nationalism based upon ethnic identity.

Although globalization is often portrayed as an integrative force in world politics, nations and nationalism are usually seen as fragmentative. Nationalism becomes a potent political force when ethnic leaders use or manufacture a strong sense of identity against other groups to push for change or to even create a new state. Unwilling to be ruled by another ethnic group within a state, a nationalistically driven people can shake the state to its very foundations. It is therefore perhaps surprising that even more multinational states have not been dismembered so far.

Even in relatively homogenous North America, ethnonationalism has made its presence felt. Canada's state is besieged to the extent that French-speaking Quebec and English-speaking Canada have not been able to devise a constitutional formula for keeping Canada whole. The conflict between nations and states could affect the North American region in the twenty-first century even more than it has so far.

The North American Three in the World

No moat can be dug deep or wide enough to separate any state or region from these trends in the world. North America is no exception. In fact, the seven trends in world politics are mirrored in their own way but still quite clearly in the region and in each of its three members. The United States, Canada, and Mexico must make their way in a world with a shifting balance of power, a changing role for the state, a globalized and regionalized economy, differentiated gains and growing gaps, the dynamics of North-South relations, and ethnonationalism.

The Ordeal of Primacy

Like no other state, the United States shapes the world. It remains central to the world and hegemonic in its region. It has pushed for downsizing of the state's role in economic affairs as well as for a multilateral and globalized economy. Its commitment to liberal economic market economics remains a central pillar of its leadership. U.S. leaders are true believers in capitalism's virtues to increase absolute gains for all those who play by their rules, but they also act as if relative gains are important for preserving U.S. primacy in the world. There is no doubt that the United States has a global perspective, although the particular refinements of this perspective may not always be distinct or coherent. North America serves a larger purpose for the United States.

At the end of the twentieth century, the United States may have been the world's leader, but it may not always act like it or even have the wherewithal to act like it. Primacy is the U.S. goal. It need not fear an equal challenger for the time being. Still, in a globalized and regionalized world with absolute and relative gains being more widely distributed, the U.S. share of power may erode, undercutting its primacy eventually (Posen and Ross 1996–1997: 50). Things may continue to improve for the United States for a time, but other actors may do even better than the United States in the long haul.

Globalization is a cardinal tenet of U.S. leaders, who rail against barriers to markets and decry state controls on economic activity in the world, even when their own practice falls somewhat short of their rhetoric. The trends toward markets and against state controls have generally been to U.S. liking.

Gains, gaps, and the North-South issues are secondary to globalization, multilateralism, and U.S. power. The United States remains constant in its preference for creating wealth through markets. It believes that distributive issues will fall into place if all states will get their policies on track. It is most attentive about relative gains with potential competitors. It holds open the door to limited help for those who cannot prosper under such market conditions, both domestically and internationally.

The most innovative trend for the United States was its late conversion to economic regionalism. Multilateralism had been the U.S. strategy for designing the world economy. It remains so. Although the United States had endorsed European integration since the 1950s and fostered a now largely moribund hemispheric security system through the Rio Pact and the Organization of American States (OAS), the United States had never sought to organize a regional trade or economic arrangement for itself. In attempting to understand this shift in policy, we need to keep in mind that the United States had faced some global challenges to its power and to its preferences for the world economy.

What does the regionalist trend say about U.S. power in the world? Mostly, it says that U.S. power has changed, if not actually declined. More closely tying the United States to its neighbors has sent a message. By resorting to regionalism, the United States sought to strengthen its economic leadership. It did not mean that the United States had lost its ability to lead. In fact, organizing the North American triangle of the United States, Canada, and Mexico may have signaled to the world that the United States could work on more than one level toward its global goals of U.S.-led market initiatives. But it also implied that U.S. dominance over the world economy was no longer quite so assured; challenges such as the rise of Asia and growing competition from a globalized economy required strategies on more than one level. Although many now seemed to adopt basic U.S. views about the world economy, they were also freer to challenge U.S. leadership on specific issues.

What the United States found harder to do globally—to devise a multilateral regime very much to its liking—it found easier to do on a regional level. By playing up markets and globalization in North America, the United States was reaffirming its stance within the world economy. North American regionalism became a version of what the United States would like to see happen on a global level.

Looking South

The seven world trends also came to Canada. The unipolar balance of power during the late twentieth century drew Canada even closer to the United States. The weakening state affected Canada more than the United

States, although it has been able to preserve largely intact some of its most cherished features, such as its health care system. Canada has been a major proponent of multilateralism from the very beginning (Keating 1993: 18). Canada nevertheless regarded the challenges in the world economy as an ominous blip on the radar screen. Globalization raised questions about Canada's ability to compete. Regionalism and closer ties to the United States are a Canadian response to these challenges.

Gains and gaps have always been critical to Canada. The trends in the world political economy threatened to widen the gaps through shifts in relative gains. Canada was having a hard time becoming more efficient and proficient in a bare-knuckled, competitive environment (Britton 1996: 450). More than either other North American state, Canada faces severe ethnonationalist challenges. Canada mirrors in its own way the global trends.

For years, Canada has held membership in a rather exclusive club of states. Certainly no world power, Canada was a "middle power" with important access to the great powers of Britain and then the United States. As a constructive junior partner with the Anglo leaders of the world, Canada did not tip the balance of power but rather was a constant supporter. It was a dependable ally with an independent voice.

Canada has made some adjustments to these world trends rather than abandon its foreign policy altogether. Long committed to a balance of power centered around the North Atlantic, Canada remains a part of the dominant coalition of countries to emerge from the global wars of the twentieth century. As it adds what weight it has to the economically powerful of North America and Europe, it also buys into a view of the world that is reformist, liberal, and multilateral. Taking the moral high ground, Canada has contributed more than its share to peacekeeping, development aid, and other "good works." In other words, it is a member of the establishment, but it can afford to be more tolerant and scrupulous than its larger ally to the south. Canada's voice often echoes some of the sentiments of the minority within the U.S. foreign policy establishment.

When all is said and done, Canada has clearly edged closer to the United States. Even without a Soviet threat, Canada remains the closest U.S. ally. Drawn further into the orbit of the United States, Canada at the start of the twenty-first century seeks a new balance between U.S. domination and Canadian independence. At times, Canadian nationalist fears are publicly vented in different quarters. But as it is holding the United States at bay, Canada is also resisting Quebec separatism.

More and more, Canada regards the U.S. view of the world as largely its own. Canada counts on U.S. leadership, accepts reluctantly the shifting role of the state, is adjusting to the realities of globalization, and follows a regionalist path to multilateralism. Although sympathetic to the global South, Canada still clearly puts first its own concerns about absolute and relative gains. It reaches out to the United States to avoid the erosion of its world position. Yet Canada's multinational plight is unique in North America if not the world. For the most part, Canada's relations with the world have come to mean that it looks to its southern neighbor.

Looking North

Mexico's place in the world has evolved gradually since the 1910 revolution. Like many countries in the global South, its primary goals are domestic rather than international. It strives for domestic political stability, sustained economic growth, and national independence. For much of the twentieth century, its most important challenge was not the world at large but the United States in particular. Keeping the United States at arm's length while relying on the largesse of its economy became the delicate balancing act for promoting Mexico's viability as a Third World state.

The basic trends in the world political economy no longer allow Mexico the luxury of business as usual. The unipolar moment meant that Mexico more than most global South states had become a U.S. dependent. It is drawing closer to the economic power and to the economic orthodoxy of the United States. The Mexican state has also evolved dramatically in recent years. Mexico's "stabilizing development" during midcentury relied upon heavy state intervention in the economy, and it also practiced state-sponsored protection against the international economy (Hansen 1971). This is no longer true. During the 1980s and 1990s, Mexico overhauled its economy in ways that have downsized the state and essentially abandoned policies such as state ownership of many businesses and large state subsidies of some private firms. What is more, Mexico has gone beyond domestic defensiveness in the world. It has officially adopted multilateralism: Mexico now emulates the domestic and international policies of those high-income states it once suspected and criticized.

The globalization of the world economy altered Mexico's institutions and economy to become more accommodating to the transfer of capital, investment, and technology. Indeed, globalization and NAFTA, its regional cousin, were a way to lock in Mexico's domestic reforms (Bosworth et al. 1997: 11). As the sole member of the global South in North America, Mexico is the region's fulcrum for blending the issue of gains and gaps within North-South relations. Mexico's international strategy is to make Mexico a high-income country along the lines of U.S. preferences. Mexico's leaders seek to make their country more like the United States.

Mexico's adjustments to world trends have not been made easily. Nor are they complete. With a smaller, less-developed economy than that of either the United States or Canada, Mexico has risked a great deal. The perils of adjustment to the changing world have been keenly felt. The Mexican economy is not as competitive as it needs to be; more disturbing is that it is even more vulnerable to the world economy under globalization. Unable to suppress political challengers as it once did, the state is going through a slow democratic transition away from authoritarian politics. Domestic uncertainty is greater than it has been for decades, but Mexico's path toward greater openness and liberal economic practices seems basically entrenched for now.

Mexico's new response to the world stems from a realization that there seems for the time being to be no other viable option. Since Mexico needs external support for its ambitious goals for the twenty-first century, it had to become a card-carrying member of the exclusive club led by the United States and other countries of the Organization for Economic Cooperation and Development (OECD). Naturally, some nationalist angst about this reversal of strategy surfaces within the more emboldened domestic opposition in Mexico. Yet Mexico's liberal insertion into the world and especially into North America in ways that would been thought inconceivable in the first half of the twentieth century is part of the emerging domestic consensus of liberal Mexico.

As Mexico moves closer to the open, globalized, market-oriented world, it is actually moving closer to the United States. Domestic shifts in economic and other public policy made possible a new partnership with the country that more than any other had traumatized Mexico in the past. Even now, this world of liberalism and globalization still mostly means the binational relationship with the United States. In the past, Mexico had mixed success in defying the hegemonic presence. At the dawn of the century, Mexico also seems to welcome it. This more than almost anything else shows how Mexico's approach to the outside world has changed. Whether this dramatic shift in perspective will prove well founded only time will tell.

2

The Three States of North America

North America is a premier region in a world of regions. Asia Pacific, Europe, and North America are linchpins of the global economy. Asia is much larger, more diverse, and complex than North America; it is actually made up of several regions, centered on several great powers and would-be great powers. Europe is about the same size as North America economically, but it is expanding and deepening its regional commitments in ways North America is not.

Two basic conditions affect North America as a region. First, the three states have a standing or place that somehow sets them apart from the rest of the world. Second, they have enough in common upon which to invent a region.

Standing

How do the United States, Canada, and Mexico stack up to the rest of the world? Size of state, population, economy, political rights, ethnic diversity, and income (equality) can serve as points of comparison. These features reveal that North America is a rather unusual, even privileged collection of states.

All states have territory. As a vast continent occupying the northern half of the Western Hemisphere, North America has two of the world's largest states; even the smallest of the three ranks among the top twenty states in terms of area. Even more impressive, all three are transcontinental. That is, the United States, Canada, and Mexico all have coastal boundaries on two or more oceans or major bodies of water. They are large territorial states in geographic isolation from the rest of the world.

The territorial giant is Canada. Occupying 9.9 million square kilometers, Canada's vastness spans five time zones. Only Russia is larger. The United States is Canada's only contiguous neighbor. Not far behind is its southern neighbor. The United States is the world's fourth largest state, occupying 9.6 million square kilometers. It, too, is bounded by three major bodies of water (the Pacific, the Atlantic, and the Gulf of Mexico). It has long borders with Canada and Mexico—two of the longest, largely undefended borders in the world. More compact than the other two, Mexico ranks fourteenth in size, with 1.9 million square kilometers. The home of three large states, North America as a continent is larger than South America.

Population is another distinguishing feature. The United States and Mexico have among the largest populations in the world, ranked fourth and eleventh. Canada is thirty-first. All three states are fairly urbanized, Mexico less so than the other two. The average size of households is relatively small in the United States and Canada. Reflecting its poverty, Mexico's household size is larger.

Economic prowess is also important. The United States has the largest gross national product (GNP), the third highest GNP per capita, and ranks number one in economic capability in the world (see Table 2.1). Canada is also part of the world's economic elite. It ranks seventh in size, eighth in GNP per capita, and fifth in economic capability. Of course, Mexico is North America's anomaly. As a large developing economy, it is the thirteenth biggest economy in the world, but its average individual income ranks it much lower. Even so, its economic capability puts it among the top three dozen national economies in the world. Mexico's relative poverty is the central challenge for inventing North America as a region.

The political environment is critical. Political freedoms place North America well within a small elite of the world's states. The rights of Canadians are better ensured than the rights of people living in all but a handful of states. Of the three in North America, Canada leads the way, ranking fifth and sixth on civil and political rights. The United States does not fare quite as well, but it does rank among the top twenty on both counts. Not known for its scrupulous commitment to democracy in the past, Mexico nevertheless scores relatively well in a global context. The gap between Mexico and the rest of North America, although considerable, is not as great as the gap between Mexico and

Table 2.1 World Rankings of the United States, Canada, and Mexico

	United States	Canada	Mexico
Size of state	4	2	14
Length of borders	5	8	37
Population	4	31	11
Urbanization	33	30	44
Household size	200	191	64
Homogeneity	82	116	64
Christians	71	72	43
Political rights	18	6	50
Civil rights	17	5	47
GNP	1	7	13
GNP per capita	3	8	58
Percent of national income received by the wealthiest 10 percent	60	52	24
Percent of national income received by the poorest 20 percent	67	32	93
Economic capability	1	5	31
Education spending per capita	7	3	61

Source: Data adapted from Kurian 1992.

the rest of the world. Mexico ranked forty-seventh on civil rights and fiftieth on political rights out of two hundred states. On a global scale, the United States, Canada, and Mexico compare very favorably, to varying degrees, with the other states of the world.

Ethnic diversity makes North America more similar to the rest of the world. Mexico is the most homogenous of the three. Over the centuries, Mexican culture and society have experienced a blending of racial and ethnic backgrounds. Still, Mexico ranks sixty-fourth in the world on ethnic homogeneity. But it leads North America on ethnic cohesion. The two "immigrant" societies of North America, the United States and Canada, rank lower than Mexico. Their societies are more complex and less cohesive. With minorities constituting about 20 percent of its population, the United States ranks eighty-fourth in the world on ethnic homogeneity. Divided by language and culture, Canada ranks 116th in the world.

Income equality sheds further light on North America. Although all three states rank among the upper half of all states on income equality, none claims a leading position in the world. Canada does the best on this score, with the United States falling somewhat lower. Mexico is twenty-fourth in the world in the percent of income received by the wealthiest 10 percent.

Income concentration is relatively high. Canada ranks thirty-second in the world for the share of income that the poorest 20 percent receive. Once again, the United States and Mexico are not listed as high because their lowest-income people receive a smaller share of the national income.

Overall, then, the states of North America to some extent stand apart from much of the world. Their distinctiveness lies with their favored place in the world in terms of territory, economics, and political freedom. In this sense, the three are a plutocratic club. But ethnic diversity in the United States and Canada makes them more like many other states. The same can be said of income inequality.

Inside North America

Within all regions and within all states, unity and diversity play off against each other. History, culture, people, economics, and politics shape the prospects for regionalism.

Three Paths

North America went through several epochs. The precolonial era lasted for several millennia. Peoples from Asia migrated to North America during a prehistoric ice age, 11,500 or more years ago. One of the earliest groups was the Clovis people, but recent theories, based on evidence such as Kennewick man (in Washington State) and Monte Verde in Chile, suggest a more complex picture of early settlement (Wilford 1999: D1).

The indigenous peoples of North America were greatly affected by the occupation from the east. Europeans came to North America not so much discovering as subduing precolonial peoples. In the United States, Manifest Destiny was not to be foiled by the "Indian problem": The original inhabitants were "in the way" and had to be killed off or removed to reservations.

In Canada the aboriginal peoples were dealt with in roughly similar fashion. The Inuit (or Eskimo), the First Nations (aboriginals in the sub-Arctic area), and Mètis (mixed blood) were seen as problems rather than assets. Their numbers and their influence dwindled well into the twentieth century. In Mexico, too, the policy toward the Indian civilizations was one of conquest, but it had a different twist to it. The colonizers conquered expansive, well-established civilizations with urban centers and complex societies. And when in the early 1500s Hernán Cortés beheaded the Aztec empire, he did so without exterminating most of its people. This had very important consequences for Mexico's culture and development during the centuries to follow.

Each state had a parallel but distinct experience in the next stage, the colonial period. Although the United States and Canada are "children of a common mother" (Harrison 1997: 43), the United States had a somewhat different relationship to its parent. One and a half centuries of colonial rule ended with a war of national liberation. The United States bolted from the empire; Canada did not. Indeed, it was not until 1980 that "O Canada" finally replaced "God Save the Queen" as the national anthem (Lipset 1993: 652). And unlike the United States, with one dominant colonizer, Canada had two. The French empire in North America came to an end in the eighteenth century, but the Francophone influence lingered. The loyalists of British descent in North America found Canada to be a refuge from liberalism, egalitarianism, revolution, and Americanism.

Farther south, Mexico was a jewel in the Spanish empire for three centuries, giving it by far the longest colonial experience in North America. Colonial Mexico was run by the conquistadores, the church, and the large landowners (or *hacendados*). As a semifeudal society, Mexico produced great wealth for the Spanish empire through a system of land tenure and social control that stymied the rapid emergence of a modern society. A handful of Spanish and colonial elites controlled a vast number of indigenous peoples.

When independence did come to North America, it came relatively quickly for the United States and Mexico, but it took longer for Canada. In Mexico the struggle for independence (1810–1821) offered the promise of an end to harsh colonial rule. But independence brought major problems of its own. More than any other North American state, Mexico struggled long and hard in the postindependence period. For one thing, Mexico lost a war in 1848 as well as approximately half of its original territorial claims, including Texas, California, and much of what is now the American Southwest. As if that were not enough, the French Bourbon intervention in the 1860s threatened Mexico's newly won independence. After five years of Maximilian and Carlotta, the Mexicans were able to rout the French attempt to regain a toehold in North America.

In its first years of independence, the United States struggled to find a workable formula for self-rule. Even when it succeeded, there remained domestic and foreign challenges. Sectionalism and the slavery issue were not resolved until the Civil War, and if the War of 1812 had turned out differently, the United States would have failed in its entire experiment in sovereignty.

Canada achieved its independence gradually, through negotiation, distinguishing it from the other two. Unlike its rebellious colonial sibling to the south, Canada was compliant. It sought protection from the British in its effort to stand apart from the United States. The British North American Act of 1867 and the Charter of Rights in 1982 symbolize Canada's approach to loyalty and independence.

Cultures and Peoples

The cultures and values of North America also suggest how the three states converge and diverge. The United States, Canada, and Mexico have broad cultural affinities, yet from inside the region the differences may stand out more than the similarities.

If culture and values had been the criteria, Mexico would not have been incorporated into North America in the 1990s (Harrison 1997: 24). The United States and Canada—with the important exception of Quebec—have Anglo-Protestant cultures, whereas Mexico is Ibero-Catholic. The differences range far beyond sectarian ones. A little more than one half of all Americans are Protestants, and 38 percent are Catholics (Banks et al. 1997: 899). In Canada the French Catholics of Quebec are proportionately a smaller group, but they are more cohesive culturally and linguistically. As for Mexico, the Ibero-Catholic culture is even more dominant, despite the growth of evangelical sects in Mexico and in the rest of Latin America. The two dominant cultures differ over life's basic values, such as time, work, frugality, education, merit, community, justice, authority, and secularism (Harrison 1997: 31).

Given the roots of both, it is to be expected that the two cultures do share some specific traits. The United States, Canada, and Mexico show a marked preference for authority based on rationality rather than tradition, especially when compared at the global level (Inglehart et al. 1996: 20). Authority is more accepted in North America than in most regions, but those in Mexico and the United States are more skeptical of authority than are Canadians. North America is also a very religious region. The emphasis on traditional religious values spans the three states and two cultural traditions. Accommodation between Anglo-Protestant and Ibero-Catholic North America might therefore be easier to achieve than it would between Christian Europe and Muslim Turkey, an associate member of the European Union (Huntington 1996: 150).

The cultural differences among the three states vary in importance and indeed may even be eroding (Inglehart et al. 1996: 13). For example, the differences between English-speaking Canada and the United States are less dramatic than are differences within Canada. Many Canadians "want to be different [from Americans] only to the extent of being called Canadians" (Bell 1992: 56). Culturally, Mexico is the most distinctive in North America. In some ways its culture, a vibrant amalgamation of two major cultural groups, may be closer to Quebec's than it is to the dominant English culture in North America. Its blend of European and Iberian culture with indigenous cultures sets Mexico apart from the United States and Canada, in which native cultures were less important to the overall life of the societies.

Political culture in North America has European roots. The U.S. political tradition gravitates to John Locke, the Canadian to Edmund Burke. The United States is liberal, Whig, individualistic, antistatist, populist, and ideological. Without rejecting Locke, Canada is slightly more in the Tory tradition. It is more mercantilist, group-oriented, statist, deferential, and socialist (Lipset 1990: 212). The United States has moved further away from European philosophy, whereas Canada, with a history of social democracy, more closely resembles Europe (Lipset 1996: 23, 26). The United States and Canada may be siblings, but they are certainly not twins.

Mexico is a different story. It is culturally closer to Latin America than to the rest of North America. As an American journalist once observed, "Probably nowhere in the world do two countries as different as Mexico and the United States live side by side" (Riding 1984: ix). In fact, Mexico, Chile, Brazil, and Argentina and much of Latin America have values that set them apart from other areas, making Latin America a single cultural area (Inglehart and Carballo 1997: 41; Harrison 1997: 26). For Anglo-Protestant North America, political values such as individualism, liberalism, achievement, egalitarianism, diffused authority, progress, and antistatism are paramount (Lipset 1990: 212; Harrison 1997: 46). In other words, Locke and Thomas Hobbes are the European parents of Anglo North American political culture. For Ibero-Catholic North America, patrimonialism, centralism, caudilloism, statism, and corporatism are more ingrained (Dealy 1992: 209; Harrison 1997: 87; Wiarda 1995: 86–88). Thomas Aquinas and Jean-Jacques Rousseau are its intellectual parents.

North America, made up of three states, is also the home of several peoples or nations. The United States is multiethnic. Its population of 280 million is growing slowly, much of the growth coming from immigration. Four-fifths of Americans are white or Anglo, many descended from British, Irish, and German forebears. But the United States is a home for increasing numbers of other ethnic groups. As 12 percent of the total, African Americans form the largest racial minority. The ethnic minority of Hispanic or Latino Americans are about the same size (Banks et al. 1997: 899) and will surpass African Americans in numbers some time in the first part of the twenty-first century.

Although ethnicity plays a major role in defining the United States as a plural society, the situation in Canada is more complicated. The particularism of the group has long been Canada's central civic value (Bell 1992: 86). It is not hard to see why. Quebec and the rest of Canada give the state a binational character that finds no equal in the United States. Quebec's troubled marriage with English Canada may dictate the future of Canada as a state. Beyond Quebec, Canada is also multinational. Inuit, First Nations, and Mètis, not to mention the recent immigrants from Hong Kong, Asia, Latin America, and Eastern Europe, give this state a decidedly multicultural cast. Canada's pragmatic live-and-let-live approach to diversity seeks a mosaic society rather than a melting pot in which diversity is tolerated. Yet Canada, like the United States, has struggled over its multinational identity.

Despite its geographical area, Canada has a low population. One-third as populous as Mexico, Canada has 29.7 million people (1999 estimate) more divided by culture and language than any other place in North America except possibly for the state of California (see Table 2.2). More Canadians live in central Canada than in all the other provinces combined. This stretch of Canada, especially Ontario and Quebec, also accounts for 60 percent of the national income and the same percentage of representation in the House of Commons, Canada's most important legislative body (Brooks 1996: 139). Almost nine out of ten Canadians live within 100 miles of the U.S. border.

One-fifth of all Canadians speak French, most speak English, and some speak both. The Catholics of Canada live mostly in Quebec. English-speaking Canada is largely Protestant. If Quebec were independent, it would be the twenty-fifth largest state in the world. The place of Quebec in Canada remains Canada's most fundamental issue.

Table 2.2 North America in Brief Statistical Profile

	United States	Canada	Mexico
Land area in region (%)	45.1	45.4	9.5
Population in region (%)	68.1	7.4	24.5
Under age 14 in region (%)	22.0	21.0	36.0
Labor force in region (%)	73.1	8.3	18.6
Net national migration per thousand	3.1	4.5	–2.9
GDP per capita (1996 U.S. dollars)	$27,246	$20,006	$3,292
GDP growth (1996)	2.4	1.5	8.6
Unemployment rate (1996)	5.4	9.7	5.5
Gini coefficient[a]	0.42	0.36	0.48
Male life expectancy at birth	72.5	75.3	69.5
Population growth rate	1.0	1.2	2.1
Foreign born (%)	7.9	15.5	0.8
Births per thousand	14.8	13.2	31.2
Employed in manufacturing (%)	15.3	14.7	31.2
Defense as % of all federal spending	15.3	6.6	4.4
Manufacturing as % of all economic activity	17.4	17.4	21.1
Current government spending as % of GDP	16.2	19.6	10.6

Sources: Calculated from Cremeans 1998: 85–87; United Nations 1997: 34, 122, 196; *The World Europa Yearbook 1997:* 780–783, 2224–2227, 3477–3481; OECD 1997b, "Basic Statistics: International Comparisons."

Note: a. Gini coefficient is a measure of income inequality with 1.0 indicating the highest degree of inequality.

The Quebec issue goes to the heart of Canadian identity and survival. Many Quebecois see themselves as a "distinct society" whose culture and language is threatened by assimilation with the Protestant Anglophone majority (Lemco 1996: 12). The problem with a distinct society is that it contravenes the equality of all groups. To Quebec nationalists such as René Levesque, Canada is like "two scorpions in a bottle" (Lamont 1994: 108). The culture war is mostly a war over language (Brooks 1996: 315). Officially bilingual, the country is actually divided between Francophone and Anglophone Canadians.

Quebec's demands for special recognition and protection of its language and culture have stirred the political cauldron. In fact, culture and language may be the Achilles' heel of Canada's future as a united state. In the 1990s constitutional initiatives such as Meech Lake and the Charlottetown Accords failed to devise a solution once and for all to the problems of federal powersharing and Quebec's status. A political solution for the binational state has been illusive. The cultural impact on national unity and diversity continues to be the most serious challenge facing the Canadian state. Consequently, it is not inconceivable that one day North America may have four independent states.

Multinational Canada also insists on being heard. Albeit small, the indigenous Canadian nations are seeking recognition, redress, and even self-government. Indigenous Canadians make up 2.7 percent of the Canadian population (Doerr 1997: 280). The Inuit of the Northwest Territories (about 30,000 in total) achieved majority rule in the territory of Nunavut; they have a fair degree of autonomy over their own affairs. The First Nations (aboriginal or Indians) also lay claim to greater self-rule. These native nations are concerned about their future role in Canada whether it stays united or breaks apart along the Francophone-Anglophone fault line. Although the Inuit and Cree have voted to stay in Canada, they reject Quebec's efforts to expand the number of non-aboriginal people, mostly Quebecois, into their territory around the James Bay area of the province (Aubry 1997: B9). Federal and provincial policies also may be in flux with respect to aboriginal peoples (Abele 1997: 126). A good example of this is the unprecedented treaty negotiated in 1998 to grant self-government to the Nisga'a tribe in British Columbia (De Palma 1998: A1).

Mexico is more unified ethnically than the other two North American states. Although much divides the population of about 100 million, the people do broadly share a culture and an identity that sets them apart from the United States and Canada. The dominant identity is mestizo, a blending of Indian and European blood and culture. Education, urbanization, economic development, and the media since the revolution of 1910 have created a more integrated society. Still, Mexicans are not a homogenous people. Sectionalism and cultural nuances play a part in Mexican unity. The *chilangos* (the residents of Mexico City) are seen as different from the *norteños* of Monterrey. Mexicans are united in language, religion, and national myths; the differences among them remain regional, economic, and to a lesser extent cultural.

Divided between the haves and have-nots, Mexico is becoming a contested arena for the rich, who increasingly adopt the values of North American liberalism, and the poor, who have yet to benefit from neoliberal change. Monterrey in the north and Chiapas in the south symbolize this cleavage. Mexico is torn between its traditional national and cultural heritage and the attractions of Anglo-Protestant culture of the United States (Huntington 1996: 149–151).

National Politics

The three states have constitutions, federalism, political parties, Western-type government institutions, and democratic ideologies. This is the political basis for unity in North America and is as close as it comes to a general consensus about the nature of national politics in North America. Yet politics embodies differences as well, making it more difficult to find common ground in a more integrated North America.

A constitution is basic to each of the three states but in each serves a unique purpose. The U.S. Constitution, the "supreme law of the land," found innovative solutions for governing a new state in the late eighteenth century. As a Lockean contract of popular will, the Constitution strikes a balance between unified and limited government. It divides power at the national level, protects minority rights, balances the three branches of government, and shares powers between the federal and state governments. Skeptical of governmental power, the framers preferred a rather weak, divided state over a strong, unified one. Following Locke and Thomas Jefferson, the U.S. Constitution enshrined the belief that good government governs least.

The constitutional framers in Canada had a different vision. The goal of their constitution was not to limit government but to establish "peace, order and good government" (McNaught 1993: 200). Somewhat like Britain, Canada has a constitution that is made up of multiple documents and relies on custom as well. Its evolution over a century has been more organic than contractual. What is more, Canada's constitution, especially the 1867 and 1982 acts, has been a lengthy process of the country's finding its way, securing independence from Britain, and struggling toward a sense of political community. Most recently, constitutional reform has become embroiled in the central problem of Quebec's place in the federation.

Ironically, the revolution breathed life into Mexican constitutionalism. The oldest in Latin America, its 1917 constitution was written to help end a decade of revolution. It reads like a conventional liberal, federal document, but its more radical purpose was to change Mexico (Hansen 1971: 88–91). The constitution did not aim to limit government but rather to create a stable political order that would be broadly acceptable to the factions and coalitions that had toppled the old system. It is less an accurate guide to the workings of Mexican politics than a verification of Mexico's standing as a modern and stable state.

Federalism is no stranger to North America. Each state practices federalism of some kind. A federal system divides power between the national and local (state or provincial) levels, taking into account the large size and great diversity of such states. The struggle over how centralized or decentralized these federal systems should be remains a constant feature of North American politics.

U.S. federalism was a genuine constitutional innovation in the eighteenth century. In the beginning U.S. federalism steered a middle course between a weak national government of the Articles of Confederation and a centralized system favored by Alexander Hamilton. With the arrival of large government programs in the 1930s, the balance tipped away from the states and toward the federal government. More recently, there has been a debate about a "new federal order" that would recalibrate the balance once again. Today federalism provides a constitutional battleground for waging cultural wars, welfare reform, and a host of other policy causes (Schram and Weissert 1997: 1–31).

Canada is incorrigibly a federal country (Smiley 1993: 247). More than that, it is a "regional country" (Francis 1993: 229). Domestic regionalism (or sectionalism) has greatly affected Canadian federalism and will likely do so in the future even if part of the federation cracks under the strain of cultural diversity. The strong sense of regionalism within Canada made federalism more decentralized than in the United States.

Canada has ten provinces and two territories. Within this loose federalism, the gap between levels of government and even among political parties is large (Stewart and Stewart 1997: 97). It is hard to envision how Canadian federalism could tolerate even more decentralization. Native demands for self-government have joined with the Quebec issue and other regional tensions to imperil Canadian unity and community (Brooks 1996: 45). A strong national government would allow one region (Ontario, for example) to dominate the others (Francis 1993: 230).

Centralization has long held sway over Mexican federalism, although it now seems to be going the other way. Rather than restraining the national government in favor of adamant regionalism, federalism historically allowed the centralization of power after the revolution.

Until recently, state governors were of the same party as the national government party that has ruled Mexico since the revolution. Governors did what presidents wanted. A president has constitutional authority to remove a state governor. As Mexican politics becomes more open and competitive, Mexican federalism will no doubt begin to resemble more closely the two other federal systems in North America.

Political parties are no strangers to the political landscape of North America. Party systems reflect national differences and converging trends. Despite its critics, the two-party system is a durable feature of U.S. politics. Strong interest groups and weak parties allow little political space for third parties. When they do arise, they are unable to challenge them for long. Although the Reform Party of the 1990s may be a party, it has not dislodged the two major parties; the party system is a tango for two. Republicans and Democrats alternate control of the presidency and the Congress, but rarely does one party hold onto both. The dominant party in the Congress is more effective when it reaches out to the other party in a "constructive partnership" (Dodd and Oppenheimer 1997: 410).

Two parties tend to be the most competitive, but in Canada there is some fluidity. A host of smaller, regional parties register limited gains at both the national and provincial levels from time to time. Reflecting the regionalism within Canada, the parties are disparate and nonideological. In the federal Parliament, party discipline is much greater. During the last three decades of the twentieth century, two parties in particular, the Liberals and the Progressive-Conservatives (or Tories), dominated the national elections. The former is center-left; the latter is center-right. Some parties, such as the Quebec Bloc and the Reform Party of Canada (now the Alliance), are regional more than national.

Mexico's party system has been about one horse winning most of the races. Only one party, the Institutional Revolutionary Party (PRI), ever held the presidency until 2000. As part of a one-party dominant system, Mexico's parties reflected the traditional authoritarian nature of power (Handelman 1997: 66–85). Single-party dominance is on the wane, however. During the 1990s modest electoral reform opened up the system. Opposition parties such as the National Action Party (PAN) and the Revolutionary Democratic Party (PRD) made some headway in state governor races, and the PRI lost its majority in the lower house of the legislature, failed to put itself in power in the Mexico City government, and could not hold onto the historical center of power in postrevolutionary Mexico.

Governmental institutions in North America reveal similarities and differences, not to mention a partial common debt to European influences. In the United States, executive power is separated from legislative power. This bestows more independence on the U.S. Congress than the legislatures of either Canada or Mexico have. Divided government is an artifact of the Constitution and a reality of contemporary politics.

Only twice during the second half of the twentieth century has the same party controlled the presidency and both branches of the Congress. Still, the presidency remains relatively strong, an institutional legacy of the New Deal. Even Republican conservatives such as Ronald Reagan and Richard Nixon wielded the powers of a strong president to pursue their own anti–New Deal agendas (Milkis 1993: 302). The U.S. Supreme Court is relatively independent from the other two branches. Although it may defer to them on certain issues of legislative and administrative expertise, it defers to no one in interpreting the law and the Constitution (Cheney 1998: 6).

On paper, Mexico resembles the United States. Like the United States, Mexico has a presidency, a bicameral legislature, and a judicial branch. But Mexican institutions operate differently. Given its history, culture, and politics, the Mexican system is far more presidential than even its counterpart in the United States. Until recently, the Mexican congress was merely a rubber stamp for the ruling party. The judiciary has never been truly independent of executive power. Cliques and factions rather than institutions and agencies are most important in Mexico. The rule of law is sporadic. Still, if gradual liberalization takes hold, its institutions will probably experience a more balanced distribution of effective power (Poitras 1998).

Borrowing from the British, Canada's representative institutions at the national level fall outside the normal experience in the Americas. The parliamentary system of the national government in Ottawa is genuinely unique for North America. The system unifies rather than divides legislative and executive power in what once was called a "constitutional monarchy." The prime minister is the head of the majority party in Parliament's House of Commons. (The Canadian Senate is not elected, resembling the House of Lords in Britain.) But as in Mexico and the United States, the executive power in the prime minister dominates the legislative body. Constitutional powers and weak parties solidify executive dominance in Canada.

Each state is democratic, but each in its own way. For example, in the United States individual rights are given priority over collective or group rights. In Canadian history collective rights under a mantle of tolerance have received more attention. Despite the Charter of Rights and Freedoms of 1982, Canada's protections for individual rights are not as strong as those of the United States (Lipset 1993: 656). And all three states have been globally criticized for mistreatment of minorities.

Traditionally, North America varied in its emphasis on individual rights. The United States stressed civil and political rights; for Mexico and Canada, democracy goes beyond such a view of rights to include social and economic ones. The 1917 Mexican constitution enumerates such rights. Recent constitutional processes in Canada have split the difference. The 1982 charter focuses upon political, legal, economic, language, aboriginal, and equality rights but not on social rights (Brooks 1996: 273). For its part, the United States trumpets equal opportunity but is less committed to equality of results. Canada has historically sought to address this very problem.

The big question is Mexican democracy. Until recently, Mexican politics was widely regarded as elitist, centralist, authoritarian, patrimonial, corporatist, and corrupt. With the 2000 election, a full-scale transition to democracy seems to be under way, bringing a possible end to the traditional paradox of Mexican politics in which democracy and authoritarianism coexisted (Poitras 1998: 63). Mexico may one day join the rest of North America as a full-fledged democratic state.

The Three Economies

Capitalism rules in North America. Markets, the price system, private ownership of production, individual property rights, and other tenets of classic economic liberalism are pervasive in all three states.

There is more to it than this, however. The United States, Canada, and Mexico have national economies that blend differently the liberalism of free markets and the neomercantilism of state involvement. The U.S. economy stands apart from the other two because it has a highly market-oriented approach to the economy. Over the years Canada and Mexico were less enamored of free markets.

Economic values, structures, and policies are currently coming together around the liberal tendency toward markets. Banking and other financial institutions have largely been in private hands, although Canada and the United States have strong central banks. Privatization of ownership and government restraint in the economy are important points of economic convergence in recent North American history (Bell 1992: 56).

Economic structures in Canada and the United States are growing more similar as time goes by (Lipset 1990: 216). The economies of all three are industrial or even postindustrial. The U.S. economy remains the world's largest, most industrialized, and advanced economy. Ironically, the postindustrial evolution of this economy has shifted the emphasis away from manufacturing to the high-skilled and low-skilled service sector where most workers are employed. As large and wealthy as the U.S. economy is, it has not been able to raise real personal incomes substantially since the early 1970s.

The U.S. economy has also been unable to lessen relative inequality. This is the most glaring flaw of the U.S. market-style capitalism. The United States has one of the highest levels of income inequality in the developed world. Since the early 1970s, the poorest 20 percent of the population have claimed a smaller share of the national income whereas the top 20 percent has increased its share by 15 percent (Birdsall 1998: 76). Size and diversity have something to do with this, but so, too, does the growing reaction in the United States against the New Deal liberalism that tried to ameliorate growing inequalities through welfare programs. As the most market-oriented economy in the developed world, the United States has a relatively small and still shrinking social safety net.

Canada's economy is similarly advanced and developed. It has produced a high standard of living, rivaling the United States in per capita income. During the 1990s, Canada was often ranked first in the world on the Human Development Index, a UN measure of livability. By contrast, the United States was fourth (in 1999) and Mexico was forty-seventh (Economist 1999: 26). The historic comparative advantage of the Canadian economy has been natural resources or staples, but Canada is moving toward the production of services characteristic of postindustrial economies.

The end of the twentieth century was somewhat difficult for Canada. During the late 1980s and early 1990s, the economy performed below expectations. Unemployment was stubbornly high at a time when the social net sagged. It also lagged in technology, suffered from relative inefficiency, and experienced waning international competitiveness. Still, Canada has dealt more successfully with inequality of incomes than has any other North American state, although social and economic policy has been unable to shield the country from persistent inequality. The top 20 percent of the people controls 47.2 percent of the national income, whereas the bottom 20 percent has 1.2 percent of the national income (Shifrin 1993: 611).

Canada lives with an unusual fate: It may be the most-developed economy in the world to be so dependent on one other national economy. Tied as it is to the U.S. economy through natural exports, it was once dubbed a "banana republic without the bananas" (Bell 1992: 178).

Mexico is once again the economic outlier. Historically, the government took an active role as "rector" of the economy's development

(Hansen 1971; Wilkie 1970). It regulated foreign investment, tightly controlled trade, regulated and protected national business, set prices and wages, and engaged in other neomercantilist practices. After three decades of impressive "stabilizing development," Mexico's economy suffered greatly from the "lost decade" of the 1980s, with declining incomes, a large foreign debt, inflation, and underemployment. The economic traumas of the 1980s had much to do with ending the government's traditional role in the national economy.

Mexico is caught between two worlds. In terms of policy and aspirations, Mexico is economically North American. In terms of structural realities, it is not. With Mexico, North America is the global North but it is also the global South. After the cycles of boom and bust, Mexico remains the poor cousin in North America, but it is blessed with enormous potential. Despite its well-publicized economic ordeals in the 1980s and the 1990s, the Mexican economy is not submerging but emerging. Mexico's economy has real strengths and a promising future within North America and even the world.

For the time being, Mexico's economic place in North America must remain problematic. Mexico has a relatively fast-growing population with many potential workers under the age of fourteen and a low-skilled workforce with high levels of underemployment. It suffers from a severe concentration of wealth, one of the worst in Latin America. It suffers from deficiencies in basic infrastructure. It has a large but poor domestic consumer market. It has an antiquated banking system. Like its neighbors in North America and like many of its cohorts in the global South, Mexico has a burgeoning income problem. Individual incomes in Mexico are about one-tenth of those in the United States. In the 1990s alone, the income gap between the top 20 percent and the bottom 20 percent of the population grew 25 percent (Birdsall 1998: 78).

Unity amid diversity in part defines North America. History, culture, and politics tend to heighten differences as well as provide some bases for greater cooperation. But it is the convergence and integration of national economies, as different as they are, that are driving the momentum behind a new North America.

Does North America Exist?

Does North America really exist? The standing of North America within the world and the unity amid diversity within this region suggest that the answer is at most a tentative yes. What sets North America apart and what brings it together are indispensable for its status as a region.

North America is a region of a few big territorial states that adhere to a set of basic ideas about ways of life and particularly about how to organize governance and how to produce wealth. With some exceptions, its legacy is Western, Christian, democratic, and economically liberal. Its plural societies are made up of ethnic majorities that are mostly European in background and traditions, although Mexico's cultural mosaic is more indigenous and somewhat less European. So, too, do these states have similar national dilemmas: problems of community and governance, ethnic identity and cultural conflict, wealth and inequality. Mexico's membership in this exclusive club called North America is probably the most important challenge to its prospects for regionalism.

At some point North Americans must begin to think and act as if they are more than neighbors living behind their own fences. Rather, the triumvirate must do things with one another that they do not do with others. Or they may do these things more intensely or do them in ways that are somehow distinctive. The North American region will emerge from not just what they are but what they do together.

3

Neighbors and Partners

The three states of North America are neighbors. At times their leaders and peoples have appreciated this situation and even made the most of it. But like neighbors everywhere, they have had their ups and downs. Tension, indifference, and engagement have pervaded the region from time to time.

North America is a zone of peace. In the late twentieth century, the three states found more to bring them together than to drive them apart. Grievances and irritations persist, but the relations are too valuable to be put into jeopardy. Tending to the neighborhood is in everyone's interest. Being a regional neighbor has come to mean building at least some degree of trust.

But what kind of neighbors are they? At the dawn of the twenty-first century, this has become a question very much worth reconsidering. What is clear is that the triumvirate is not made up of adversaries, although their tactics in dealing with each other may sometimes seem that way. Conflicts are bounded and contained. What is more, the three no longer can afford "splendid isolation" from each other or from the world for that matter. Benign indifference does raise its head now and again.

The United States and Mexico have worked on a "marriage of convenience" (Weintraub 1990). At their worst, they are "distant neighbors" (Riding 1984). To the north, the United States and Canada are perhaps closer (Kirton 1993: 37). Although North Americans may not know each other as well as they should, it is becoming untenable for them to see each other as complete strangers. North America is moving in a direction that makes hostility and indifference a no-win situation for everyone. But that still leaves the matter of how this partnership will be devised and how it will address the durable issues facing the region.

The idea of a North American partnership is appealing. In general, partners agree on how to achieve mutually important goals through rules about consultation, compromise, and conflict resolution. Partners usually accept and trust one another. Mutual sensitivity, vulnerability, and dependence encourage such a relationship. They may not always agree, but, to borrow a cliché, they can usually agree to disagree. Partners work on those problems that imperil the relationship or those problems that can be addressed. Harmony and accommodation are highly prized, although conflict and confrontation are by no means absent. Partners accord each other respect and even some measure of equality. Partners in the neighborhood still build fences, but they also build gates in those fences.

The essential features of North American relations make a partnership both desirable and difficult. First, the United States, Canada, and Mexico adopt perspectives on the evolving relationship that do not always coincide. Although all three are moving toward a convergence of views, their very different places within the region's structure make some variance almost inevitable. Second, relations among the three are greatly affected by power asymmetry. The large disparity of power between the United States, on the one hand, and Canada and Mexico, on the other, creates challenges for developing a genuine partnership. Third, North American states are bonded together at common borders and border regions. This is the mortar with which to cement a partnership of neighboring states. Finally, the prospects for North American relations rest on the collective ability to grapple with abiding issues confronting two or more of the states. It is sometimes less important that these problems be solved outright. Since some of them are more dilemmas than problems (such as immigration), they may not be solvable in any ultimate sense. Almost as important for the relationship is how they are addressed.

A Triad of Perspectives

How leaders and people in North America see each other depends to some extent on the region itself. Perspectives of the neighbors also emerge from history, events, and aspirations. There is thus some divergence over the region but a good deal of growing convergence as well.

The U.S. perspective is crucial. But it hardly stands alone as the only important perspective. Historically, U.S. views were not always widely or deeply shared in North America. The United States has held to the view through policy and preference that North America is for North Americans. All others should be held at arm's length. Peace, democracy, and capitalism are North American icons. For Americans, the self-evident premise was that all North Americans subscribe to these U.S. precepts, whether or not they actually did.

U.S. views of its neighbors and the region are largely positive and benign. The United States is North America's sentinel rather than a threat to its neighbors. What the United States wants for its neighbors is what they want for themselves. Stability, prosperity, democracy, and free markets are on the U.S. wish list for its neighbors. It is important that Canada and Mexico be in agreement with the United States on important issues.

The United States sees its neighbors as independent but like-minded allies. Their differences are relatively small, at least compared to global standards. Canada and Mexico are, or should be, loyal and beholden to the United States. What is more, its neighbors will do better than they have so far when (not if) they follow U.S. rhetoric and, even better, when they emulate U.S. practice. Good relations emerge not when the United States dictates to its neighbors. Heavy-handed meddling is generally unwise but occasionally necessary.

North America is no utopia. Conflicts do obviously occur because of misunderstandings and lack of sensitivity, straining relations that at times may be taken for granted. For example, faced with the burdens of global leadership, the United States has sometimes overlooked its neighbors' interests or took actions globally without fretting too much over adverse regional repercussions. In 1971 the United States imposed a 10 percent import surcharge. Such unilateralism was devastating to Canada and Mexico, whose trade with the United States was of overwhelming importance to them. Even if its neighbors felt the blow more keenly than others, the U.S. view is that it must do things for "larger" reasons as it looks beyond the region. In this view, the leaders and peoples of Mexico and Canada misperceive U.S. intentions and actions because they do not fully comprehend the unique and burdensome role the United States must play on the world stage.

The United States is also more inclined to view closer ties and even integration throughout the region with a benevolent eye. It therefore regards fears of U.S. paternalism and domination as groundless. The central issue is how to allow the three states to draw closer together without abandoning national sovereignty. In particular, the United States argues that free market capitalism and democracy break down barriers that stand in the way of greater regional prosperity.

Policies encouraging regional competition rather than national distance better serve all three national economies. As the United States sees it, Canada and Mexico have nothing to fear in the long run; their political economies will be stronger if they adopt these policies. Weaker, smaller economies have more to gain potentially in relative terms than does even the United States from a regionalism based upon openness, competition, and interdependence. With the United States as the mainspring of this triumvirate, everyone wins.

This U.S. outlook does not always coincide with those of Canada and Mexico. But it is not necessarily in conflict with them either. Although some mistrust of the United States still lingers, its neighbors are now less skeptical of the United States and of its views of the relationship than at almost any time in history.

Canada has its own perspective on the partnership emerging from Canada's long-standing relationship with the United States and its growing expectations about this bilateral relationship within the context of a competitive world economy. As the only other developed country in mainland North America, Canada regards North America as the basis for a unique partnership. Some Canadians once entertained the vision of a trilateral alliance of Canada, Britain, and the United States (Haglund 1990–1991: 89). But today its vision has become more telescoped. Canada's aspirations for North America rely on the idea that the United States is and will remain Canada's lifeline to a highly competitive, globalized world.

Canadians historically saw the United States as a friendly giant sometimes prone to error. But another view competes with this one. The Canadian perspective on North America revolves around how to preserve Canada and make it prosper even as U.S. involvement expands into Canadian society. To ardent nationalists, this is a Faustian bargain that may mean the end of Canada as a distinct nation. To the internationalists, this is the only viable strategy to ensure Canada's survival and prosperity. Canada's star is hitched to the United States, and the new partnership deepens and reinforces Canada's fate.

Canada's actions reflect this view. Canada has adopted a worldly approach to international engagement for many years. For many years, it has committed itself to multilateralism, morality, and peacekeeping.

Although far weaker than the United States, Canada has an international perspective more in tune with that of a great power. Even so, Canada's internationalism cannot hide its increasing focus on the United States.

As long ago as the 1920s, "a powerful United States held the continent in its hand. It needed only to squeeze" (Granatstein and Hillmer 1991: 72). Canada accepts the first as self-evident. But now it hopes to avoid the squeeze. Canada seeks closer ties, but it wants to be cautious. If Anglophone Canada is preoccupied with distinguishing itself from the United States, a greater embrace with economic and political implications may make this even harder to do. The Quebec issue also looms on the horizon for the new partnership. Closer to the United States culturally than they are to the Quebecois, the majority of Canadians may find themselves drifting toward the United States and away from an independent Quebec state.

Despite the warmth radiating throughout the relationship during much of the decades of the twentieth century, Canadians do not always see the United States the way Americans do. Canadians are not always convinced that the United States always knows what it is doing or that it has Canada's national interests at heart. In other words, the United States may at times be indifferent to Canada's most central aspirations; there are even those times when U.S. interests collide with—or at least may not be compatible with—those of Canada.

Whatever second thoughts it may have, Canada has cast its lot with the United States. There is far more to gain from becoming the closest ally of the United States than from remaining more distant and independent. Although Canadians think of themselves as the moral conscience perched on the shoulder of this great power (and therefore in some fashion superior to it), Canada must remain vigilant about its own identity. The Canadian perspective will remain distinctive from that of the United States, even as it converges with it to an extent barely imaginable in the twentieth century.

Mexico has its own perspective. The Mexicans and Canadians even now remain mostly distant from each other. And like the Canadians, the Mexicans think of the United States when they think of North America. They have traditionally referred to U.S. citizens as *norteamericanos*.

For much of the twentieth century, the Mexican perspective was quite nationalistic. The United States was seen as anathema to Mexican integrity, pride, and security. In the traditional view, Mexico needed the United States economically. Still, the "barbarian of the north" could not be trusted to serve the interests of Mexico. Distance, indifference, and even hostility permeated the official relations of Mexico and the United States even as both would quietly seek accommodation across a shared border almost 2,000 miles long.

History gives some reason for wariness. Mexico's attitude was influenced by the "bad behavior" of the United States, especially in the late nineteenth and early twentieth centuries. A volatile blend of attraction and hostility colored U.S.-Mexican relations almost from the very beginning. Mexican hesitancy about a full embrace *(abrazo)* with the United States was best captured in the saying, "Poor Mexico: so far from God, so close to the United States." Even in its most nationalistic periods, especially in the 1930s and the early 1970s, Mexico understood its national dilemma. On the one hand, it relied heavily on the United States for tourism, markets, capital, and technology. On the other, it would strike defiant poses of nationalistic independence.

But the official perspective shifted markedly toward the end of the twentieth century. Mexico openly embraced the United States and North America in 1990. Mexico no longer portrays itself as a principled and sometimes feisty Third World counterweight to the heavy-handed United States. Rather than standing on the outside looking in, Mexican leaders saw themselves as fortunate insiders within North America, a privilege its Latin American neighbors did not enjoy. With Mexico's status as partner and insider, North America's southern border has become Mexico's southern border. The Mexican perspective coincides with the U.S. perspective more than it has ever done before. Mexicans do not want to be part of the United States, but they would like their country to be more like it in some ways. Their cultural, economic, and political differences with the United States still shape a distinctive view.

Pyramid or Triangle?

North American relations are mostly about the structure of power among the three states. In classic realist terms, North America is a very lopsided balance or distribution of power. To put it another way, the United States is the wealthy and hegemonic core. Canada is a wealthy but dependent partner. Mexico is the poor and weak newcomer to the region.

The United States is the regional hegemon. For more than a century, it has had the capability and the will to act like one. No one really doubts that the United States has a preponderance of power in Latin

America (Poitras 1990: 2, 29, 43). It sets the rules and insists on its privileges, but it also provides benefits to its dependent allies.

In North America this is even more true, and it carries with it some significant consequences. First, the region accords special privilege to the United States. It is the dominant rulemaker. Conflict occurs not over basic shifts in power but over enduring issues within a skewed distribution of power. Second, this asymmetry of power leads to an asymmetry of priorities: Canada and Mexico are much more attentive to the United States than the other way around. On a similar note, although all three have a lot at stake in the region, Canada and Mexico have relatively more at stake than does the United States. Finally, reciprocity dilutes raw power. Weaker than the United States, Canada and Mexico are far from powerless in their relations with it because most issues cannot be tackled let alone solved by just one state.

The U.S. public and, even more so, its leaders understand the vital interests that the United States has in its less powerful neighbors. Only Japan, Russia, Saudi Arabia, China, and Israel are ranked ahead of Canada and Mexico on this list in the 1990s. Toward the end of the 1990s, U.S. leaders and the public were slightly less likely to believe that Canada and Mexico were as important to the United States as they were at the beginning of the decade (Rielly 1999: 103).

The basic architecture of North America is straightforward. Hegemony and asymmetry make unilateralism and paternalism the classic approaches to managing the region. The United States is the hub; Canada and Mexico are the spokes. There is no important connection between the spokes except through the hub. To use another image, the relationship is a pyramid. Nothing important is done without U.S. approval or acquiescence. In this view, North America remains a sphere of influence, a unipolar system and a hegemonic one to boot.

But North America is more than a simple unipolar hegemony, for the asymmetry is filtered through a more complex way of managing relations. In this view the region is an emerging triangle. Crude power differences simply do not determine exactly how things are done all the time in North America. Rather, a partnership between mutually dependent, unequal states gives all three states at least some voice. True, the triangle has a weak leg: Canada and Mexico are still not coequal partners, and they have not as yet established strong ties between each other. One of their strongest bonds is that they are both tethered to the same hegemon. Mexico even officially suggested once that they become "strategic allies" in the region and in the world (Covarrubias Velasco

1996: 491). Shared views on U.S. policy toward Cuba and OAS involvement may turn indifference and reluctance into joint action. This would help make the triangle a more credible construct for North America. As it now stands, however, the triangle points to a possible future of genuine partnership. North America is at most a limited, unequal partnership.

Borders and Region States

The United States, Canada, and Mexico have large territories and long borders. Territorial states stress security, arms, power capabilities, and conflict. Trading states stress economics, trade, business, and interdependence (Rosecrance 1986: 136–155). If the North American states were only territorial states, they would think of their mutual borders as fences or even walls. But they also think of them as gateways and checkpoints between trading states.

As important as the borders are, not every state sees them in the same way. The Canadian-U.S. border and the Mexican-U.S. border are largely undefended. This may explain why most take them for granted. Although Mexico City, Ottawa, and Washington, D.C., perceive the borders as necessary but peripheral to their states, the people of the border regions, especially the U.S.-Mexican border, see their destiny as tied to the "other side." El Paso, Texas, is closer to Mexico City than it is to Washington, D.C.; the closest large city to it is not Dallas but Ciudad Juárez, its twin city of almost 2 million just across the Rio Grande. These borders and the regions on either side of them are key to the neighborhood.

For some, ties across borders are just as compelling as ties within a country. Private groups (nongovernmental organizations, or NGOs) are increasingly networking across both borders, especially on commercial and environmental issues (Thorup 1995: 157). Business clearly motivates the most important of these ties, but labor has begun to forge alliances as well. In 1997 the president of the AFL-CIO for the first time went to Mexico to encourage Mexican and U.S. unions to work together and to organize across the border (Dillon 1998: A3).

People and businesses in border regions come to depend on those on the other side. In the 1990s some hotels in Washington State gave a discount to Canadian visitors because of the declining value of the Canadian dollar against the U.S. dollar. Likewise, the boom-and-bust cycles of the Mexican economy over the past few decades had consequences for U.S. retailers in border towns like Laredo, Texas, whose shoppers are as likely to come from Monterrey as they are from San Antonio.

So-called region states may inhabit border areas. Region states are areas or locales of economic activity and other intense interaction among nonstate actors that often span borders (see Ohmae 1993). For example, take the Pacific Northwest Coast region of Canada and the United States. Vancouver and other areas of British Columbia strongly gravitate southward. Vancouver increasingly orients itself toward Seattle and other U.S. centers in the region as well as toward the Asia Pacific. Its identity with eastern or central Canada is compromised by this pull toward the south and west. Another region state is the south Texas border region. North–South relations are critical to this region. People and goods move north and south from one country to the other (see Table 3.1). Monterrey and San Antonio in some ways have more in common with each other than Seattle has with either. These region states increasingly take their cues from the other side of the border or the global economy.

In a similar vein, the entire U.S.-Mexican border runs east and west across a quasi nation. In the southwest United States, the Mexican tradition in culture, food, life-style, language, and society remains a vibrant force. This is "MexAmerica" (Garreau 1981). Extending from the Gulf of Mexico to the Pacific on both sides of the U.S.-Mexican border, MexAmerica has a feeling all its own. Anchoring the eastern section on

Table 3.1 Export Shares as a Percentage of Total Exports, 1990–1999

	1990	1991	1992	1993	1994	1995	1996	1997	1998	1999
U.S. to Canada	26.4	20.1	20.1	21.5	22.2	21.5	21.2	21.7	22.5	23.4
U.S. to Mexico	9.0	7.8	7.8	8.9	9.9	7.7	9.0	10.3	11.5	12.4
Canada to U.S.	74.5	75.1	77.2	78.8	80.5	79.5	81.6	82.7	85.3	87.2
Canada to Mexico	0.3	0.3	0.4	0.4	0.4	0.4	0.4	0.4	0.3	0.4
Mexico to U.S.	69.4	79.5	81.1	83.0	85.3	90.8	84.0	85.6	74.3	72.7
Mexico to Canada	0.8	2.6	2.1	2.9	2.4	2.7	1.2	1.9	4.2	4.5

Sources: Calculated from IMF 1997: 318–319, 148–150, 452–453; IMF 1999b: 156, 273, 467–469; IMF 1999a: 72–72, 167–168, 246–247; IMF 2000, 168, 247–248, 72–73.

the U.S. side is south Texas. If it were a separate U.S. state, the border counties of south Texas would be the fifty-first in terms of individual income in the United States. In that sense it is part of the global South. It thus may have more in common with northern Mexico than it has with New England.

Enduring Issues

North America is in many ways quite fortunate, but it does have impressive problems, which are different in magnitude but not in kind from those facing Europe and to some extent the Asia Pacific. Perhaps more than anything, problems and issues facing North America put to the test the idea that neighbors can be partners.

Unlike those of northeast Asia, the Indian subcontinent, the Balkans, or the Middle East, North America's issues rarely are matters of life and death on a large scale. Still, they are important. Some of the issues facing North America arise from the close proximity of the states. Many are also the consequences of modern, interdependent economies. Some emerge from regional peculiarities and national differences. More than that, the North-South divide in North America puts its own imprint on some of these issues. Although many are economic and political, others are more cultural and political in nature. Some issues bedevil policymakers on a day-to-day basis. Others are the backdrop of the North American stage, occasionally reaching the agenda of one or two states. The issues of North America are concerns and even threats. But there are few readily identifiable villains. For North America, the issues revolve around the quality of life as well as who may win and lose from the choices to deal with these issues. If North America is unable to make progress on intraregional problems, then it is hard to be optimistic that any other region in the world could.

Trade

The intense exchange of goods across borders is part and parcel of North American relations (see Table 3.2). This was not always the case. During the twentieth century, all three states shifted their focus. They are prone now to look toward each other rather than to turn inward. Instead of threats to security and territorial integrity, the United States, Canada, and Mexico are more concerned about competing more effectively in the world's political economy.

Table 3.2 Ranking of North American States on Six Trade Dimensions

Size of exports in U.S. $ volume
1. U.S.
2. Canada
3. Mexico

Growth of intraregional exports (1990–1996)
1. Mexico
2. U.S.
3. Canada

Growth of trade dependence
1. Mexico
2. Canada
3. U.S.

Top U.S. trade partners
1. Canada
2. Japan
3. Mexico

Top Canadian trade partners
1. U.S.
2. Japan
3. United Kingdom

Top Mexican trade partners
1. United States
2. Canada
3. Japan

Sources: Data calculated from United Nations 1997: 122, 34, 198; Cremeans 1998: 318–319, 148–150, 452–453.

Manufactures and commodities (especially energy and agriculture) are the key components of North American trade (see Table 3.3). The most important exports among the three are equipment or machinery (especially autos and electronics), chemicals, petroleum, minerals, and food. Trade in services (banking, consulting, financing, etc.) are also increasing under the more liberal rules of NAFTA.

Investment and Jobs

Trade and foreign investment go hand in hand, at least in North America. A firm with operations in two or more North American countries will trade its own products or parts of products across borders to its other operations. This intrafirm trade makes up about two-thirds of all trade between Mexico and the United States (Gonzalez and Velez 1995). The story is largely the same with Canada and the United States (Blank 1993: 2). In the past, U.S. firms often set up assembly plants in Mexico, for example, through the *maquiladora* program, and in Canada,

Table 3.3 Rankings of Commodities in Intra-North American Trade, 1996

Exports	Imports
United States	
1. Transportation equipment	1. Transportation equipment
2. Electrical and electronic equipment	2. Electrical and electronic equipment
3. Industrial and commercial machinery	3. Crude petroleum and gas
4. Chemical and allied products	4. Industrial and commercial machinery
5. Primary metal products	5. Primary metal products
Canada	
1. Transportation equipment	1. Transportation equipment
2. Crude petroleum and gas	2. Industrial and commercial machinery
3. Primary metal products	3. Electrical and electronic equipment
4. Paper and allied products	4. Chemical and allied products
5. Industrial and commercial machinery	5. Miscellaneous
Mexico	
1. Electrical and electronic equipment	1. Electrical and electronic equipment
2. Transportation equipment	2. Industrial and commercial machinery
3. Crude petroleum and gas	3. Transportation equipment
4. Industrial and commercial machinery	4. Chemical and allied products
5. Apparel and related products	5. Agriculture and livestock

Source: Adapted from Cremeans 1998: 80–82.

for example, through the auto agreement of 1965. Parts manufactured in the United States could be sent to these assembly plants. Or parts manufacturing could be carried out in Mexico and in Canada. U.S. firms found it more cost-effective to move assembly and parts operations away from the traditional centers for car manufacture in the United States. This has fueled a regional trend; the auto industry is becoming increasingly "continentalized." General Motors is a major player, especially in the Mexican border region with the United States. In the 1990s the GM parts subsidiary, Delphi Automotive Services, was Mexico's largest private employer (Dillon 1998: C4). Such trends mean that the border region in Mexico attracts investment, reducing Mexico City's role in the national economy, and the border area offers higher wages than other areas of Mexico (Hanson 1997: 131).

Jobs are a highly charged issue in all three countries. It goes beyond numbers of jobs; it is also about "better" jobs created by investment. In the 1990s Canada feared that U.S. plants were more efficient than their U.S. subsidiaries in Canada and jobs would therefore be lost through plant closures. U.S. opponents of trade and investment liberalization fretted about the transfer of jobs to Mexico from the United States. We return to the auto industry on this point. Relocating plants from the United States to Mexico and Canada has created an issue out of jobs. In 1998 the strike by United Auto Workers (UAW) against General Motors was motivated in large part over the fear that U.S. workers would eventually lose out to Mexican workers. In the 1990s GM auto parts plants in Matamoros paid Mexican workers $1 to $2 an hour, whereas GM's Delphi East Factory in Flint paid its workers an average of $22 an hour. General Motors has fifty such plants in Mexico and sought to close two plants in Michigan (Dillon 1998: C1).

The job issue can cut both ways. The United States must also live by its own standards or be called to account if it does not do so. Of course, NAFTA was mostly written for the benefit of business and in the defense of national sensitivities (Stevis and Boswell 1998: 10). It was not a social contract. Each country retains its own domestic standards of wages, safety, and working conditions. There are no "common minimum standards" for North America.

Although most of the early complaints about treatment of labor were filed against Mexico, enforcing domestic standards is not just a Mexican issue. In 1998 four Mexican unions filed a complaint with their government that the U.S. government, Washington State, and U.S. apple growers did not uphold rights guaranteed under the labor accord of the NAFTA because Mexican workers were alleged not to have been adequately protected from the use of pesticides under U.S. law (Greenhouse 1998: A14). Without common standards, the labor issue becomes a matter of each country's living up to its own standards in the eyes of its North American neighbors. Different standards, labor mobility, and growing interdependence promise to keep labor issues at the top of the North American agenda.

Immigration and Human Rights

The movement of people is another issue—primarily how it should be regulated but also about how people from one country should be treated in the other country.

Immigration can be temporary or permanent. Within North America it is both. For more than a century, Mexicans have gone to *el norte* to seek wages unavailable to them in their own country. They may return to Mexico with remittances for their families, or they may stay in the United States for years. Income gaps and the North-South divide in the region guarantee that this issue will not soon evaporate. Canada and the United States import workers; Mexico exports them.

The leading North American state for immigration is Canada. Canada has twice the percentage of foreign-born than does the United States. What is more, Americans, Canadians, and Mexicans choose other North American countries after their own as a preferred place to live. Decades ago, as many as one-fourth of all Canadians migrated to the United States. More Americans live in Canada than in any other foreign country; Mexico is a distant second choice for Americans living abroad. Although human mobility in the region is quite high, the essential controversy exists on the issue of net migration from Mexico to the United States.

Many Mexicans go north legally, entering under provisions of U.S. immigration laws about family unification, skilled labor, and the like. Many gravitate to California, the Southwest, Texas, and the Midwest. Legal immigration, too, raises issues for the United States, but the binational issue that mars cordial relations between the United States and Mexico is not the fine-tuning of the laws on immigration but the issue of illegal or unauthorized migration of Mexicans to the north.

The U.S.-Mexican border is often the focus of attention. Each year the U.S. Border Patrol detains more than 1 million people coming into the United States from Mexico. (Some of these are not Mexican nationals.) The total number of illegal Mexican immigrants in the United States at any one time can only be guessed, but it probably does not exceed several million by much.

U.S. efforts to restrict immigration are an uphill battle. Steps to tighten up the border have often been perceived as anti-Mexican south of the border. Beefing up border enforcement, emphasizing work skills over keeping families together in U.S. immigration law, and treating Mexican immigration on a par with that from other countries signal the unwillingness of the United States to take dramatic steps to legalize in large numbers this flow of people to the north. At times the United States has allowed amnesty for undocumented aliens (which allows them to legalize their status in the United States) and even encouraged legal aliens with permanent residence in the United States to become citizens.

Immigration has become wrapped up with human rights. The Mexican government has spoken out on the treatment in the United States of illegal Mexicans, arguing that their status should not be taken to mean that these individuals do not have human rights. They are not legally criminals under U.S. law. The issue was further inflamed when local and state initiatives, especially in California, sought to restrict the benefits of legal immigrants and to abandon bilingual education programs. Of course, Mexico is hardly a paragon of human rights protection. U.S. critics have certainly made that point many times, as have groups such as Amnesty International. Torture, imprisonment, and other acts against Mexican citizens have come to light time and again. Canada and the United States, as I have mentioned, have also been criticized internationally for their treatment of minorities.

Narcotics and Crime

Narcotics trafficking is a major regional issue for which there seems to be no easy answer. It involves economic consequences, political will, and criminal activity in and out of government. Illegal drugs usually flow north toward the wealthy, consuming markets. Mexico is a leading supplier or at least the principal intermediary for these drugs from Latin America. More than half the cocaine, 80 percent of the marijuana, and about one-fourth of the heroin that flows into the United States come from or through Mexico (Schultz 1997: 5). Narcotrafficking across borders is a problem no single state is capable of solving on its own.

The drug trade is viewed differently across North America. The United States regards narcotrafficking as a law enforcement problem and a major health and political issue. Professional law enforcement, interdiction of supply, high-tech equipment, an effective judiciary, and sting operations are the preferred U.S. weapons in the drug war. Without Mexican cooperation, however, this strategy of going to the source is myopic. Mexico agrees that such tactics may be necessary, but its position is that it is not enough. Focusing on the flow of narcotics north is not going to work. The United States must do more to dry up demand for these drugs. Narcotic flows northward are also economically and politically driven.

One thing is for certain: Narcotrafficking is a vast enterprise. In 1994 Mexico earned between $7 billion and $30 billion from the drug trade. Drugs are the country's major export crop (Schultz 1997: 2). The drug trade has a vast impact on Mexico's economy, and the war on drugs may have a major impact on its politics. The involvement in drug trafficking extends high into the upper reaches of government, police, and military. The Guadalajara and Tijuana cartels in particular may have vast political influence in Mexico. Even the army is not immune. General Jesús Gutiérrez Rebollo, head of an antidrug agency, was arrested and convicted of protecting one of the drug cartels in 1997.

Corruption by itself does not cause drug trafficking, but it does allow it to continue. Corruption weakens the coordinated efforts of Mexican authorities and U.S. officials to enforce drug laws. Drug enforcement, not just the drug trade, can have a major impact on Mexican politics as well as on Mexican-U.S. relations. The U.S. Congress has at times sought to decertify Mexico as an ally in the war on drugs. Taking umbrage at this, the Mexican president assailed the U.S. legislature for scapegoating and for its insensitivity to Mexican sovereignty (Clymer 1997: A7).

Tension and conflict between the United States and Mexico erupted more than once over drug issues. In the late 1990s, a particularly serious incident illustrated how relations can be affected. A U.S. drug sting operation (Operation Casablanca) was carried out in Mexico without prior knowledge or approval of the Mexican government. U.S. authorities were targeting some Mexican bankers who were laundering drug money. Mexico's foreign minister charged that the operation had harmed "our mutual confidence" (Sheridan 1998: 7A). As a result, the United States and Mexico signed a pact in 1998 about cross-border undercover operations (True 1998: 1A).

Crime in general is also a permanent challenge for these neighbors. Counterfeiting, smuggling, and money laundering are only some of the issues that the judicial authorities of the United States, Canada, and Mexico are constantly trying to deal with on a joint basis. The picture is clouded by federalism, as Canadian provinces and U.S. states have considerable authority to enact laws on criminal matters, complicating attempts at cooperation.

Greening the Borders

In the 1990s the environment came to the fore as an issue among the North American states. Water pollution, sewage treatment, air contamination, and the like are the major environmental problems along the borders, especially the U.S.-Mexican border. The high growth of assembly plants (or *maquiladoras*) on the Mexican side of the border went hand in hand with environmental contamination. U.S. businesses with plants in Mexico avoided U.S. pollution laws and counted on Mexico's lax enforcement of its own environmental laws. Prior to 1994, the North American approach to border environments was weak, haphazard, decentralized, and fragmented. One result was that the U.S.-Mexican border witnessed a free trade boom accompanied by environmental degradation. In the immediate post-1994 era, things were slow to improve. Promises to clean up the environment were made to secure free trade. The trade has come; the environmental cleanup has not.

Cultural Identity

Some issues are not always on the front burner of all three domestic agendas in North America. Cultural identity is an example. Even so, cultural identity sets the tone or context for North American relations; people more than states are sensitive to cultural identity. At times, especially in Canada, cultural identity can surge forward as a public issue with the potential to affect North America.

Growing economic integration may perhaps awaken cultural insecurity. It may call forth a sense of popular unease about sustaining a distinct cultural identity. To use Barber's terms, McWorld confronts Jihad (Barber 1995). North America is moving toward a more integrated, consumer society in which products and life-styles become more standardized and less unique. Identities may seem overwhelmed by economic trends. The Canadian sense of identity has spawned anti-American feelings from time to time (Doran 1984: 100). The debate over NAFTA in the early 1990s simply highlighted the growing concern over the issue. Canada's civil society rather than Canadian leaders forced the issue of placing identity and culture on the nation's foreign policy agenda (Belanger 1998: 18).

English-speaking Canada is more sensitive to the intrusions of U.S. culture and mass media than are the Quebecois. The fear is that Anglophone Canada and the United States will become essentially indistinguishable in a more economically integrated region. Anglophone Canadians may have more in common culturally with Americans than they do with Francophone Canadians. Sharing language with the Americans, many Canadians are a convenient market for U.S. mass media.

As the larger of the two, the United States has a greater capacity to absorb cultural influences from the outside without the same sense of concern. Canadian culture is more influenced by the United States than by any other outside factor. Of course, Canadians have made their way into U.S. popular culture as well. Celine Dion, Jim Carrey, Peter Jennings, Michael J. Fox, Alanis Morrisette, and Shania Twain have carved out personal niches for themselves in the entertainment industry. Vancouver and Toronto have become important centers for the filmmaking industry largely controlled by U.S. interests or oriented to that market.

Mexico's identity may be less of an issue. After all, it does have a cultural identity distinct from the rest of North America. This puts some distance between itself and any cultural imperialism from the north. Mexicans admire and resent U.S. cultural influences. Books, magazines, films, and television programs from the United States find their way into Mexican society. The vibrant cultures of Mexico are the most important antidote to U.S. cultural imperialism. Still, the influence of U.S. culture, especially as mediated through the entertainment and publishing industries, is growing in Mexico. Like France, Mexico has tried in the past to restrict English in several public venues, such as trademarks and advertising. None of this has had a major effect. With the deregulation of the Mexican state in the more recent neoliberal era, U.S. culture along with U.S. consumerism will grow in importance for Mexican society.

The United States is also culturally sensitive to regional trends. A cultural identity crisis of sorts appears in the United States in a somewhat different guise. Ethnicity, language, and culture are becoming issues within some segments of U.S. civil society. The debate over NAFTA in the early 1990s had a strong undercurrent of cultural and ethnic politics. Nativist and populist resentment against Mexico bubbled to the surface within domestic fora. The emotional tenor of the debate in some circles clearly went beyond the economic issue of jobs and job displacement.

Autonomy

In a hegemonic region such as North America, the issue of sovereignty and independence lurks just below the surface. Liberalism has been stronger than nationalism in much of the region for more than a decade. This has meant that Canada and Mexico have jumped on the U.S. bandwagon rather than try to balance against encroaching U.S. power. Yet fears of U.S. domination have not entirely evaporated. It is simply that the benefits promised from engagement and accommodation with the United States are more seductive.

The regional tilt toward the United States has yet to lead to a severe nationalist backlash within Mexico or Canada. Canada and Mexico have expressed their positions; they have insisted on independent stands on some regional issues. What is more, they have at times sought to stake out independent foreign policies on some issues. The leeway for displaying such autonomy is not great, but it does exist. As the idea of a new, limited partnership comes to dominate North American regionalism, Canada and Mexico may be expected to be more rather than less assertive, especially on issues peripheral to the growing economic interdependence of North America. Although neither may actually form a bilateral alliance that smacks of an attempt to balance or offset the United States, they may assert independent positions in the absence of Cold War rigidities. Shared interests and grievances may make it easier for Canada and Mexico to work more closely together. Canada and Mexico do share an affinity for Europe, Latin influences, and state activism. They also have common interests in joint peacekeeping efforts, inter-American diplomacy, and having extrahemispheric influences serve as counterweights to the United States (Spicer 1995: 26–27). They have been particularly vocal in their opposition to the Helms-Burton provision in U.S. law that attempts to restrict third-party economic relations with Cuba.

North America Rising?

The process of inventing North America involves many nuances. The rise of North America as a region is about unity amid diversity. It is also about getting along and dealing with issues under sometimes trying circumstances. Perspectives, power, equality, and partnership must be juggled within a unique region in the face of enduring issues facing the welfare of all three states. That the states of North America are working with and through their peculiar endowments to address common problems is a sign that they may be on their way toward inventing North America.

The three states of North America have long been neighbors. Now they are also becoming partners in a limited and perhaps unique fashion. The national perspectives on the region reveal diversity as well as convergence. Although U.S. power in the world may be ambiguous in the post-Soviet world, it is not so in North America. Yet U.S. hegemony does not mean that paternalism, unilateralism, and domination are strategies for regional management. It may mean, however, an inordinate influence for the hegemonic state over how things are done. This is why the partnership is limited. A partnership of unequals must still be based upon the realities of an interdependent neighborhood.

4

GLOBAL FORCES

By the late twentieth century, potent influences began to shape the world system. The end of the Cold War, new relations among advanced capitalist states, the increasing globalization of trade and production, shifting patterns of international finance, and new ideological currents favoring more openness and less regulation were strong impulses sent throughout the world's political economy. There were many ways for states to respond to these trends. One was regionalism.

Responding to change carries with it great uncertainties and opportunities. Because globalization, multilateralism, and regionalism affect both absolute and relative gains, they promised to help some states and not others. Shifts in power were on the horizon. Increased competition on a global plane might call for extraordinary responses. And since not everyone agreed on how to participate in this brave new world order, reactions to the global trends varied. For North American leaders, a regional response to global trends made sense. The United States, Canada, and Mexico wanted to have their cake and eat it, too.

The global trends of the late 1980s and early 1990s posed important challenges. Wary but hopeful, North America faced two essential facts of life. First, as impressive as it was, U.S. power to manage the tripolar world economy was limited. The United States was the last superpower, but it did not exercise global hegemony. Second, U.S. frustrations with multilateralism pushed a regional response to the forefront. The slow progress in the Uruguay Round motivated the United States to find a lever for tilting multilateralism in a U.S. direction. The United States wanted globalization on its own terms and by its own rules. The U.S. shift toward regionalism was a way of making a statement on this point and, in a limited way, even living by its own version of globalization in North America. In the early 1990s, these factors helped to drive the regionalist response for the United States and to some extent for the other two states. By the end of the century, some of these began to change again, affecting perhaps the commitment of all three to the future of North American regionalism.

U.S. Power

Much—perhaps too much—has been made of the United States' status as the last superpower. The collapse of the Soviet Union is less important for the world political economy than is the shift in power among advanced capitalist states. It is on this score that U.S. power remains formidable but by no means overwhelming.

With the end of the Cold War, the United States searched for a new strategic vision. So far, it has not had much luck. Nothing with the panache or appeal of "containment" has been devised as a post–Cold War touchstone for U.S. strategy in the world, though not for lack of trying. In the mid-1990s, the United States did embrace "democratic enlargement" (Brinkley 1997: 117–127). This implied that the former Soviet Union and its allies, as well as large segments of the global South and Asia, would jump on the bandwagon. A world that practiced democracy and capitalism of some sort would be congenial to U.S. interests. But this sidestepped some issues about how the global economy would work in a world of differing interests and systems of capitalism.

U.S. power in the world is tied more and more to political economy and less and less to grand strategy of peace and war affecting the balance of power among great powers. The world of the trading state is the world the United States must deal with. Less than one-fifth of the U.S. economy depends on world trade, but the United States is rapidly immersing its economy into a world political economy. Better-paying jobs are tied to U.S. economic activity abroad. International financial centers are now scattered across the world; equity markets in Asia and Europe are watched as carefully as Wall Street. Even an economy as large as the United States is so intermingled with the world that it is misleading to talk about Ford or Coca-Cola as really "American." Electronic money, outsourcing of production, and international finance make it difficult and even arbitrary to speak of truly national economies. The line between U.S. economic power and that of the world is becoming blurred. Although the U.S. economy accounts for about 22 percent of the world's economy and is twice as large as the next biggest economy, that of Japan, globalization dilutes the role of any one economy or any one state in the world economy. Being number one does not carry the same weight it once did.

North American regionalism is a response to U.S. power in this world. It is an attempt to bolster U.S. leverage and influence. Its economic power is potent but, whether emanating from the U.S. Treasury Department or from Wall Street boardrooms, it is sometimes a dubious tool of leadership and management. One way to deal with this is to think globally but also act regionally. A formalized region of North America does not enhance U.S. power in the world to any great extent because Canada and Mexico are so much smaller than the United States. But it does afford some marginal advantages. By creating a regional arrangement in North America that it can dominate, the United States is able to convey its message about power, competition, and its rules of the game. Canada and Mexico are there to validate U.S. credibility.

Multilateralism

In the 1980s and early 1990s, slow progress in the Uruguay Round of GATT made the regional option more attractive. Regionalism could also be used as a lever to push ahead with the multilateral negotiations. North American regionalism thus came to the fore at the same time as the GATT negotiations were going through the final stages. In 1994, the year NAFTA came into force, the new era in the GATT began with the creation of the World Trade Organization. North American regionalism must be understood within the context of multilateralism.

The United States never really wavered on multilateralism, or at least on what it generally sought from multilateralism. When the current multilateral movement began in the 1940s, the United States had more economic power relative to its allies than it did in the late twentieth century. The Bretton Woods system devised in 1944 fashioned an architecture for the world economy. It called for a multilateral system and set of institutions to create a more liberal world economy, underwritten by the U.S. dollar. A few years later, the GATT established the foundation for a liberal trading order based upon the most-favored nation principle. But it was not until the collapse of the socialist bloc and the gradual conversion of the Third World to its principles that GATT became as universally accepted as it now is.

The multilateralists strove for consensus. GATT members live by rules applied to all states without discrimination on the basis of preference or situation. And all accept the principles of indivisibility, joint action, and a wide distribution of gains to states (Ruggie 1996: 20). The economic ethos was a community of like-minded states even when disagreements erupted among some of the members.

Although broad, the consensus was not always very deep. To keep multilateralism on track, national differences over world economic policy were tolerated up to a point. This meant that the varieties of capitalism in the advanced economic world would be allowed to participate in the multilateral movement. At this point multilateralism was made safe for diversity. Early on, negotiated trade agreements under the GATT sought incremental gains that would preserve the consensus. These were inclusionary. They made room for the liberal market economies such as the United States, the developmental capitalism of Japan, and the social market economy of Germany (Garten 1992: 108–109). The global economy was gradually multilateralized without becoming harmonized. For example, no GATT policies regulated domestic relations between state and market; no common trade policies were mandated (Goldstein 1993: 225).

Regionalism was also allowed under multilateralism. At the height of the Cold War, Europe's road to regional integration was widely applauded in the advanced capitalist world. The Soviet bloc would have little or nothing to do with economic multilateralism, but the United States was willing to make economic concessions to its allies during the Cold War to gain their fealty over military and strategic issues. During the Cold War, it accepted GATT rules that were not in its own best interests (Goldstein 1993: 222). Although the United States may have had the power to impose its will in the late 1940s, it was sometimes reluctant to do so.

It was when U.S. relative power began to fade in later decades that the conflict over multilateralism became more pronounced. The end of the Cold War put multilateralism to the test. Differences over more advanced levels of multilateralism and the harmonization of policies around market precepts became a trial by fire for the GATT. As time went on, the United States and other market-oriented states began to press for more liberalization of the multilateral regime. Disputes became fissures in the late 1980s and the early 1990s over the multilateral trade negotiations (MTNs). Multilateralism was being tested as more and more was expected of it.

Quarrels with Europe were particularly difficult. U.S. frustration over the Uruguay Round centered on liberalizing agricultural trade and ending nontariff barriers (NTBs) and in particular state subsidies. The EU worked toward a regional position on these issues, but national politics interceded. For example, French farmers remained particularly adamant in their opposition to further liberalization of agricultural trade. For their part, Japanese negotiators also resisted the end of NTBs. All told, the Uruguay Round dragged on for eight years during the 1980s and 1990s.

Frustrations with multilateralism encouraged the United States to consider alternatives. To move MTNs closer to its own positions, the United States turned to regionalism in the 1990s. Multilateralism might turn out to be more to its liking if it were linked to two other strategies. First, regionalism could be a faster track toward liberalization because the United States had greater control over trade and trade-related issues in its own bailiwick (Bhagwati 1995: 13–14). Regional integration agreements such as NAFTA could proceed more rapidly and with more far-reaching liberalization among fewer members (Caporaso 1993: 61). Second, a regional agreement might also be the leverage needed to make the multilateral negotiations more fruitful (see Hoekman and Kostecki 1995: 214). Regionalism could hedge U.S. bets against multilateralist stalemate or perhaps make multilateralism more friendly to U.S. preferences.

Multilateralism and regionalism at the turn of the century were similar in a key respect: They were international policies about liberalization and globalization. Therefore one cannot be understood without the other. Indeed, Article 24 of the GATT allows for regional trade. There are two conditions: Completely free trade must occur within the region; trade barriers to nonmembers do not have to be eliminated but they cannot be raised (Hoekman and Kostecki 1995: 218). North America aspired to meet these two conditions.

Regionalization

The world economy is built upon economic regions. Most world trade takes place within regions rather than between them. The most dynamic and advanced economies of the world are located in one of three regions. The lion's share of the world's GNP comes from this tripolar economy, concentrating world economic power in North America, the Asia Pacific, and Europe.

Such regions do not have to become economic fortresses. Rather, it may mean that economic power has moved away from one pole or center and is dispersed or diffused among three power centers. The United States anchors the "dollar bloc" in North America, although the dollar remains a preferred currency in much of the world. (More than half of all U.S. currency is held outside the United States.) Germany, along with France, is the core of the "euro bloc." Despite the economic travails of Asia during the 1990s, Japan's "yen bloc" anchors the Asia Pacific. Each region conducts important economic relations with one or two of the other regions. North America trades more with Asia and Europe than either of those two does with the other. In other words, the world economy rests on the pillars of tripolarity.

The world's three most important regions straddle two fundamental realities. The first is that a multilateral, interdependent world feeds off cooperation and absolute gains (Caporaso 1993: 63). The second is that the world of regional economic areas is centered around trade and investment and based upon discrimination and relative gains. The first reality is free market globalization. The second is the reality of distinct, preferential regions (Stallings and Streeck 1995: 67). One is the world of competitive firms in the unfettered market. The other is the world of competing states and firms. The world economy is therefore a stage for paradox. The forces pulling toward unity coexist with those of diversity. Linkage and rivalry likewise mark the global economy. This blend of forces makes for a "difficult coexistence" (Grilli 1997: 194–233).

It is no wonder, then, that in this way the rise of North American regionalism makes sense in a global context. Caught between these two realities, the North American states opted for playing both ends against the middle. Faced with a more modest role in the world economy and confronting fierce competition from the east and west, North America began to think of itself as an economic region within a larger, very competitive economy.

The United States had geoeconomic strategy in mind. North America served larger goals. But why did Canada and Mexico go along rather than remain firmly tied to multilateralism? Like the United States, Canada and Mexico sought to hedge their bets in a new high-stakes game. All of North America has been solidly in the multilateral camp since Mexico joined the GATT in 1986. Their leaders recognized many of the opportunities and threats ahead.

In the fiercely competitive world beyond North America, it was better to find a refuge than to face the challenges alone. If Canada and Mexico did not find a regional refuge, then they would be left to navigate the multilateral seas on their own. This meant that Canada and Mexico came to regionalism out of necessity and out of hope. It was not a goal so much as it was a strategy. Canada had sought a new partnership with the United States in the 1980s. Europe and Britain were out of the question for Canada. The same was true of Japan and the rest of Asia. It could have good ties with them, but it could not be in their club. Unsurprisingly, it sought and found sanctuary close to home. To the extent that even open regionalism implies differentiation, exclusion, and discrimination, Canada wanted to be in a region that would protect its relative gains.

Mexico's understanding of world economic change was little different. When President Carlos Salinas visited Europe early in his administration, he realized that Europe put Europe first. Asia was much the same. Mexico had nowhere else to go. In 1990 Salinas asked the United States for a bilateral trade agreement similar to the one Canada had struck with its neighbor in 1988. It is from such initiatives based on the regional trends in the world that North America backed into regionalism. Canada and Mexico were not interested in each other; they were interested in the United States (Eden and Appel Molot 1992).

Asia Rising

The general trend toward regionalization in the world economy eventually engulfed North America. But it was the looming importance of Japan as a competitor that also helped to inspire North American regionalism in the early 1990s. U.S. leaders in some circles came to see Japan's ascent during the 1980s and early 1990s as predatory. Led by the United States, North America adopted an ambivalent approach to Asia. It needed the economic prowess of Japan and its Asian neighbors, but it also sought to curb Japan's role in the region. North America would be largely an "open region," but it would also attempt to deal with encroaching Japanese influence.

There is more to Asia than Japan, of course. China; Southeast Asia; the tigers of Taiwan, Singapore, Hong Kong, and South Korea; and some island states in the southwest Pacific are becoming more important as time goes on. These trading states use a particular strategy to export aggressively to the world and to curb imports from the world. In this sense, the United States has some reason to be concerned about Asian trade practices and economic policies.

With Japan leading the way, the Asia Pacific's ascent was indeed impressive. Between 1980 and 1994, Asia as a whole increased its status as a world exporting region faster than any other. In 1980 Asia accounted for 15.6 percent of the world's exports; by 1994 this had risen to 27 percent. The growth rate of the leading trading states was even higher. By way of contrast, the North American triumvirate went from about the same world share (15.4 percent) to 18.1 percent during the same time interval (WTO 1995: 38). Relative gains shifted to Asia. Yet even as the "Asian miracle" began to wear a little thin in the 1990s and Japan entered a recession, other players stepped forward. China is the most dynamic in the region, with annual growth rates during much of the 1990s averaging about 10 percent or more, or three times the U.S. growth rate.

Japan remains the preeminent influence in this loose-knit Asia Pacific region. Japan was even more dominant in the Asia Pacific than the United States was in Latin America. In 1994 Japan's exports to the Asia Pacific were about 40 percent of its world exports; U.S. exports to Latin America were $92 billion, close to 18 percent of its total exports and about the same as its exports to the Asia Pacific (excluding Japan) (IMF 1995: 436–438, 261–263). Japan's neighbors admired and even emulated the Japanese model of developmental capitalism and export-led growth. Yet Japan rejected official regionalism in Asia, even though the Asia Pacific emerged as a commercial and economic region in terms of actual activity.

With the ascent of the Asia Pacific, the "Pacific century" supplanted the "American century" in the 1980s and early 1990s. Even so, the Asia Pacific and the Americas have become more interdependent. This Pacific Rim of both Asian and non-Asian states is a transoceanic collectivity of shared economic power. Although conflicts and differences abound, the rim accounts for more than 40 percent of the world's gross domestic product. By the mid-1980s, transpacific trade between the Asia Pacific and the United States outstripped transatlantic trade between Europe and the United States. There was even speculation at the time about a global duopoly: Japan and the United States would constitute a G-2, a kind of global partnership, for management of important economic global issues (Langdon 1993: 96). But Japan is reluctant to step up to that challenge (Johnston 1991: 33). On a less ambitious level, the Asia Pacific and North America (plus Chile) in the early 1990s agreed to use the Asia Pacific Economic Cooperation forum (APEC) as a vehicle to bring free trade to the rim by 2010 for developed countries and by 2020 for developing ones. Asia and the Americas are coming together within a transregional economy.

Not all is sweetness and light, of course. That is why tension and rivalry help to explain North American regionalism. Asia's rising had something to do with inventing North America. North America, especially the United States, was alert to the westward shift in relative gains and therefore sought regionalism to keep Japan at a disadvantage in North America. Trade imbalances became crude measures of East-West animosity. The United States was combative on trade deficits. It insisted that the Asian trading states, especially Japan, open up their economies to greater imports. The trade deficits did not go away, however. The United States has also pressed for its own liberal views on protection of intellectual property rights, labor relations, and subsidies and other nontariff barriers. Even after recession in Asia, surpluses and deficits still cast a pall over North American relations with Asia, and as one might expect, most of the U.S. trade deficits with Asia are with Japan. U.S. deficits with Japan are larger than with any other state or with any other region in the world.

The conflict with Japan had all the earmarks of a classic struggle over relative gains and the role of the state in the economy. Years of public recriminations, negotiations, settlements, and renegotiations between the two did not produce a solution. The United States points to Japanese protectionism; Japan points to U.S. structural problems. They have therefore come up with different diagnoses of what is wrong. Japan charges that the United States has refused to discipline its fiscal budget, to increase its savings rate, and to live within its means. For its part, the United States says that Japan discriminates against U.S. exporters and investors by using nontariff barriers and traditional business practices that do not allow fair competition. Japan practices capitalism differently than does the United States (Thurow 1992: 118–120; Garten 1992: 109). By the mid-1990s, when North America was organizing formally into a region, neither had taken steps to fully appease the other.

As a response to Asian trade and economics, North American regionalism was forged in the crucible of transpacific acrimony. Under the guise of regionalism, the United States could decide how Japan could deal with North America. The United States insisted that certain benefits be reserved for North America. Take autos, for example. Both

Canada and Mexico wanted lower hurdles for Japanese and other "non–North American" auto manufacturers so they would qualify for national (preferred) treatment as North American businesses. The United States demanded higher hurdles. Nor did the United States believe Japanese investment should be granted the same privileges in North America as investment from within the region. NAFTA's rules on investment were tailored to fit U.S. preferences, making the United States a more desirable target for Japanese investment than Mexico or Canada (Orme 1996: 265). In 1993 the Japanese prime minister voiced his concern that NAFTA would turn North America into a "fortress." Japan was skeptical about North America's enterprise. Reading between the lines, Japan believed the message was that North America would moderately restrain Japan. Indeed, Japan was the hidden target of NAFTA (Orme 1996: 274–275).

Mexico and Canada were caught in the middle. Desiring greater Japanese involvement in the region but dependent on the U.S. economy, they were in no position to intercede as mediators between the two leviathans. Nor could they expect that Japan would run the risk of irritating the United States. Besides, Japan was more interested in the rest of Asia than in Canada or Mexico. The ascent of Japan and the Pacific Rim and their disagreements with the United States on trade and other issues made it easier for North America to become a contender in global competition.

The European Track

Europe was a stimulus for North American regionalism as well. By the early 1990s, the European Union had adopted a course of action that promised to deepen considerably European regionalism. With the end of the Cold War in Europe, it also faced the prospect of widening its experiment to include new members in central Europe. The EU had a full agenda as it made its way toward greater supranationality through monetary union. Europe's track was unique.

Through its evolution from a free trade area to a monetary union, European regionalism was something that the United States applauded in principle but chose not to emulate in practice. In fact, the other North American states also saw Europe as an exception with little to teach North America. For example, the EU sought to coordinate and harmonize domestic and monetary policies, to pool sovereignty, and even to delegate some basic prerogatives of states to a supranational authority. This remained an alien idea in North America during the early 1990s. In Europe, regional integration is the goal; in North America, modest regionalism is a strategy of independent states. The North American states stopped short of harmonizing national policies even on such matters as competition, subsidies, or antidumping (Lawrence 1996: 72).

Europe did convey across the Atlantic the idea that North America had to think about its priorities. Europe's main priority was Europe. North America had some reason to think along the same lines. The EU could become an ally as well as a rival of North America in the twenty-first century.

The EU did not withdraw from multilateralism. Still, national policies and EU policies on multilateral issues were hard to thrash out. Striving for a coherent approach, the EU had a difficult time with issues from the Uruguay Round such as liberalizing the service sector and curbing agricultural subsidies. It was not just that the Europeans did not always agree with the United States; it was hard to come to a consensus among themselves. National politics, policy divergences, and a unified European stand on multilateral issues tugged at the dynamics of the EU and made relations with the United States more problematic.

EU dynamics and multilateralist frustrations aside, North America was also responding to the idea of Europe as an economic competitor. The economic size of the EU in the aggregate is about the same as North America's, but Europe is the world's largest trader. Western Europe, which includes much if not all of the EU, accounted for more than 40 percent of the world's total merchandise exports between 1980 and 1994 (WTO 1995: 38). Not surprisingly, much of this trade is within the EU. EU trade with other regions pales in comparison. And the EU is becoming even more self-involved.

Halfway Globalization

Regionalism allows North America to take what it wants from globalization but also to practice its own variant of state and market relations. North American regionalism splits the difference between market globalization and state protection. Unable to buy into full globalization and unwilling to stay with state regulation alone, North America is taking a middle path. It becomes North America's version of globalization writ small. Managing the global economy from one center is not feasible.

Managing a smaller part of it may be. Regions are less remote for states; states with a say in globalization have more opportunities to play a role if economic relations are managed closer to home.

Globalization and regionalization may coexist. After all, they embody the same trends. But globalization dilutes the influence of any one state; states, even important ones, cannot make their preferences heard or felt so easily. Managing international economic relations in a more confined space may therefore be an option. Regions may allow for the management of economic influences in ways that cannot be done so easily on the global level (see Fishlow and Haggard 1992: 12–13). The internationalization of money and capital markets since the 1970s has made it harder for North American states as well as others to control their economies (Hirst and Thompson 1996: 196). Regionalism allows states to have more control over some areas, such as trade and investment.

Approximately half of all world trade is covered by regional trading arrangements (Lawrence 1996: 96). Regionalism relies on markets, but it does not give them free rein over international economic relations. Globalization backs the state out of managing the global economy. A region opens the door to allow the state back in. Regionalism is half a loaf. It stands between the all-or-nothing approach of extreme globalization and of national autarky. Regionalism affords states a refuge in a globalized world. North America apparently needs this as much as almost anyone.

Outside In

Why did North America launch an initiative to draw closer together toward the end of the twentieth century? The simple, quick answer may just be that it inhabits the world it does. Looking outside North America helps us to grasp why the three states of North America took official measures to move closer together.

The United States, Canada, and Mexico are more dependent upon the world economy than they ever were. They simply do not want to face alone the challenges and opportunities afforded by the international economy. The rapid changes in the world economy have prompted them to reconsider their own relations and to respond accordingly. To some extent regionalism confirms the liberal premises of globalization, but it is also a political reaction to the unnerving challenges facing them in a global economy. The competitiveness, fluidity, and complexity of the world economy have encouraged regions to exist as marginal safe havens. They provide refuge in the familiar and more manageable relations of neighbors. North America responded to power shifts, globalization, regionalization, and the changes in the other two legs of the tripolar world. By embracing regionalism, the North American states carved out a slight advantage by treating themselves more kindly than they would treat others who they know less well and who compete with them more directly. North American regionalism responds to world trends by balancing globalization of free markets and the security of preferential treatment. In that way all three states may be able to prosper in the increasingly strong crosscurrents of the globalized world economy.

5

Regional Factors

Inventing North America was a response to global forces in the late twentieth century. Yet it was about something quite a bit more than that as well. What also made regionalism possible was that it was nurtured within the region itself.

Three vital trends within North America moved the three states toward regionalism. First, the United States, Canada, and Mexico converged on important ideas and issues. Of course, seeing things in the same light did not always or even usually mean seeing eye to eye on all matters. Still, this growing convergence on economic liberalization, the role of the state, and trade relations did make it possible to move closer together.

Convergence was one thing, but politics was another. Domestic or national coalitions favoring free trade regionalism came to the forefront in all three states. The proponents of liberalization and free trade got the upper hand within national policymaking institutions, at least for a while. Without this political momentum at the time, regionalism would not have been possible.

The third factor in fostering stronger ties within North America was regionalized interdependence. In other words, the policy of regionalism was following the structural change of regionalization. The interdependence within North America gave regionalism a major boost.

Convergence

Historically, national differences and nationalist sentiments stood in the way of convergence of the North American states. Indeed, adopting U.S.

views of liberal economics was political heresy and therefore a political hot potato in nationalistic circles north and south of the United States. Canada and Mexico could not do without the United States, but they also sought in their own ways to offset U.S. domination in the region. Playing by U.S. views and rules was considered for many decades to be a slippery slope to national subservience.

Convergence no longer carries such historical baggage. Although defensiveness, wariness, nationalism, and protectionism still retain some vibrancy, to some extent they have given way to liberal, open, market-oriented views. Some see this as the Americanizing of North America; others prefer to see it as the evolution of convergence among three neighbors.

Two tendencies in North America pulled in opposite directions for more than a century. The nationalist, defensive tendency sought to keep the United States at bay. It was a strategy of balancing against U.S. power. In contrast, the liberal, integrationist tendency kept Canada and Mexico within the U.S. orbit. It was a strategy of bandwagoning in which Canada and Mexico sided with the United States in their own national interest. Trade was a barometer for these tendencies in relations within North America.

Canada and Free Trade

In the first century of U.S.-Canada relations, the nationalist tendency strongly influenced North American relations. In this formative period, economic ties were subordinated to larger goals. As U.S. power grew in the nineteenth and early twentieth centuries, some U.S. circles suspected that Canada was a Trojan horse for British interests in North America. Thus, the U.S. sought not to create a cooperative economic union with Canada but rather to disengage Canada from the British empire (Stewart 1992: 185). For Canada, the United States was an economic magnet, but it was also a political hazard. Canadians entertained fears of domination and even absorption by the United States. As early as 1818, John Quincy Adams claimed that the United States had its "natural dominion in North America." By retaining its European connection, Canada could hope to offset U.S. aspirations for a continental sphere of influence.

Of course, this was not the whole story. Mutual necessity was ever present in these bilateral ties. Economically, this meant that the liberal tendency was not entirely suppressed. In the nineteenth century, the

United States focused on tariffs as a protectionist weapon; Canada focused on reciprocal trade agreements as the Holy Grail of Canadian policy. In 1854, however, a reciprocal trade agreement between the United States and Canada allowed for limited free trade in natural resources. This was a modest step toward liberalism and cooperation. And yet politics once again intervened. In 1866 the United States abrogated the treaty. Domestic pressures and national antagonism over Canadian actions during the U.S. Civil War made it politically expendable (Doern and Tomlin 1991: 57–58). By the late nineteenth century, resentment and antagonism on both sides had led to higher tariffs and protectionism. The nationalist tendency had recaptured the high ground.

The oscillation between the two tendencies continued well into the twentieth century. By 1910 the administration of William Howard Taft had come out in favor of reciprocal free trade with Canada. The next year national elections in Canada made free trade with the United States a central issue. Framed as a choice between "Canadianism or Continentalism," however, free trade with the United States was decisively rejected at the polls. Fear and wariness carried the day once again: Even some south of the border worried that reciprocity would enhance U.S. domination of Canada.

U.S.-Canada economic relations went ahead anyway. Both economies were becoming more tightly linked. By the 1920s, U.S. economic penetration into the Canadian economy, including investment, had eclipsed the British presence. Despite high tariffs, bilateral trade boomed. A "cash nexus" cemented strong bonds between the two economies (Granatstein and Hillmer 1991: 86). Canadians welcomed the economic ties with their southern neighbor even as they disdained its crass materialism and immorality.

Early in the world depression of the 1930s, nationalist tendencies gained the upper hand. The United States and Canada slapped high tariffs on imports through the Smoot-Hawley Act and the Ottawa agreements of 1932, respectively. Yet President Franklin Roosevelt and Prime Minister MacKenzie King were able to pursue bilateral tariff reductions on lumber, fish, livestock, and other commodities. The window on trade liberalism had been opened slightly, despite U.S. isolationism and Canadian resentment over U.S. condescension. In 1938 the United States and Canada came to an agreement that lowered tariffs and excise taxes covering 60 to 80 percent of the export trade (Granatstein and Hillmer 1991: 116). Still, each saw this step toward liberalism differently. Canada tended to regard this exercise in bilateralism as a limited but practical approach to critical trade issues during the economic crisis. More visionary perhaps, the U.S. negotiators also regarded it as a small step toward eventual economic integration of the two economies (Diebold 1988: 24).

The post–World War II era was a blend of both tendencies. Close allies in World War II, both states were major supporters of the Bretton Woods system put into place after the war to promote economic liberalism. But except for a sector agreement on autos in 1965, there were no major comprehensive bilateral free trade agreements between Canada and the United States until 1988. Substantial breakthroughs in bilateral agreements were stymied over differences about trade, security, and domestic policy. For example, Canada was openly critical of the U.S. role in Vietnam. This strengthened the nationalist tendency. Canadian nationalism peaked during U.S. interventionism in the Asia Pacific and elsewhere.

Bilateral tension also grew over economic issues during the 1970s. The United States and Canada clashed openly over protectionism and U.S. power. Canadian nationalists regretted U.S. insensitivity, immoderation, and its backhanded approach to Canada's needs with the 1971 tax surcharge on all imports imposed by the administration of Richard Nixon. Growing U.S. power also fed Canadian fears about its very existence, leading President Nixon to promise Prime Minister Pierre Trudeau that the United States would not "gobble up" Canada (Granatstein and Hillmer 1991: 250).

The Canadian response was defensive. In 1971 Trudeau implied that the United States presented more of a threat to Canada than did the Soviet Union. Subsequently, Canada sought to regulate U.S. involvement in its economy through the Foreign Investment Review Agency (FIRA), created in the early 1970s. Later it created the National Energy Program to preserve national control over oil and gas. On a broader front, Trudeau sought to diversify Canadian dependence on the United States. Still, nationalism, fears, and politics made an open embrace of free trade liberalism difficult to sell in Canada and in the United States during the economically troubled 1970s.

The tide began to turn with the new decade. By the mid-1980s, the bilateral climate had warmed markedly. The United States shifted its political center to the right. Reaganism became the mantra for free market capitalism. A large state role in the economy was out of favor in the United States. Although the "imbedded liberalism" from the New Deal would survive the Reagan revolution, it was scaled back through reduced social spending, decentralized federalism, and greater advantages bestowed on the private sector.

In Canada there was a similar shift toward liberal market economics. The welfare state remained a Canadian fixture, but Canadians also welcomed economic liberalism. A more open and unregulated economy was necessary for Canada in order to sustain its productivity and high standard of living. The nationalist tendency began to recede. For example, the FIRA, created to balance against U.S. domination, completely reversed course. It was renamed Investment Canada. Its goal was to encourage foreign (mostly U.S.) investment rather than to regulate and screen it. The rise of economic liberalism in both countries at about the same time meant that convergence had replaced divergence as the dominant motif of U.S.-Canadian relations.

Mexico and Free Trade

Convergence in the south was even more dramatic than in the north. During the 1980s and 1990s, the wholesale conversion of Mexican leaders to U.S.-style economic prescriptions bordered on the counterrevolutionary. Not since the Mexican revolution in the early twentieth century had there been such a massive shift in official ideology. True, the Mexican economy from the 1930s until the 1980s had relied heavily on the United States for markets, capital, technology, and investment. Indeed, the Mexican economy had been tied to that of the United States during the prerevolutionary dictatorship of Porfirio Díaz (1875–1910). Despite these structural links, Mexican nationalism unleashed during the revolution essentially blocked any official willingness on a policy level to allow Mexico to enter the realm of market and free trade economics between the two countries. U.S.-style liberalism was often portrayed as the villain behind Mexico's underdevelopment rather than as Mexico's savior.

The nationalist tendency clearly stood in the way of official liberalism in U.S.-Mexican economic relations for much of the twentieth century. To downsize the Mexican state would have been ideological heresy as well as political suicide until the 1980s. Convergence was out of the question; U.S.-style capitalism was to be held at arm's length. Rather than exploring how to break down economic barriers between the United States and Mexico during the first half of the twentieth century, Mexican leaders gained domestic approval if and when they stood up to U.S. abuses, real or imagined, of Mexican economic sovereignty.

In Asia the Great Wall was meant to keep the Mongols out of China. In North America the Mexican state had raised its own wall to keep out the "barbarians" to the north. Even as late as the 1970s, the Mexican state erected barriers or reclaimed national patrimony in the name of state-led import substitution. This strategy took credit for some of the "Mexican miracle" by fostering industrialization during much of the twentieth century. It did this by imposing high import tariffs. The ostensible purpose of this import substitution policy was to protect Mexican businesses and to develop a national industrial economy. The Mexican state also employed subsidies, nontariff barriers, anticompetitive policies, state ownership of major businesses, and a host of interventionist strategies. This role of the state as rector of the economy collided very clearly with the free trade and open market philosophy of the United States.

After the 1910 revolution, the most volatile clash of the nationalist and liberal tendencies came in the 1930s. Petroleum was the battleground. In the 1920s Mexico was the leading producer of oil in the world. The oil industry in Mexico was owned largely by foreign investors, mostly U.S. and British firms. During the presidency of Lázaro Cárdenas (1934–1940), the Mexican state challenged the power of the foreign oil companies. The dispute peaked in the late 1930s when the foreign firms defied a Mexican supreme court ruling on behalf of striking oil workers. That prompted the government to "seize" the oil firms by invoking Article 27 of the Mexican constitution, which states that all subsoil minerals are the property of the Mexican people. Nationalization with compensation is a right of any state, but the United States was obviously displeased with this fateful step. Nevertheless, despite U.S. sanctions, including the embargo of Mexican oil exports until 1942, the Mexicans had secured their triumph.

Although the United States and Mexico were usually not so combative, the nationalization of Mexican oil did highlight the strong presence of the nationalist tendency, especially in some key areas of U.S.-Mexican economic relations. The nationalist, populist, statist tendency called for a large role for the state in the economy; it also involved a very ambitious redistributive land reform program during the 1930s. Even after World War II, Mexico's rapid development was tied to industrialization behind tariff walls and favored with government regulation.

By the 1970s and early 1980s, the nationalist tendency began to lose momentum. The "Mexican miracle" began to look a little frayed around the edges. The "stabilizing development" of the 1950s and 1960s produced high economic growth rates with government encouragement of foreign investment aimed at manufacturing for the domestic market. A stable, friendly, growing Mexico was all to the good, in the eyes of U.S. leaders. But when Mexico began to experience severe economic distress, the United States became more concerned about its traditional approach for dealing with its economic problems. Not only were Mexico's nationalist, populist, and statist tendencies at variance with U.S. wishes, but they were not working.

The mounting failures of Mexican economic policy and the resistance to liberal prescriptions for addressing these deficiencies drove a deep wedge between Mexico and the United States. In the early 1970s, the administration of Luis Echeverría (1970–1976) launched fiscally unbalanced programs to sustain growth. The state also antagonized the private sector and made huge mistakes in trying to manage the economy. The next president, José López Portillo (1976–1982), did not do much better. He poured old wine into new bottles. The nationalization of the banks and rejection of membership in the GATT in 1982 revealed that Mexico was farther than ever from the way the United States wanted it to act. In the summer of 1982, Mexico defaulted on its foreign debt. The nationalist, statist tendency was by that time in ruins.

The year 1982 was a turning point: It marked the beginning of the Mexican state's conversion to markets and free trade. Although it was not quite ready for U.S.-style capitalism, Mexico was beginning to move in that direction. First came harsh austerity in government budgets and then came neoliberal reforms of the state and the economy. Mexico was entering the liberal camp, out of desperation as much as out of conviction. Mexico cut its tariffs unilaterally from 50 percent to 12 percent on average and reduced import licensing to 20 percent of the total possible exposure. Domestically, the inflation rate was pared down from 132 percent in 1987 to 7 percent in 1994 (Bosworth et al. 1997: 4). By the late 1980s and early 1990s, the official orthodoxy was no longer government ownership, state subsidies, import restrictions, anticompetitive policies, and the like. Rather, the Mexican state had downsized and liberalized. Instead of refurbished protectionism, Mexico had embraced market economics, including the price system, deregulation, privatization, fiscal restraint, and export competitiveness. In other words, Mexico had gone from a highly regulated economy to one of the most liberal.

There was an international dimension as well. In one decade Mexico had reversed its official position on trade. Four years after refusing to join the GATT, Mexico decided to do just that. The Mexican state opened the economy, improved competition, and attracted foreign investment (De Mateo 1988: 175). In addition to the unilateral reduction of many tariffs, Mexico signed framework agreements called "understandings" on trade and other matters with the United States in 1985 and 1987. These proved to be a bridge to the eventual free trade agreement. By 1990 Mexico had decided to go all the way; it proposed that the United States sign a comprehensive free trade agreement with Mexico. This was a major breakthrough; it was also the most singular indication that Mexico had adopted free trade liberalism as its own. By forsaking the nationalist tendency, Mexico had adopted the very policies it had quite often rejected since the revolution. Mexico and the United States were now on the same wavelength.

* * *

The convergence of the United States, Canada, and Mexico was vital for North America. Without it, regionalism would have been impossible. For the United States, it required very little soul-searching. Although the United States had not always practiced free trade, it usually advocated it. The U.S. public is for greater economic ties with its neighbors (Inglehart et al. 1996: 41). For Canada and Mexico, the convergence over free trade and liberal reforms in general required some adjustment. A continental free trade agreement represented a basic shift, especially for Mexico. But convergence did not mean complete Americanization of economic thought. Canadians and Mexicans favor almost as much as Americans greater economic ties, but Mexicans in the 1990s were still more inclined to accept state intervention and non-market options (Inglehart et al. 1996: 106–108). Yet the lure of free trade with the United States was stronger than were lingering differences or the fear of U.S. hegemony. Market economics and free trade became in the 1990s a more widely shared ideology in North America. By the late twentieth century, the liberal tendency had come out on top.

Coalitions

Coalitions favoring free trade and liberalism were also responsible for bringing about a change in policy on North American regionalism. Without liberal ruling coalitions in all three states, an indispensable ingredient for making a regionalist commitment would have gone missing. As it was, the rise of such domestic coalitions at approximately the same time in the United States, Canada, and Mexico made it possible to transform convergence on economic issues into a regionalist policy.

The U.S. domestic scene proved crucial. Ronald Reagan, the "godfather of NAFTA," gave the concept of North America some support (Doern and Tomlin 1991: 105). Within Reagan's inner circle, the idea of North American convergence rested on national interests. The imperatives of energy supplies for the United States in the late 1970s partially motivated such an idea. John Sears, a Reagan adviser, argued that Mexican oil could be swapped for freer market access to the United States. Martin Anderson, another adviser, went further by making a very general case for a North American accord (Orme 1996: 35). Reagan and later George Bush invited Mexico to take the initiative by requesting such an agreement (Orme 1996: 39).

The dominant coalition of the 1980s was conservative politically and for free markets economically. After the inflation, unemployment, and recession of the 1970s, Republicans were able to capture the presidency in 1980. This is important, because without a president committed to free trade there is not much chance for its success. In fact, Reagan had given an inkling about his own views when he agreed with some of his advisers shortly before his bid for the presidency in 1980 that a North American accord should be a priority. Still, the idea stirred little interest in the early 1980s. The two U.S. neighbors were hesitant at first. In the early 1980s, Trudeau of Canada and López Portillo of Mexico were not prepared to accept such a plan (Barry 1995: 6). At this point neither Canada nor Mexico had fully embraced the market orthodoxies long defended by those in the Reagan-led conservative coalition.

The U.S. position was slow to develop as well. The conservative coalition in the early 1980s did not put free trade that high on the list. The top priority was domestic. Tax cuts, social spending reductions, deregulation, deficit reduction, and military spending were accorded the greatest importance in domestic economic policy. Still, free trade did make some sense within this ambitious agenda. The Reagan revolution's domestic agenda and the high-profile Cold War policies of the early 1980s pushed regional free trade to the back burner.

The United States left it to its North American neighbors to seize the initiative. If bilateral or even regional free trade were to move to the front burner, Canada and Mexico would have to accept the diffuse offer made earlier by the United States for a free trade agreement.

Canada responded first in the mid-1980s. It took Mexico another five years to follow suit.

The Tories and Free Trade

The emergence of the free trade coalition in Canada began unobtrusively enough. Unlike in 1911, there was no national election to put such a coalition into power. Most Canadians probably would have rejected such a move once again. Rather, the Progressive Conservatives (or Tories) under Brian Mulroney took power in 1983 without a free trade program. Indeed, before becoming prime minister, Mulroney had defended some of the protectionist sentiments of previous Canadian governments and even opposed free trade with the United States (Lusztig 1996: 72). Once in power, he was not quick to abandon the Foreign Investment Review Agency or the National Energy Program that he had opposed (Kirton 1993: 28).

By 1984 continuity gave way to a fundamental change in Canadian policy (Doern and Tomlin 1991: 16). Mulroney was at the center of the transformation. In the Canadian parliamentary system, a change of heart in the majority party leadership instantaneously created a dominant free trade coalition within the federal government. Mulroney's view of the United States and Canada helped him to arrive at the conclusion that a free trade agreement was the best thing for Canada. Acting as his own minister for U.S.-Canadian relations, Mulroney saw the United States as a benign presence; he was also the most pro-U.S. Canadian prime minister in recent memory. He believed that Canada was a mature, confident nation with nothing to fear and perhaps a great deal to gain from greater integration with the United States (Granatstein and Hillmer 1991: 293). Years after leaving office, Mulroney never regretted free trade, only its timing within the larger agenda of Canada.

The free trade coalition in Canada had foreign allies. With the conversion of the Tories to free trade, Mulroney forged a personal relationship with Reagan. The summitry between Mulroney and Reagan led to a binational coalition for free trade. The "two Irishmen" were able to create a working relationship that eventually allowed both countries to negotiate the Canada-U.S. Free Trade Agreement (CUFTA) during many months of hard bargaining in the mid-1980s.

Free traders in Canada needed all the help they could get. Free trade with the United States was politically risky. Although most Canadians were lukewarm to a trade deal with the United States, the politics of free trade in Canada must be understood within a larger context and a broader political agenda. Canadians still feared absorption by the United States and believed that a free trade deal could overwhelm Canadian social programs, identity, and culture. For some, free trade meant the beginning of the end for an independent and strong Canada. There were also worries about economic impact. Predictably, labor unions, academics, artists, women's groups, churches, charitable organizations, and even some industrial and agricultural interests as well as the Pro-Canada Network opposed the free trade negotiations. Fears about jobs and social programs motivated much of the anti–free trade forces during the 1980s. Drawing on anti–free trade sentiment in Ontario and elsewhere, the Liberals staked out their position against the agreement. The CUFTA met strong opposition.

The domestic coalition behind free trade had support, however. The pro–free trade Tories had control of the government, for one thing. For another, it could count on the support of business, bureaucrats, the press, Quebec, and the western provinces, especially Alberta and British Columbia (Bothwell 1992: 149). The government's most important single ally was no doubt the private sector. An important about-face had occurred among the business elite in Canada (Vernon et al. 1991: 27). In fact, the conversion of Canadian business interests to a free trade agreement with the United States was pivotal to the shift in coalition politics.

Two business associations were critical to the private sector's support for a free trade agreement. The Business Council on National Issues (BCNI) and the Canadian Manufacturers Association (CMA) came around to the free trade cause (Doern and Tomlin 1991: 46). The CMA experienced a remarkable turnaround. In 1980 one-third of its members favored a free trade deal with the United States. Four years later three-fourths of them did (Bothwell 1992: 144). The 1982 recession, opposition to Liberal policies in the waning Trudeau years, and fear that sector agreements with the United States would not protect Canada from U.S. "fair trade" retaliation against Canadian exports were decisive in converting powerful Canadian business interests to this departure from Canadian policy.

Other factors strengthened the hand of the free traders. The prestige of the MacDonald Commission in the 1980s added weight to their cause. The commission was a blue ribbon effort to reassess Canada and its basic public policies. The commission's recommendations supported "a leap of faith" in favor of free trade; it sought to "demythologize" free trade in Canada (Doern and Tomlin 1991: 53–54). Business support rested on the argument that Canadian business had to become more competitive and that free trade would help that come true. As time went on, free trade advocates in Canada saw the United States and continentalization of Canadian trade policy as their country's most viable option. "Canadian policy was multilateral and nondiscriminatory by preference, but manifestly North American by default" (Muirhead 1992: 182).

Canadian Politics and Free Trade

The Tories' ruling coalition had more than trade on its agenda. Mulroney was engaged in a complex game with three interrelated goals: The first two were to implement constitutional reform as a response to the Quebec issue and to bring free trade with the United States to Canada. These were to serve another goal: a durable electoral realignment in favor of the Tories. This political entrepreneurship was meant to preserve Mulroney's power in a Tory-led coalition by creating an electoral base in Quebec on the constitutional reform issue and by creating an electoral base in the west by pursuing free trade with the United States (Doern and Tomlin 1991: 50). By reconciling Quebec within a united Canada and by strengthening ties with the United States, as favored by western Canada, Mulroney hoped to set up a governing coalition that would endure (Lusztig 1996: 71).

This was not to be. Constitutional reform in the 1990s failed; Quebec's tenuous relationship with the rest of Canada still hovers ominously on the political horizon. The grand strategy of Mulroney and the Tories had come to naught. By the early 1990s, the Tories had lost all but a handful of seats in the Parliament in Ottawa. The ruling coalition had collapsed.

Only the free trade agreement with the United States, which was so bitterly debated, was to bear fruit for the domestic coalition. Canada's parliamentary system gave the free trade coalition its victory. The Canada-U.S. Free Trade Agreement of 1988 was the only success in the grand strategy of the coalition.

In the 1990s the ruling coalition in Canada got the NAFTA approved as well. Since the United States rather than Mexico was the center of free trade debate in Canada, NAFTA was easier for the ruling coalition to pass. Before leaving power, Mulroney wanted Canada in NAFTA, for defensive reasons. Being left out would risk the gains the coalition hoped to reap from its own trade agreement with the United States, signed a few years earlier. The ruling coalition in Canada had won on free trade, but the price had been steep.

Free Trade and Reform in Mexico

The free trade coalition in Mexico emerged from a very different domestic context. In the 1980s and early 1990s, Mexico's one-party system was still mostly authoritarian yet capable of some adaptability (Teichman 1997: 142). But it faced mounting pressures, both political and economic. The emergence of free trade within the existing dominant coalition was critical to domestic economic reforms. The traditional political game would be put in service to both liberalism and free trade. For President Carlos Salinas (1988–1994), free trade with the United States was the crowning achievement, and it was the fail-safe device to protect economic reform in Mexico.

The domestic ruling coalition in Mexico reinvented itself. It had gone through a gut-wrenching experience in the 1980s, almost losing the presidential election in 1988. The conversion to economic liberalization had forced political realignments and institutional change on a country that had largely stagnated politically since the 1930s. By the late 1980s, Mexico had launched a neoliberal reform with earthshaking impact. It reduced the state, privatized its holdings, deregulated the economy, opened itself up unilaterally to import competition, and joined the OECD and the GATT countries.

These policy upheavals in Mexico put a great deal of stress on the ruling coalition and on the country. The so-called lost decade of the 1980s had severe repercussions on business as usual. Economic nationalism, corporatist relations, populist programs, and state dominance of the economy were now discarded as liabilities from an era of massive macroeconomic miscalculations. The austerity programs of the mid-1980s gave way to the neoliberal programs of the late 1980s and early 1990s. Mexico had become a convert to market economics and free trade.

The political fallout was painful. The PRI had held national politics in its powerful grip since the 1920s. But the reversal of policy meant a political bloodletting. Some populist, nationalist, statist elements bolted from the party in 1987 in order to oppose the neoliberal ruling coalition of the PRI in the 1988 election. Those who remained fought for their cause within the party. Nevertheless, the new breed of young, neoliberal technocrats assumed the top positions within the party and the government. The ruling coalition was thus still in power, but it had a distinctly different political hue. The traditional power base of the PRI lost favor. Labor unions, peasant groups, and the "popular sector" of the party were shunted to one side as business and other economic elites assumed a privileged place within the new ruling coalition.

The ruling coalition in the late 1980s and early 1990s was committed to economic liberalism and free trade. It cemented together into a multiclass alliance. Elites from the public and private sector as well as traditional supporters of the old coalition were its main pillars. A duopoly of public and private elites who favored market economics domestically and free trade internationally led the coalition (Poitras and Robertson 1994: 5).

The coalition used political authoritarianism to support economic liberalism. Free trade was pursued through largely traditional means of influence and control. Salinas was the premier free trader in the coalition. But he had a formidable coterie behind him. Key ministries were instrumental in the free trade negotiations. The private sector largely rallied around the cause. Major business confederations recognized by the government, from the Employer Confederation of the Mexican Republic (COMPARMEX) to the National Chamber of Transformation Industry (CANCINTRA), either strongly backed or went along with the NAFTA negotiations. In 1990 a special coordinating agency served to link business and government in the negotiations. State-controlled labor organizations and other corporatist bodies fell into line, as expected. With party discipline largely intact, the PRI supported the president's initiative for free trade, whereas the opposition parties, whose backing was not critical to passage, were split on the issue. The public sang the praises of the coalition's cause, although typically it had little to do with such issues. The timing was fortuitous. The economic recovery in the early 1990s, after the previous lost decade, provided enough popular support for the Salinas initiative for free trade (Philips 1991: 205).

The free trade coalition had an agenda and a message. Its interests were to defend the economic reforms by locking them into an international agreement so that they could not be reversed. This meant that Mexico's economy would remain open to foreign influences. It would signal to foreign creditors and capitalists that Mexico could once again be trusted as a reliable place to invest. It would also send the message that Mexico would reciprocate and would play by the same general rules on trade and investment that the United States and Canada did. In the long haul, Mexico would be the great winner in a free trade deal including the United States. It would receive access to U.S. markets, and it would get the capital it could no longer borrow. Free trade would raise profits, competitiveness, productivity, and eventually incomes.

The opposition was no match for this juggernaut. Weak and off balance, it was marginal to the policy process or could raise only minor objections. The congress was essentially superfluous in the debate. It was excluded from most of the important deliberations. Nationalists, populists, academics, independent unions, and environmentalists objected more to the coalition's methods than to its purposes. Throughout civil society in the early 1990s, the view was that Mexico had no other choice. Despite the short-term pain for some, a free trade deal with the United States was inevitable. It simply confirmed what was already happening between the two economies. The hope was not to derail the free trade agreement with the United States and Mexico but to get the best deal possible. The opposition had been outflanked.

U.S. Politics

The free trade coalition in the United States was powerful, but it faced stiffer opposition than in Mexico. By the early 1990s the initial momentum of the Reagan revolution had lost some of its punch. Although a backer of NAFTA, President Bush was vulnerable in the 1992 election and rarely mentioned the NAFTA negotiations. A mild recession coupled with a mounting protectionist and nationalist backlash, especially in the Congress, served to make the NAFTA debate acrimonious and the vote a close call.

Free trade coalitions in the United States must be led from the top, or else they are doomed. Historically, the president is a proponent of free trade (Goldstein 1988: 180). Bill Clinton's support of NAFTA was firm, in keeping with history. But it was also qualified. In the 1992 presidential campaign, he insisted a few weeks before the November vote that side agreements on labor, environment, and import surges be incorporated into the overall package.

The pluralistic structure of the government and civil society gave the opponents ample opportunity to attack the free trade initiative. Trade had once again become a focal point for special interests (Krueger 1992: 109–111). A Democratic president in favor of free trade could not persuade most of his party to vote for it. Republicans tended to stay with the coalition, unless they were from states with significant opposition by organized labor (Conybeare and Zinkula 1996: 1).

Organized labor was the core of the opposition. Although its members would not be as adversely affected as would the lower-skilled workforce, the issue for them was the principle about the redistribution of employment within the United States rather than the issue of the net national benefit accruing to the United States from free trade. An alphabet soup of labor and other groups opposed NAFTA, and 90 percent of the top forty congressional recipients of labor political action committee (PAC) money opposed it as well (Conybeare and Zinkula 1996: 5). Environmental groups were split on NAFTA, but some did support it. Those opposed to it felt that free trade undermines local environmental regulations. Since NAFTA did not harmonize environmental rules, NAFTA was portrayed as a pollution promoter.

In the end, the free trade coalition prevailed. The main hurdle was in the House of Representatives. Under a fast-track procedure, the NAFTA agreement passed by thirty-four votes, after considerable pressure from and logrolling by President Clinton. The bitterness and acrimony over the vote was not lost on the victors or the defeated. The experience would steel resistance to the free trade coalition in the future. By late 1997 the coalition was not strong enough to authorize fast-track authority for another round of free trade agreements with other countries in the Americas or elsewhere. Domestic politics and the dominant coalition within the United States had prevailed on behalf of free trade regionalism in the early 1990s. The domestic struggle over free trade regionalism in the United States, however, has cast a pall over its immediate future.

Interdependence

North America is developing a regionalized interdependence that gives a structural foundation for the task of inventing North America.

Regionalism is the deliberate act of policymakers. The state is being used to shape and guide a process. But the process itself is broader and deeper than that. Regionalization is the process of tying together the economies and societies of a region. But regionalization is going on at many levels, in large ways and small, with or without states. Regional change and structural factors must be in place if the whole enterprise is to move ahead.

In North America, interdependence is being regionalized. This is a profound process of basic economic, technological, and developmental changes. As such, these changes are beyond the control of a few policymakers. Although these trends and changes also drive globalization, they surface within North America in ways that they do not elsewhere. For one thing, borders make a difference. Greater border transactions and economic and political ties evolve together (Deutsch et al. 1957). This gives momentum to broader and even deeper ties. As the old saying goes, familiarity may indeed breed contempt—but it can do something quite different. It can bolster trust and convergence, both of which can "gear" the process as well (Nevitte 1995: 205).

Taking Care of Business

The prime movers for regionalizing interdependence are no surprise. Businesses, especially U.S. multinationals, are the driving forces behind the growing economic integration of the region. Most large firms have global ambitions; still, North America is very important for manufacturing and marketing. Multinational firms are increasingly becoming dependent on North American markets to improve their bottom lines. Bankers, portfolio investors, and fund managers are very busy in a more fluid capital market in North America. U.S. dollars are a large part of the everyday transactions in all of North America, especially in Mexico. Investors and manufacturers rely on labor and markets of the other countries for assembly work and coproduction arrangements. North America is not one economy, but it seems to be moving in that direction.

To its consumers, North America is gradually becoming a single vast supermarket. Wal-Mart, one of the largest discount retailers based in the United States, set up outlets in Mexico and Canada in the 1990s, competing with national retailers. In Canada Zeller's, a subsidiary of Hudson's Bay, competes head to head with Wal-Mart for the same customers. The Canadian firm pitches to its customers the advantage of "buying Canadian," although many of their product lines are produced elsewhere in North America or by firms with operations in Canada and the United States. Whether produced in one or two countries, North American goods are usually marketed in three languages. Whirlpool, a trade name in household appliances, packages instructions in English, Spanish, and French. Many other consumer products are also being marketed in this way.

By the early 1990s, Canadian firms invested more dollars in the United States than the other way around (Harrison 1997: 59). Even so, the share of U.S. investment in Canada and Mexico is very large, although Canada's share of incoming foreign investment in the United States is relatively modest, at 14 percent, and even more so for Mexico, at 2.5 percent (Weintraub 1994: 21). What regionalized interdependence has done so far is to reinforce the structure of North America. Although Canada and Mexico are important to the United States, the

United States is far more important to Canada and Mexico. In this sense, the more things change, the more they stay the same.

Foreign investment in the three economies is more and more becoming North American. Trade, investment, and finance from the United States loom large in the two smaller economies. Between 1981 and 1991, U.S. manufacturers increased their share of investment in Canada. Canada's share of all manufacturing in the United States rose slightly (2.6 percent) during the same period. For their part, U.S. manufacturers in the United States had a declining but still large share of all manufacturing. It dropped from 90.7 percent in the early 1980s to 85.4 percent in the early 1990s. On the other side of the border, U.S. manufacturing in Canada rose from 24.5 percent to 27.4 percent during the same period (Statistics Canada 1993: 32–33). Foreign investment is frequently North American, but it is becoming so at differential rates.

The Mexican financial crisis in the mid-1990s illustrates quite well the mutual dependence of the region. The U.S. loan allowed Mexico to service its debt, which was owed to U.S. banks. U.S. investors and Mexican debtors were able to get the U.S. taxpayers to protect their mutual interests. Mexico had become too important to fail. Its macroeconomic mistakes had led to an ad hoc policy of state protection of private investments in Mexico. The interconnectedness of U.S. capital and Mexican financial stability was the structural reality of regionalization; the financial rescue was a regionalist response. Capital and state action had come together over the problem of Mexican financial stability. The same cannot be said for movement of labor. Capital moves without as many legal hindrances as does labor within North America.

Regional Politics

Markets may rule, but they do not rule to the exclusion of states. States find it in their own interests to cooperate with each other from time to time. North America is no exception. The ideal of sovereignty is cherished in North America, but it is not always something that can be strictly practiced. Americans, Canadians, and Mexicans put national independence above a political union of North American states (Inglehart et al. 1996: 144). North America is not Europe. But there is room for political institutions or at least rules for cooperation.

Canada and the United States have dealt with neighborhood issues in a typically low-key fashion. In a North American style, they have kept bilateral institutions weak and modest. Almost a century ago, Canada and the United States signed a treaty to create a binational commission. The International Joint Commission is specialized, advisory, and politically circumscribed (Granatstein and Hillmer 1991: 44). In 1912 it addressed the growing problem of pollution in the Great Lakes. At times the United Kingdom was asked to arbitrate or mediate disputes over fisheries. The two countries aired and made progress on conflicts regarding fisheries, boundaries, and water. As economic interdependence mushroomed in the 1920s, the United States and Canada extended their cooperative efforts to cover defense and overflight issues. Cooperation on mutual interests also led to a permanent change in U.S.-Canadian relations. The two neighbors built the St. Lawrence Seaway. There are many such examples of neighborly cooperation prior to the trilateral institutions built into NAFTA in the 1990s.

Like the United States and Canada, Mexico and the United States have cooperated largely through private negotiations, bilateral treaties, binational commissions, and ad hoc arrangements. Since the early 1980s, the Mexico-U.S. Binational Commission has met annually to discuss issues such as agriculture, culture, customs and duties, labor, science and technology, trade and investment, border cooperation, education, energy, environment and natural resources, migration and consular affairs, fishing, business promotion, transportation, and tourism. In this sense, NAFTA had its precedents. Bureaucratic alliances have developed between executive departments in both governments to deal with common problems.

Still, regionalizing interdependence does not mean the end of conflict. Politics allows for official cooperation, but interstate cooperation can run into serious problems. Although Mexican drug enforcement authorities have long cooperated with the U.S. Drug Enforcement Agency (DEA), for example, the relationship is affected by different perspectives. The Mexicans tend to believe the United States should do more to curb demand. For its part, the United States believes Mexico should do more to curb the supply (Del Villar 1988: 191–208).

At times cooperation can be hard to sustain. Frustrations over narcotrafficking can boil over. In 1997 the U.S. House of Representatives voted to impose sanctions on Mexico for its failure to make progress on the drug war (Clymer 1997). Mexico was quick to condemn the vote, officially and unofficially. Protesters in Mexico City "voted" to "decertify" the United States for its failure to slow the demand for illegal drugs.

Cooperation on the environment is another sign of state involvement. Long before NAFTA linked environmental concerns with trade,

Mexico and the United States had cooperated on transborder environmental issues. In 1889 they signed a treaty creating the International Border and Water Commission (IBWC), the oldest and most established environmental agreement between the two. Both have worked together as well through the El Paso–Ciudad Juárez common air-quality management basin and the Border Environmental Cooperation Agreement signed in La Paz, Mexico, in 1983 (Belausteguigoitia and Guadarrama 1997).

Politics is also taking place increasingly across North America's borders. Organized interest groups are working with each other across national borders. This "transnationalization of civil participation" is the venue of NGOs (Thorup 1995). Such groups have evolved to deal with commerce, immigration, human rights, and the environment.

Although politics can tap nationalist and protectionist sentiment within North America and therefore stand in the way of a more integrated region, politics is necessary to carry out the integrative process. The states of North America have a history of consultation and cooperation despite the difficulty of the problems the states have tried to manage. The state has not stepped aside in the integration process but has made modest efforts to devise mostly bilateral, cooperative ways to deal with mutual concerns in the neighborhood.

Fateful Attraction

Outside and inside North America, important forces are at work. Global and regional factors have come together to reinforce each other and to make it a distinct possibility that North America may become a more integrated region.

This fateful attraction in North America is by no means predestined. Still, pressed by their own national problems and the problems they share, Canada, Mexico, and the United States have become more aware of how they can affect, improve, or harm one another's prospects. Living in a regional neighborhood of considerable diversity but also of converging trends and interests, the leaders and peoples of the region have potent reasons for finding ways to invent a more coherent region. For North America, coming closer together does not mean the replacement of national legal independence; rather, it seems to mean the modest accumulation of regional efforts to supplement national ones.

The rise of free market ideology, the emergence of dominant coalitions in favor of free trade, and the regionalized interdependence of North America moved Canada, Mexico, and the United States toward a more self-conscious awareness of common bonds and mutual interests. What the three states do in the twenty-first century could be even more crucial. One thing is certain: The fate of North America lies at least as much within the region as it does outside the region—and perhaps more so.

6

Trading Places

Global and regional forces drove the North American three toward a closer embrace in the 1990s. Even so, a threshold for inventing North America, or at least to advance the process, had to be crossed. The United States, Canada, and Mexico had to take deliberate steps to bolster the cause of North America as a region. These measures came in small and large doses, but by far the most important were two free trade agreements. One was signed by two, and the other was signed by all three. Taken together, they signaled an unprecedented commitment to a regional agenda in North America.

"Free trade," "freer trade," or even "open trade" became touchstones for constructing a new regional experiment around these agreements. The trade agreements were more complicated than that, however. For one thing, they were imbedded with regulation. Like regional arrangements, they deregulated the regional economy at the same time they erected barriers to make sure that outsiders did not enjoy some advantages of regionalism (Fishlow and Haggard 1992: 12–13). For another, to say that the agreements were about trade was to overlook a great deal. The North American states were clearly "trading places," but they had more on their agendas than just trade.

FTA or PTA?

To their supporters, the Canada-U.S. Free Trade Agreement of 1988 and the North American Free Trade Act of 1993 are not merely regional integration agreements but free trade agreements. They argue that free trade and other market principles incorporated in the pacts reduce barriers and open up economic relations. To their critics, the two RIAs, especially the first one, are actually preferential trade agreements (PTAs) rather than free trade agreements. They include barriers to discriminate preferentially against nonmembers. One observer even labeled the NAFTA as the NAPTA (for North American Preferential Trade Agreement) (Bhagwati 1995: 2). Depending on one's vantage point, the glass is partially full—or partially empty.

Both views have something to be said in their favor. After all, markets and states alike are allotted some role in regionalism. The new regionalism espouses free market ideas, but it also allows the state to set rules governing some aspects of markets. Regionalism plays both ends against a middle position. It gives the nod toward market liberalization, but it keeps the state in. RIAs are shades of gray rather than starkly black and white on the free trade/preferential trade issue.

The RIAs of North America are also important for what they do not do. The goal behind both was freer trade (and investment). It was not a high level of integration going beyond an FTA or PTA. For example, a customs union was out of the question. That would have required that all goods and workers be allowed to flow freely across borders. It would also have required a common external tariff (CET) of all three states. What is more, a common market was more than anyone wanted. It would go too far in ending national policies and differences. Naturally, the European integration movement toward an economic union was also not in the cards for North America. To follow Europe would have meant pooling sovereignty among the North American members. Each would have surrendered a bit of sovereignty to achieve a regional goal. The North American RIAs stress something different: They are about relatively modest but significant efforts to create a regional market without moving toward a very advanced scheme of economic integration.

North America does not put regionalism on a pedestal. The national and global economies are simply too important to make regionalism the epitome of its foreign economic policy. Global trade and investment cannot take a backseat to regionalism. The United States can be regional without sacrificing the global context (see Fishlow and Haggard 1992: 11). In Europe regionalism has usually come first; in North America it does not—at least not yet.

GATT-ability

Just how do North America's RIAs fit within the multilateral picture? RIAs are permitted under Article 24 of GATT. They must meet loosely defined requirements, however. RIAs must eliminate within a "reasonable" length of time "substantially all" the trade barriers within the region (Bhagwati 1993: 27; Hoekman and Kostecki 1995: 218). "Reasonable" and "substantially all" are politically useful but maddeningly vague. Another condition in Article 24 is about outsiders: Barriers to outsiders can exist, but they cannot be increased through the RIA (M. Smith 1993: 99).

Article 24 is very broad. It is also very tolerant. Its vagueness allows virtually all regional agreements. A free trade area, customs union, common market, and economic and political union are all permitted as long as they meet this nebulous standard. For example, under Article 24 a customs union must not raise its common external tariff to levels higher than before the customs union came into existence (Bhagwati 1993: 35). For a free trade area without a CET, duties are not to be raised (Article 14, 5b). This was intended to make regional agreements compatible with later multilateralization.

Article 24's softness on regionalism did not go unnoticed. In 1994 a GATT "understanding" on Article 24 among many members attempted to deal with its leniency toward RIAs. This understanding about Article 24 cautioned members of GATT to be wary of regionalism and its impact on multilateralism. RIAs should facilitate trade among members rather than raise barriers to nonmembers. Members of RIAs should avoid creating adverse effects on the trade of other members of GATT, and a transition period of ten years should be used to implement such agreements. What is more, the discrimination must be "explicit" if nonmembers are to be compensated for losses under GATT (Hoekman and Kostecki 1995: 219–220, 222).

How do the two North American RIAs stack up? They are "GATT-able." That is, they arguably fall within the guidelines of Article 24. Certainly, CUFTA and NAFTA are no more, and probably a good deal less, toxic to multilateralism than are either the EU or Mercosur, the Common Market of the South. The North American RIAs reduce barriers within the region, though CUFTA is less GATT-able than NAFTA on this crucial point. They also set up barriers for nonmembers, adopting investment restrictions for outsiders. But the GATT did not cover such rules at the time the two agreements were approved. The NAFTA is also theoretically open to new members outside North America. North America opted for a blend of free trade and trade preferences acceptable under the GATT.

First Step

The Canada-U.S. Free Trade Agreement was the first RIA of its kind in North America. Perhaps no one really knew at the time that it would become the building block for the second RIA involving all three North American states. It was bilateral rather than regional. Trading more with each other than with any other countries, these two states with a strong basis of friendship set a new course for North America.

The agreement promised to weld more firmly together the largest and the seventh largest economies of the world. It was a plus for both, but it did fall somewhat short of what each would have ideally preferred. And of course, it was about more than just trade. It was also an attempt to deal with some economic issues beyond the pale of multilateral negotiations during the 1980s. As the forerunner of NAFTA, CUFTA tackled problems of economic interdependence while acknowledging the sovereignty of both partners. Therefore, it struck an acceptable balance between free markets and state regulation and between a large affluent state and a smaller affluent one. Tilting toward free trade, the agreement did not go that final mile toward a completely free trade agreement between the two neighbors.

The Canada-U.S. Free Trade Agreement of 1988 reaffirmed GATT principles. It incorporated GATT's principle of nondiscrimination (Article 1), national treatment of foreign investment (Article 3), and reduction of quantitative and some nonborder measures (Article 11). The pact also dealt with rules about how Canada and the United States would treat each other. It did not, however, seriously curb domestic restrictions on trade in either country (Windham and Grant 1995: 25–26).

Freer trade was a major goal. The pact sought to end tariffs on many traded items over a ten-year period. It also provided for the elimination of some nontariff barriers, such as quotas. But some sectors were exempt in this compromise. Agriculture, textiles, and beer were excluded from the agreement. By not being more inclusive, the CUFTA was barely consistent with GATT rules on RIAs (Lawrence 1996: 65).

The RIA did not throw open the doors to free trade because states and protectionism were part of the agreement. For example, antidumping provisions in domestic legislation permitted both governments to impose duties on imports (countervailing duties) that are dumped or sold at below-market prices prevailing in the country of origin. This was a disappointment for Canada because its agenda for the bilateral agreement was to have guaranteed access to U.S. markets. Still, Canada was granted some preferential treatment in U.S. contingency protections (Lawrence 1996: 64). Likewise, government subsidies to private businesses were not adequately dealt with in the pact. This has long been an issue for the United States in bilateral relations with Canada. Neither party to the agreement could agree on common standards or harmonization. This would have required deeper commitments to integration than either wanted to make at the time.

Dispute settlement was also part of the agreement. Procedures over trade disputes were institutionalized in CUFTA. Binational panels would have the power to make binding decisions about trade disputes. Each state could challenge domestic rulings on trade disputes through binational dispute settlement procedures, but neither had the right to challenge the laws themselves. Through these binational panels, states could raise objections to domestic trade laws that might contravene the trade pact (Lawrence 1996: 63, 65). Dispute settlement clearly tilted toward sovereignty over supranationality. In other words, states rather than new supranational institutions would retain control over trade policy under the pact.

Selectivity further dampened the pact's commitment to free markets and economic liberalism in other ways. In addition to textiles and agriculture, some manufacturing sectors such as steel and energy were excluded from CUFTA. Canada's domestic policy on energy would be permitted to protect national interests from U.S. control. Only limited steps were taken in the pact toward liberalization of trade in services such as basic telecommunications, transportation, culture, media, professions, and child care.

Foreign investment was liberalized to some extent, although CUFTA made Canada more open to U.S. investment. Large U.S. investments would come under review by Investment Canada, the successor of the FIRA. Financial services, transportation, Crown corporations, and government procurement were also exempt under CUFTA. Yet Canada could no longer generally screen U.S. acquisitions of Canadian businesses as it once did, and U.S. investors were afforded some preferential access to the Canadian market (Lawrence 1996: 63). The 1965 auto pact, a sector agreement predating free trade regionalism, continued in force under CUFTA.

Notwithstanding these limits, foreign investment was more open under the principle of national treatment. U.S. firms in Canada would receive the same treatment as Canadian firms in Canada and vice versa. Nondiscrimination within the region was to be guaranteed, unless specifically exempted. Of course, investors from other states would not be treated so kindly. Liberalizing foreign investment within the bilateral economy therefore meant protectionism against outsiders. To do this, the agreement included provisions on rules of origin (ROOs). Since a regional free trade agreement does not have a common external tariff for imports from nonmembers, it sets content requirements so that nonmembers cannot take advantage of reduced tariffs without fully reciprocating with similar privileges (Whalley 1993: 354). To be eligible for the reduced tariffs, goods must be mostly "North American" (that is, made in Canada and the United States). In this way as well, CUFTA set the stage for NAFTA's approach to investment a few years later.

The agreement between Canada and the United States started the ball rolling toward regionalism in North America. Despite its limited openness, the pact affirmed the growing interdependence and emerging convergence over economic policy within bilateral North America. True, CUFTA was in some ways symbol more than substance. Trade barriers were already low before the two agreed to the trade agreement. What it did suggest, however, is that initial measures toward regional integration must strike a balance between markets and states. In the larger scheme of things, freer trade and investment was adopted officially as the operating code between two very highly interdependent economies.

Three's Company

The CUFTA was only the first step, as it turned out. Seen from the United States, the pact was really about Canada. The second RIA a few years later was about Mexico; with NAFTA, North America became a threesome. As the bilateral forerunner for an even broader, deeper, more liberal, and more innovative RIA, CUFTA helped to make NAFTA a reality. This was hardly the original intent, however. For Canada, North America stopped at the Rio Grande (Orme 1996: 53). With NAFTA, North America had become a tripartite partnership.

By regional and even world standards, the North American Free Trade Agreement was remarkable. If CUFTA was barely "GATT-able," NAFTA is a GATT-plus agreement (Hufbauer and Schott 1993: 289;

Lawrence 1996: 72). For its time, it went beyond GATT in trade liberalization, foreign investment, services, and intellectual property rights, making it a "pleasant surprise" for free traders (Hufbauer and Schott 1993: 261). But its boldest departure was that NAFTA found a way to bring a developing country into an RIA without making important concessions to Mexico's relatively poor economic status. Reciprocity among unequal partners was a cardinal premise. Through NAFTA, North and South met, but the South was not able to plead for concessions. NAFTA was for the consumer, the taxpayer, and interfirm competition (Weintraub 1997: 86).

To claim that NAFTA is merely an FTA (or even a PTA) is to view it perhaps too myopically. Indeed, its real significance may be understood only more broadly—and over the long haul. NAFTA is about a vast spectrum of economic activities, infused with strong symbolism and political implications. The key components of NAFTA include agriculture, automobiles, dispute resolution, energy, financial services, government procurement, intellectual property, investment, standards, tariffs, textiles, and transportation. It also includes the environment within the North American "neighborhood," especially along the Mexico-U.S. border (Grayson 1995: 101–105; Weintraub 1994: 2). With tariff barriers already low before NAFTA, the North American triumvirate clearly had more in mind than merely reaping the traditional benefits of a classic free trade area.

Like its predecessor, NAFTA strikes a balance of interests. At the same time it symbolizes the regionalization that had already taken place in North America, it also mirrors the priorities of the three states. Even as it acknowledges the goals of the private sector for greater efficiencies and larger economies of scale, it implies something quite basic about North American relations. NAFTA reflects convergence over economic policy and especially over U.S. approaches to trade, investment, and other issues. It is an agreement that rests upon growing mutual interests.

There are other parallels as well. Like CUFTA, NAFTA wears two faces. On the one hand, it exalts markets, globalization, interdependence, trade, and other trends of economic liberalization. The eventual goal of NAFTA is to let markets rule. On the other hand, it incorporates the state. NAFTA is a state-led agreement for regionalism. The state regulates the transition to a freer, more regional economy. What is more, regionalism requires that only some can enjoy the advantages of the region. NAFTA keeps the state in.

Even so, at its most basic, NAFTA aims to liberalize and open economies. It seeks to end tariffs and other barriers to trade. This goes for merchandise, including textiles, field crops, and autos. Yet it does not stop there. The reciprocity principle in foreign investment means that foreign (North American) investment is to be treated like national investors (Windham and Grant 1995: 26–27). The national treatment idea was strongly pushed by the United States (Arsen 1996: 44). It is the investment version of the most-favored-nation clause under the GATT for trade.

The immensity of North America's task made a transition period an absolute necessity. NAFTA was to open economies—after a fashion and after a time. The 2,000-plus-page text of the agreement sets up schedules and procedures for the transition. The state's imprint is thus clearly visible on the transition period as North America moves gradually toward greater liberalization. The state is supervising its own retreat from managing the regional economy.

A ten-year transition, for example, will lead to a fully integrated market for automobiles, an important industry in all three countries. The same is true for discontinuing quotas on North American textiles. NAFTA went beyond GATT in agriculture. In two separate agreements on agriculture, Canada, Mexico, and the United States will rescind all import restrictions. The United States and Mexico were originally scheduled to end such limits within fifteen years. Even before this comes to pass, both countries agreed to major changes in agricultural trade. The United States lifted barriers on imports from Mexico of horticultural products, cotton, and sugar. In turn, Mexico ended import restrictions on some field crops from the United States (Hufbauer and Schott 1993: 263). Still, the transition could be bumpy. A few years after NAFTA came into force, U.S. displeasure with Mexican exports of tomatoes to the United States led to a managed solution: Mexico agreed to a minimum price for this export (Weintraub 1997: 50). These episodes may interrupt the process from time to time, but NAFTA will gradually bring free trade in agriculture to North America, probably long before it comes to the world through the World Trade Organization.

Following U.S. preferences, trade and investment in services are part of NAFTA; new services are to be liberalized. Financial services are becoming the most important sector for a globalized economy. North America will have a liberalized financial sector. This puts Mexico front and center in the reform of its financial sector. Historically, the Mexican financial sector has discriminated against foreign participation. NAFTA will encourage badly needed reform in the banking sector. By 2007 all

Mexican restrictions on foreign entry into financial services are scheduled to come to an end under the NAFTA transition phase.

Transportation is vital to cross-border trade in the region. To move goods requires a more integrated transportation grid with fewer bottlenecks. About half of all U.S.-Mexican trade goes through Texas, but trucks, trains, and other land transportation have not yet been entirely deregulated. According to the transition, the United States and Mexico were scheduled to form a common network under NAFTA by 1999. The transition to deregulated transportation hit a snag, however, when the Clinton administration delayed an early phase of the plan by refusing to allow Mexican truckers deep into the United States, perhaps violating the NAFTA provision (Weintraub 1997: 50). In early 2001, the Bush administration agreed with a dispute resolution panel that keeping Mexican trucks out of the United States was a violation of NAFTA and proposed lifting the ban.

Investment therefore rivals free trade as a NAFTA priority. With already low tariff schedules in place, liberalization on investment was actually a more important goal, especially for the United States. Mexico is the most obviously on the spot to make reforms. This is critical for Mexico, whose past policies were blatantly discriminatory. Mexico's policies on foreign investment are committed to a gradual implementation of the NAFTA idea that all investment should be treated the same. This means that Mexico is required under the agreement to abandon by 2004 all restrictions placed on foreign investment that affect exports from Mexico, the Mexican content of their products, restrictions on sources, and trade balancing (Hufbauer and Schott 1993: 261–266). Exemptions in the Mexican energy sector cover only basic oil production. (Canada has exempted cultural industries and the United States labor under the agreement.) The North American three could not bring themselves to practice the ideal of fully liberalized investment: Majority foreign ownership in telecommunications, airlines, the merchant marine, nuclear power, broadcasting, and fishing was banned (Orme 1996: 41).

Intellectual property rights (IPR) have long been a favorite hobbyhorse of U.S. trade negotiators. They pushed for and got a provision about it in NAFTA. All parties pledge to vigorously protect rights to patents, copyrights, trademarks, and trade secrets. The U.S. holders of intellectual property lost about $533 million in Canada and $367 million in Mexico in 1986 alone because of infringement of intellectual property rights (Grayson 1995: 103–104).

Other provisions are less central to NAFTA. The RIA is fairly thorough in spelling out how the agreement is to be carried out. This gives some transparency and leverage to the process. It also curbed domestic discretion on customs regulations. Government procurement was not generally exempted; North American businesses may therefore bid on any government purchase, even in the Mexican oil industry (Lawrence 1996: 69; Orme 1996: 140).

NAFTA is a landmark step for inventing North America. Even so, NAFTA did not go all the way. Protectionism and preferential treatment are still part of NAFTA. In the early 1990s, NAFTA was defended in the U.S. Congress with protectionist arguments about how it would help the U.S. balance of trade (Weintraub 1997: 5). The most important elements of state involvement are the rules of origin, investment exemptions, and the trade remedy options within domestic law, such as antidumping and countervailing duties. These provisions essentially lend weight to the charge that NAFTA, despite its free market leanings, is a blend of markets and states. It is about freer trade with some state involvement.

Rules of origin (ROOs) are often written into regional trade agreements. They set content requirements for freely traded items within the region. Without a common external tariff such as in a customs union, an FTA protects its members through a rule that requires that trade and investment be basically from within the region to receive the benefits of reduced barriers. This may lead to some trade diversion because of state intervention rather than trade creation based on the market. Unfortunately, rules of origin can actually bring about what they are intended to prevent (Whalley 1993: 253).

If anything, the ROOs in NAFTA are stricter than those of its predecessor (Lawrence 1996: 70). The United States was concerned that Japan and Brazil would use Mexico as an export platform into the U.S. market in autos (Hufbauer and Schott 1992: 166). A ROOs provision would make this harder to do until it lapses in 2004 under the original terms of the agreement (Orme 1996: 149). NAFTA requires that 62.5 percent of autos be made in North America to come under the favorable treatment of the agreement. CUFTA required only 50 percent. All border barriers to this "North American" trade are to be eliminated. Rules of origin are intended to discriminate against some and extend privileges to others. Still, Mexico's pledge to end all barriers to auto and auto parts imports from the United States and Canada was a major triumph for the United States. The Detroit Big Three could not have written a provision more congenial to their interests (Grayson 1995: 102).

Rules of origin were not the only filaments of protectionism running through the NAFTA pact. Among its own members, the agreement allowed antidumping and countervailing duties in domestic trade laws just as CUFTA had done. In this sense, NAFTA did not actually exceed GATT and even fell short of the EU. Once again, NAFTA's spirit of free trade and markets was diluted a bit. Although Canadian and Mexican exporters could breathe a little easier about their access to the U.S. market under both North America RIAs, the lack of an outright ban on AD and CVDs fell short of an ironclad guarantee of unfettered access to the huge U.S. market. Article 19 of NAFTA allows Mexico and the United States to use CVDs against each other, especially in agricultural trade (Weintraub 1997: 45).

How are disputes to be handled? Leery of chipping away at sovereignty, the NAFTA members shied away from regional harmonization of standards. Still, NAFTA does not leave it entirely up to national voluntary compliance using national standards alone. It calls for outside scrutiny and even trade sanctions to encourage enforcement of NAFTA provisions (Lawrence 1996: 71). Although protective of national sensibilities, NAFTA does recognize the need for mutual consultation more than regional harmonization.

Settling disputes among parties with different domestic standards required a dispute resolution mechanism of some sort. It goes something like this. After consultation, a process to solve most disputes within ten months is put into place, first involving a review by a trade commission composed of top trade officials of each country and then through a decision made by a binational five-member panel of private-sector experts. Private parties or firms can be included in the process. The dispute resolution process is to ensure that the parties are following the agreement and that the states are following their own rules. Later in the process the three-country panels make the final determination. The tripartite nature of the process changed the dynamic as well. These panels were seen as a way to constrain U.S. power by outvoting it in the process with a two-to-one majority (Barry 1995: 12). Still, for those who had hoped for something more formidable, these "feeble instruments" fall quite a bit short of the European Union's standards (Weintraub 1997: 27; Randall 1995: 38). But it is certainly in keeping with North America's preference for minimalism in such matters.

A Shade of Green

Had it not been for U.S. domestic politics, NAFTA may never have taken a vital step toward regionalism in North America. As it turned out, three side agreements were approved to build political support for NAFTA itself. The agreements dealt with labor standards and health, import surges, and the environment. The greening of NAFTA may have set a precedent for future trade agreements, at least those involving the United States.

NAFTA's preamble pays homage to "sustainable development." As widely understood, this means pursuing economic growth and prosperity without degrading the environment. Behind this pledge was a concern about U.S. jobs lost to environmentally callous U.S. industries along the Mexican side of the border. Some opponents of NAFTA believed that Mexico had already become a sanctuary for U.S. businesses seeking to circumvent U.S. and state laws on pollution and worker safety, allowing them to pass on the costs of environmental degradation to others. The U.S.-Mexican border region attracts jobs from U.S. locales where environmental standards and enforcement are more stringent, which has turned the region into an environmental disaster area. One environmental group estimated that a cleanup of the border could go as high as $20 billion (Lott 1997: 6).

Two views of business and the environment are imbedded in NAFTA. The first is that the market will protect the environment in the long run through greater affluence and prosperity. The other is that state or transborder institutions must constrain markets when they opt for short-term profit maximization over environmental protection. Short-term political considerations in the United States require a role for states in the agreement.

NAFTA addresses the environment issue, but it does so without a highly integrated approach. NAFTA sidesteps the issue of common or regional environmental standards. Rather, each state is to enforce its own laws; no one would be expected to follow the other's standards on the environment. Environmental protection would come from consultation and compliance rather than standardization and enforcement.

Still, the RIA enumerates options. Article 904 of NAFTA allows states to stop the export of a good that does not comply with its own environmental regulations. Article 905 allows levels of government within each member of NAFTA to set their own standards of environmental conservation and protection, even if they are higher than the international standards. Article 1114 allows governments to impose regulations to ensure that investment within their borders is environmentally sensitive, but the same article stresses consultation rather than enforcement to deal with environmental violations. Trade penalties, especially nontariff barriers, may be levied if a violation of environmental laws has occurred (Weintraub 1997: 22).

The environment is also the basic issue for another NAFTA-inspired agreement. Under the North American Agreement on Environmental Cooperation (NAAEC), only upward harmonization of environmental standards is allowed, if not required. It seeks a multilateral, comprehensive, trade-linked, regional approach to environmental protection (Mumme and Duncan 1997–1998: 45). Two institutions were created to deal with environmental degradation along the U.S.-Mexican border. A Border Environment Cooperation Commission (BECC) certifies cleanup projects, and the North American Development Bank (NADBank) then provides partial financing for these projects (Weintraub 1997: 74–75; Chavez and Whiteford 1996: 27).

The Commission for Environmental Cooperation (CEC), headquartered in Montreal, is a NAFTA-based institution charged with the task of reshaping domestic practices and fostering international cooperation in environmental management. Bestowed with very modest supranational prerogatives, the CEC seeks a more integrated regional management of the environment. It faces daunting obstacles. The CEC is so weak institutionally that it must rely upon the vagaries of U.S. domestic politics to advance its cause (Mumme and Duncan 1997–1998: 54). Eventually, a convergence of views may emerge over how to minimize environmental damage (Kirton 1997: 7–9).

The Rocky Road to Regionalism

NAFTA is a complex set of bargains about trade and nontrade issues that advances North America toward closer economic ties. In some important ways, it went well beyond traditional FTAs and beyond GATT, but in other ways it is limited in what it tries to do in North America. The state remains a player for protecting state and special interests.

What has emerged from a decade or more of North American RIAs is a North American–style of regionalism. The triumvirate agreed to pool their destinies to some extent. The path of regionalism goes in two directions: It adopts liberalized policies for the region without abandoning the state entirely. It keeps regionalism well under the thumb of national prerogatives.

The two RIAs are market-friendly. The principles of free trade and markets are at the heart of North American regionalism, but they do not always serve as its road map. The provisions on tariffs and other barriers, the national treatment of foreign investment, and the comprehensive rather than sectoral liberalization of economic relations are testimony to the North American trend toward markets.

Although oriented toward the market, regionalism in North America also involves the state. The North American three embrace the liberalism of globalization in their regional enterprise, but state regulation coexists with the tendency in North America to become more open than it once was. Rules of origin, domestic trade rules, and scads of exemptions are also part of North America's more general, growing commitment to free trade and investment.

This ambivalence helps to explain North America's regionalist style. The road to regionalism in North America is more free of barriers and obstacles than it has ever been. Free markets may be the ideal, but freer trade is the acceptable reality. Freer trade means that the state is not put on the sidelines. Put another way, there is a politics to North American regionalism. States can play a role within North American economic exchange, and they can also limit outsiders in a more liberal regional economy. North America's RIAs are a unique blend of free and preferential trade.

7

Promise—and Peril

As they recast relations in North America, the two RIAs raised hopes as well as fears. The promise and peril of the RIAs lie in their impact on the lives of millions of people. Some are convinced that good will come from this venture in regionalism; others are not so sure. Where you stand on this basic idea depends to some extent on who you are and what you do.

Promise and peril are hard to pin down. Put simply, it is difficult to appraise what the impact of NAFTA and CUFTA is or will be. It takes time—decades rather than just a few years—to get results from such important steps toward a more integrated region. Merely the transition period of NAFTA extends well into the first decade of the twenty-first century. What is more, cause and effect are quite complex. Untangling the multiple and interactive causes behind changes in economic performance, growth, and income creation is a task of immense difficulty. How much can be attributed to the RIAs, and how much can be attributed to other aspects of domestic and international policy?

There is even more to it than this. The matter of gains (or losses) is also a problem. The absolute gains promised by globalization and liberalization may be one measure for assessing regionalism. But the potential savings in efficiency is not the only value of any importance, even in liberal North America. One must look at relative gains as well for the three states and their peoples. Finally, perspective enters the picture. A narrow view of regionalism as a mere business deal could yield a far different conclusion than would a broader one. Although specific and measurable effects on trade, employment, and income must be considered, of course, regionalism goes beyond this. A more expansive view would mean that assessing regionalism would lead us eventually to that classic question in studying all politics: Who gets what, how much, and when?

Expectations may set the standards for success of regionalism, but the actual record at some point must also become more clear than it is now or even will be for a time. Living with this ambiguity and uncertainty is just one of the many challenges for making sense of North American regionalism.

Promises, Promises

The lure of regionalism in North America was irresistible for some. On balance, those supporting the RIAs believed that they and their countries would be better off for having pursued regionalism. Their great expectations centered on a cornucopia of economic and political benefits. Free trade, markets, and liberalization, coupled with some state protection, would provide gains to states, firms, and peoples. Even so, the United States, Canada, and Mexico also had their own hopes for the gains to come from the RIAs.

The United States

The RIAs promised benefits to the United States and to some of its most important groups. These were not just economic promises either. In fact, a narrowly economic interpretation leaves us hard-pressed to explain why the United States saw so much potential in RIAs in the first place. The U.S. economy is too large and developed to pin a great deal of hope on one or two limited agreements with two much smaller economies. Still, firms, groups, and individuals expected to receive gains, gains that would also contribute to the economy as a whole. But the United States had another agenda as well. The United States is a great power, the hub of a major regional trade area. Its supporters viewed both RIAs, and especially NAFTA, as a geoeconomic tool, a vindication of its market ideology, a hegemonic reassurance to its neighbors, and a more diversified strategy for economic foreign policy.

In some ways the economic promise was modest. The United States had the least to gain in relative terms from the RIAs with its neighbors. With an economy more than twenty times larger than Mexico's, the United States would not reap large direct gains for its national economy from NAFTA in the short run. Mexico's merchandise exports to the United States are valued at about 25 percent of Mexico's gross domestic product (GDP). U.S. exports to Mexico are 1 percent of its GDP (Weintraub 1997: 83–84). Although less extreme, the same argument holds true for Canada.

There would be positive gains in a somewhat larger context or in particular sectors. Since Canada and Mexico are important trade partners, NAFTA could fuel economic growth and rising incomes in both, thereby creating the potential for greater U.S. exports and investment down the line. For U.S. investors and exporters, freer trade within North America could help some sectors of the U.S. economy by giving them greater access to nearby markets (Brunelle and Deblock 1992: 128–129). Greater respect for intellectual property rights, too, would translate into greater profits (Bosworth et al. 1997: 5). Many U.S. firms are more competitive than those in Canada or Mexico. In particular, the United States has competitive advantages in field crops, high-grade steel, chemicals, plastics, equipment, and transportation, and these would be favored even more if NAFTA leveled the playing field (Hufbauer and Schott 1992: 64–65).

Reaping the promise of modest positive gains was not the only hope. The economic advantages are also more compelling within a context of broader U.S. goals, especially at the international level (Hufbauer and Schott 1992: 10–11). Geoeconomic reasons blend with commercial ones; the flag and the dollar go together. NAFTA could be a safety net to make it more likely that Mexico and even Canada will be able to sustain economic growth well into the future. Growth of incomes in the North American neighborhood would serve U.S. interests. Geoeconomics is also linked to the United States' basic interest in promoting political stability south of the Rio Grande. If Mexico is able to expand and develop its economy, then U.S. leaders can be more reassured about its neighbor's stability. An economic collapse in Mexico would risk U.S. national security (Prestowitz et al. 1991: 6). Likewise, opening up to its neighbors means that the United States enhances its position. By accepting U.S. rules and standards, Canada and Mexico accept and come under greater U.S. influence.

The RIAs, too, play a global role in U.S. geoeconomic strategy. By the early 1990s, the United States had come to regard Europe and Japan as economic rivals as well as economic partners. Facing stiffer and stiffer competition from Japan, China, and other Asian economies, the United States in the early 1990s believed NAFTA could be a lever to pry open foreign markets and push everyone toward its view of multilateralism (Reynolds et al. 1991: 90). Trade conflicts with Japan, quarrels with Europe over subsidies, and the spread of economic liberalization in the Western Hemisphere during the early 1990s all made the United States more willing to consider such a regional economic policy (Morici 1992: 87). By taking a stand for North American regionalism, the United States was able to play a more leveraged form of hardball with Asia; it was also able to stake its claim once again as a leader in the Western Hemisphere. It could be the acknowledged leader of freer trade and economic liberalization (Saborio 1992: 10–11; Hufbauer and Schott 1991: 98–99). The trading agreements in North America formalized the United States as the head of a major trade region within the tripolar world (Del Castillo 1995: 97).

The promise was more golden for some than for others. But if certain firms would gain more from regionalism than others, virtually everyone would get something, according to liberal economic thinking. In order to position themselves favorably, some U.S. firms and retailers moved into Mexico with direct plant investment in order to take advantage of NAFTA even before it came into effect. U.S. firms could count on national treatment in many sectors of the economy of both Mexico and Canada. Some would tap comparative advantages like cheap labor and lax enforcement of environment laws south of the border. By exporting lower-skilled, lower-paid jobs to Mexico, U.S. firms could cut some costs and therefore compete more effectively in world markets against Asian economies, in particular Japanese firms, which have long used Southeast Asian labor markets to keep costs low.

Regional barriers to outsiders would enhance relative gains for insiders. U.S. firms would have advantages in Canada and Mexico not so readily available to nonmembers. In other words, trade diversion and investment diversion would in some ways favor U.S. firms over European, Asian, or other firms doing business within the North American market. What is more, the United States would be an attractive target for investors outside North America. Since Mexico and Canada would play by the same rules of origin as would the United States, foreign investors would have an incentive for directly investing in the United States if the U.S. market was its principal reason for relocating to North America. NAFTA would make things more predictable for U.S. investors. It would also be a credible commitment to markets necessary for building future economic ties (Weintraub 1997: 32).

Investors, exporters, and manufacturers could expect benefits from the RIAs, but so could U.S. consumers, taxpayers, and even some workers. A relatively modest increase in the number of jobs in the United States would come from more exports and better economies of scale. Certain region states and border regions would be particularly affected. Higher-skilled jobs in technology-driven sectors would stay in the United States, whereas lower-skilled jobs in assembly and manufacturing would be transported out of the United States. In other words, the more affluent U.S. workers would keep their higher-paying job and some Mexican workers would get those jobs that were previously in the U.S. economy (Reynolds 1995: 25). This could modestly raise real U.S. wages, as happened in Japan when semiskilled jobs were exported to Southeast Asia (Morici 1992: 97–98). The RIAs of North America are more sensitive to labor and environmental interests than are other fora like the World Trade Organization (Bhagwati 1995: 11).

Canada

For Canada, the RIAs unlocked a treasure trove of the vast U.S. market. This was the promise of free trade bilateralism for Canada in the 1980s. Canada wanted preferences from the United States for trade and investment that would rekindle economic prosperity threatened by the downturn of the early 1980s. When Canada came to the United States as demandeur of the CUFTA, it was the "beggar at the feast" (Bothwell 1992: 145). These hopes were coupled with fears that the United States would protect its markets from Canadian exports by resorting to the "fair trade" or trade remedy provisions of U.S. law. Although not originally popular in Canada, CUFTA held forth the promise that free trade would rejuvenate a national economy that was losing its competitive and technological edge within the world economy (Britton 1996: 450–451).

Hoping to sidestep smaller economies of scale, Canada's access to the United States and its tighter embrace with the United States could raise its standard of living and increase economies of scale. It opted for the idea that greater efficiency and integration between the two would help the economy even if it generated misgivings about the risk to Canadian identity and sovereignty. U.S. companies in Canada would help Canadian firms become more efficient and competitive (Stairs 1996: 24). Canada accepted national treatment of foreign investment, some liberalization of sectors like energy, and other provisions in the

FTA with the United States. Choosing greater dependence, a downsized role for the state, and less cultural autonomy, Canada maneuvered to offset U.S. protectionism and to guarantee access to Canada's largest export market. It also accepted the idea of a horizontal division of labor based upon manufacturing and services between the two (M. Smith 1996: 56).

Free trade promised to do for Canada what it had presumably done for others: raise consumption, lower consumer prices, broaden export markets, and exploit its human and natural resources more profitably (Lusztig 1996: 1). Canada had already achieved a great deal economically and was an attractive target for foreign direct investment. Despite the recession in the early 1990s, those in Canada enjoyed a standard of living close to that of their neighbors in the United States (Nymark and Verdun 1994: 127). To sustain this, Canadian leaders pursued openness and attracted foreign investment from the United States and elsewhere.

The first RIA was more important to Canada than the second. NAFTA was not a Canadian priority. Canada needed to be in NAFTA because being left on the sidelines would have risked its relations with the United States. Reluctant about and defensive on NAFTA, Canada became a regional player in the tripartite agreement to protect its interests rather than to embrace trilateral regionalism for its own sake. If NAFTA would solidify its economic ties to the United States, so be it. Canadian consumers, firms, taxpayers, and some workers could not safely be left out of such a pact.

NAFTA was a defensive ploy within Canadian geoeconomic strategy. If Canada stayed out of it, the United States could get the advantages of dealing with each country separately and deny these same advantages to the other. Canada has long objected to the implicit domination of this "hub and spoke" strategy (Saborio 1992: 20–21). Besides that, NAFTA improved on CUFTA (Rugman and Verbecke 1994: 94; Windham and Grant 1995: 26; R. Wonnacott 1995: 143–144). For one thing, foreign investment in services moved NAFTA beyond the CUFTA and even beyond GATT rules. For another, dispute resolution mechanisms were improved. So Canada had no choice. To be excluded was unacceptable; to be included did not promise particularly great gains. Because of Canada's insistence on being part of the pact, North America backed into a truly regional RIA. There did not seem to be a grand design behind it.

Mexico

Mexico has the most to gain in relative terms. The promise is therefore most alluring for the southernmost member of the North American triumvirate. Smaller and poorer than the other two, it could feel more acutely the impact of regionalism. What is at stake is nothing less than to change Mexico fundamentally (Orme 1996: xii). To do this means that Mexico must gain substantially in economic terms and that these gains must eventually have an influence on Mexico as a whole and on its politics as well. Relative gains are the heart of NAFTA's promise. Gains from NAFTA for the whole region could be 1 percent of GNP, but gains to Mexico could be as high as 2 to 4 percent of GNP (Weintraub 1993: 21).

To become wealthier and more developed, Mexico cast its lot with North America. It expects to receive greater capital inflows through portfolio and foreign direct investment (Hufbauer and Schott 1992: 16). It also means greater, guaranteed access to the United States, Mexico's largest export market, especially for manufactured goods (Caballero Urdiales 1991: 10). Mexico then could raise its own foreign exchange to finance its development by increasing exports, incomes, and economic growth. Greater openness to imports would force protected Mexican industries to become more efficient. It would also create more competition and therefore drive down prices. Such openness would probably spur higher growth rates in the south of Mexico more than in the north of Mexico (Ramirez de la O 1991: 25).

NAFTA promised to be a lure for foreign investment. The agreement bestows credibility to Mexico's commitment to economic liberalization; with this comes foreign investment. Investors go to Mexico to take advantage of labor costs and domestic market growth. Auto assembly is a prime example. Mexican autoworkers make substantially less than Canadian or American counterparts. NAFTA would further regionalize auto production by emphasizing the Mexican connection. If other industries relocated to Mexico, the national economy could experience an increase in real wages for skilled and even semiskilled manufacturing jobs. In the two years following NAFTA's inception, foreign direct investment in Mexico more than tripled, two-fifths of it coming from the United States (Weintraub 1997: 32).

A not-so-hidden hope was psychological. During much of the 1980s, Mexico had sullied its international reputation among those it most wanted to impress. Inflation, debt renegotiations, unemployment, impoverishment, and general economic turmoil essentially left Mexico without any viable strategy for financing its growth and development in the traditional ways. To sustain the economic reform of the late 1980s and early 1990s, Mexico had to court foreign investors. For Mexico, NAFTA was a confidence builder (Weintraub 1992: 563). If it promised to play by neoliberal rules and to guarantee that Mexico was a modern market economy, then it had some hope of attracting the capital it needed to finance its development.

Mexico had a domestic agenda for regionalism as well. NAFTA was meant to lock in the domestic economic reforms of the 1980s. There would be no going back to the old days of economic nationalism and statism, the use of government to guide and control the economy. NAFTA would make sure that Mexico honored its neoliberal pledges for years to come. Future leaders in Mexico would find it more difficult to undo the Salinas legacy of economic liberalization with NAFTA in place. Mexico's hopes for NAFTA were thus political, too.

Mexico shared with Canada the hope that regionalism would save it from U.S. protectionism. It was concerned about U.S. trade remedy laws against imports from Mexico. Although NAFTA did not provide such guarantees, Mexico assumed that it would have less to worry about if NAFTA were set up. Like Canada, Mexico was somewhat more reassured even if it did not receive the ironclad guarantees it would have liked.

The promise of regionalism also required that Mexico make a critical pledge of its own. The membership fee for admission to the North American club was the loyalty to a certain brand of economic policy. Mexico would become North American in its policy and its preferences. To reap the rewards of regionalism, Mexico had to make—and has largely kept—its promise to act more like its neighbors.

What Peril?

The idea that free trade is not really free, that it may come with a price tag, suggests that there may be more to liberalization, globalization, and markets than higher productivity and higher income as well as gains for one and all.

Apprehensions zeroed in on several specific arguments. First, free market economics and free trade would exacerbate the inequalities within all three societies, affecting Mexico most severely. Second, the same thing would also occur between states of North America because globalization, not to mention regional manifestations of it, can widen the rich-poor gap (Miller 1999: A8). Third, the market-friendly RIAs discourage states from doing very much to help those who suffer from reduced wages and job losses associated with the greater integration of markets and economies. Fourth, those most hurt in the wealthier countries would be those who were the least affluent and skilled. Fifth, differences in national standards would have a harmful impact on local efforts to protect the environment, social programs, and other nontrade issues. Sixth, free trade weakens local popular control, cultural identity, and state autonomy.

The United States

Fears about freer trade and regional liberalism went first and foremost to the pocketbook. In particular, NAFTA was seen as just the wedge U.S. companies needed to put downward pressure on employment and wages. U.S. firms would go to Mexico to take advantage of cheap labor. This relocation would raise profit margins and allow the companies to compete more effectively with Japanese firms who were using Thailand and other lower-cost labor markets in Asia. Under NAFTA, most labor could not freely move from one country to the other, but capital in search of favorable labor markets could. This tilted the agreement against labor.

The lure of cheap labor in Mexico was seen as a danger for some U.S. workers. It was particularly chilling for the unskilled and semiskilled workers in textiles, apparel, ceramics, leather goods, agricultural produce, assembled products, and other labor-intensive sectors (Hufbauer and Schott 1991). Since NAFTA is as much about investment as it is about trade, U.S. firms were suspected of exporting jobs as well as products. If U.S. firms could not compete in the low-wage industries, then U.S. workers would lose out to Mexican or Canadian workers. In 1992 Ross Perot predicted a "giant sucking sound" as U.S. firms and jobs went south to Mexico. Job losses were forecast, one early estimate putting the figure at 145,000 over a five-year period (Pastor 1993: 50).

The idea that the search for cheap labor outside the United States would most affect the poorest within the United States suggested to some that NAFTA would make the poor even poorer. Without effective adjustment programs such as retraining and income subsidies, low-wage U.S. workers would not be able to compete with even lower-wage Mexican workers. Put another way, low-wage U.S. workers would have lower incomes and Mexican workers would have higher wages, but perhaps not at the level the U.S. workers once earned (Reynolds 1995: 21–26). Of the myriad possible causes behind the growing inequality within American society, trade would be one, given the wage polarization between skill levels (Bluestone 1995: 81). What this implied is that a high-wage, high-skill economy cannot easily integrate with a lower-wage, lower-skill economy while keeping the wages as high in the wealthier economy (Belous and Lemco 1995: 10).

The health, safety, and working conditions of labor were to follow national standards, thereby prolonging differences among the North American three. Panels and commissions could study, discuss, and shed light on the failure of each country to follow its own laws, but such analysis fell short of effective enforcement of common standards or in some cases even the enforcement of national standards. Only after an elaborate process could the United States use NAFTA to penalize Mexico in trade if it continues to violate its own environmental laws.

For some, the environment was given short shrift as well. Border pollution, pollution havens, common environmental standards, and the impact of trade liberalization on the environment were critical issues in U.S.-Mexican relations (Belausteguigoitia and Guadarrama 1997: 92). Although NAFTA went far beyond GATT by including an environmental side agreement, the environmental protections in the agreement are relatively thin. Mexico has for quite a while had some strong environmental laws, but they have often been indifferently enforced. Border pollution between Mexico and the United States had raised the hackles of those who opposed NAFTA in principle. And it also worried those who believed that firms would use NAFTA to continue to take advantage of lax enforcement of pollution laws to reduce costs they would have to pay if they stayed put in the United States. Flying between Monterrey and San Antonio is a quick lesson in air quality. Even on a clear day, one cannot see the Rio Grande itself very well through the smog.

The environmental shoe can be put on the other foot. Pollution from the midwestern United States makes its way into central and eastern Canada. Lacking strong institutions and regional standards, the North American regime on the environment is underdeveloped. Whether free trade can alone solve the environmental problem is doubtful. But without NAFTA the border pollution problem would have received less attention than it has (Globerman 1993: 41). What is more, environmental agreements are to prevail over NAFTA's provisions on the environment.

The United States fears the RIAs of North America could create a win-lose situation. Or at the least they inequitably distribute gains among different groups. NAFTA would be unfair if it helped some firms and industries by hurting some workers, sectors, and regions. Federally sponsored adjustment programs would be inadequate to deal with anticipated job losses or reduced wages. Gaps between Mexico and the United States on labor and environmental standards might degrade U.S. conditions (Grunwald 1995: 71). NAFTA also played into the political equation of nationalist and protectionist sentiment among economically threatened and nativist groups. For populists, NAFTA was the unholy alliance of U.S. capital and Mexican workers to further break down the wage structure and remaining benefits available to U.S. workers.

Canada

In addition to the usual apprehension about jobs, income, and welfare, some Canadians had more subtle worries about the RIAs. In the United States, NAFTA fanned nativist resentment. In Canada CUFTA raised a sense of cultural insecurity. At its worst, regional integration could also divide Canada politically, weaken its political autonomy, and handcuff Canada's ability to use traditional social programs to make adjustments for losses. U.S. fears were about Mexican failures; Canadian fears were about U.S. successes.

In the popular imagination, full-tilt trade liberalization with the United States could be disturbing, to say the least. Some Canadians saw the agreement as a matter of winners and losers. This uneasiness stirred nationalist passions and ignited economic fears. Still, the United States was less frightening than the world as a whole. Facing the brave new world of globalization, Canada embraced the lesser evil (Doern and Tomlin 1991: 203).

The CUFTA negotiations during the 1980s failed to tether the American eagle, although the Canadian negotiating team proved to be quite capable. The primary Canadian motive for the agreement was to guarantee access to U.S. markets, but the RIAs left U.S. trade laws on subsidies, unfair trading, and the like intact. Antidumping and countervailing duties were allowed under both agreements (Safarian 1996: 43). Canada was opened up more to the United States, but the United States could still be protectionist. Even so, dispute resolution panels have sided more with Canada than the United States on trade issues during the first years of NAFTA's existence.

Rightly or wrongly, many Canadians blamed the trade agreement of 1988 for their economic troubles in the 1980s and early 1990s. Unemployment, recession, and painful adjustments in social programs were linked in the popular imagination to the free trade agreement with the United States, although deficit spending, slowing productivity, and tax problems weighed heavily on the sluggish national economy. For some, nightmares became real with job losses, especially in Ontario. The CUFTA and NAFTA were seen as a possible excuse for the United States to cut back its assembly operations in Canada. With NAFTA, U.S. automakers would have the Mexican option. Lower wages in Mexico and the threat of plant relocation could shift the North American auto industry to the south (Herzenberg 1993: 321; Reich 1993: 92).

The damage could spread even further. Canadian nationalists were concerned about what impact these agreements might have on the political and cultural life of the country. By reorienting North America on a north-south dimension, regional integration could imperil the delicate fate of Canada. As Canadian regions and provinces look more to the United States, they would have less incentive to look toward one another. Although the western provinces and Quebec were the strongest backers of the CUFTA, this was little comfort to those striving for unity.

Although closer ties with the United States did not immediately bring with them the imminent threat of political dismemberment, Canada has its own crisis to deal with. Pressured from within, Canada is reorienting its foreign commitments as well, adding another layer of uncertainty to Canada's viability. The Quebec question and the constitutional crisis added texture to nationalist qualms. A new relationship with the United States could complicate as well as help Canada work through its domestic problems.

Canada was also concerned about its remaining prerogatives. Its leaders wanted Canadian agencies and courts to make decisions about how environmental sanctions under the regional agreements might be applied. Canada allows a strong role for domestic political actors within the greater integration of North America (Del Castillo 1995: 99). Provinces have a great deal to say about issues in North American regionalism. Any perceived loss of sovereignty to the United States would be far more damaging than such a loss to a supranational or multilateral institution (Doern and Tomlin 1991: 248).

Cultural identity is another source of concern. Greater economic integration with the United States, some worry, could overwhelm the remaining national differences, obliterating Canadian cultural identity as a separate and distinct entity within North America (Inglehart et al. 1996: 35). In a legislative bill, Canada sought to curb U.S. cultural influence by using tax law to favor Canadian over U.S. advertising in Canadian media

(M. Smith 1996: 49). Cultural nationalism is still at the heart of Canadian trepidation about U.S. economic power (Rugman 1994: 113).

Mexico

With great promise comes great risk. Mexico had the most to do in order to gain entry to North America. At the time, it was not as prepared as it should have been for the quick transition mandated in NAFTA. Still, Mexico promised to do far more in the transition period than the United States and Canada to adjust its national economy to this new set of rules (Schott 1991: 272; Grayson 1995: 91). With a difficult road ahead, Mexico was facing the prospect that losers as well as winners would emerge from this rapid initiative to become more integrated economically with the more affluent North America.

Mexico must compete openly with far more advanced economies in North America. The concern was that many would be hurt in the free market melee to come. Medium, small, and even some large firms would go out of business, raising the unemployment rate among workers and others least able to adjust to these conditions. Workers in previously protected manufacturing sectors, farmers in basic grains, and consumers of exported goods were projected to be the big losers (Conroy and Glasmeier 1992–1993: 14).

The peril was magnified because neoliberal Mexico's safety net was in tatters. Mexicans would have fewer subsidies or other guarantees to cushion the fall. The most susceptible to rapid liberalization would be hurt the most. Mexico and its NAFTA obligations implied that integration would just happen rather than occur under carefully calibrated state regulation (Aguilar Zinser 1995: 108). Despite transition periods for some economic sectors, the spirit of NAFTA also meant that the Mexican state would not launch adjustment programs in education, health, and housing to deal with social inequities (Castaneda 1993: 77–78). Whatever its long-term promise, NAFTA could reduce the standard of living of many Mexicans in the short term (Krooth 1995: 219).

Politics also bubbled to the surface. The RIAs could increase U.S. domination. Neoliberal Mexico would have less sovereignty under NAFTA. It would also be more vulnerable to U.S. monetary and fiscal policies. Growing integration would mean heightened vulnerability and less monetary and fiscal independence for Mexico, even if official harmonization of Mexican and U.S. policies were not a part of the agreement. By defining the relationship in terms of reciprocity and equality,

Mexico was actually putting itself at risk. For some nationalists, this meant that NAFTA could turn Mexico into a quasi colony (Aguilar Zinser 1995: 108).

It was not clear how the domestic politics of the country would be affected. Four possibilities were suggested. NAFTA could promote democracy, revitalize authoritarianism, weaken the Mexican state, or do nothing at all (P. Smith 1992: 1–26). For those who dreaded NAFTA, it was much easier to believe that NAFTA was a crafty ruse to perpetuate the party in power and boost much-needed political credibility for the government. By 2000 the changing political landscape may have eased some concerns over the long haul about bolstering democracy in the post-NAFTA era.

The perils of regionalism were economic collapse, social inequality, U.S. domination, and political uncertainty. The Mexican state would be constrained in dealing with many of these problems even as it resisted political reform that would put the dominant party out of power.

The Incomplete Record

The promise and peril of regionalism tugged at the hopes and fears of the United States, Canada, and Mexico. Was there anything to these hopes and fears? At the dawn of the century, the record of course remained incomplete, suggesting some clues but not ultimate answers. Promise and peril are in any case refracted through a prism of perceptions.

During the 1990s, the North American states had divergent experiences. The United States enjoyed a remarkable, even unprecedented period of sustained growth and prosperity during the decade. Canada gradually pulled itself out of a stubborn recession and seemed to be facing a brighter economic future at the turn of the century. Between the two, international economic exchange leaped forward. Mexico was once again the exception. A modest economic boom in the early 1990s was deflated in 1995. After a severe contraction, the economy made a recovery, but many Mexicans are still worse off than they were in the early 1990s.

Canada

Canada has one of the most affluent economies in the world. Nevertheless, the national economy was mired in recession as the RIAs came into force in the late 1980s and mid-1990s.

Correlation is not causation. The mixed performance of the Canadian economy during the early years of the RIAs is not just about what freer trade and investment wrought but also about other trends at the time. Its recovery from recession was slow. In fact, Canada's growth rates were among the lowest of the G-7 for a good part of the 1990s. By U.S. standards, unemployment remained relatively high. Job losses due to plant closings in central Canada during the early and mid-1990s were widely publicized. In the popular mind, CUFTA and by extension NAFTA had much to do with hard times in Canada. In the three years following CUFTA's coming into force, Canada lost 23 percent of its manufacturing jobs, with a net loss of 100,000 or more jobs (Conroy and Glasmeier 1992–1993: 11).

The RIAs must be seen within a larger context. The recession of the late 1980s and early 1990s took place during budget deficits, ebbing competitiveness, and U.S. economic sluggishness, thereby depressing Canadian exports (Orme 1996: 23). Canada has also gone through domestic restructuring, partially in response to the spirit of the trade agreements. Except for cultural industries and some agricultural activity such as dairy and poultry, Canada has deregulated and privatized the economy. Investment controls and subsidies have been reduced. The Canadian dollar has declined relative to the U.S. dollar.

Although the RIAs should not be assigned all the blame for recession, they do deserve some credit for the gradual recovery later in the decade. The Canadian export sector has grown, as have U.S. exports to Canada. U.S. companies account for 90 percent of all cars and 60 percent of all computers produced in Canada. Since 1994, exports and export-oriented investment have propelled Canada's overall economic growth. Canada's tariffs on U.S. manufactures average only about 1 percent, even with "sensitive" industries being protected (WTO 1996). Canada's export economy has been able to take advantage of freer trade.

The United States

U.S. economic performance in the post-RIA period was stronger, but the impact of the RIAs was probably modest. The major signs of impact are in some specific areas. The clearest has been on U.S. trade with Mexico rather than with Canada (U.S. House Committee on Ways and Means 1997: 6). In 1996, U.S. exports to Mexico were $12 billion higher because of NAFTA. A Federal Reserve study claimed that NAFTA contributed a $7 billion increase in U.S. exports to Mexico. The short-run effect was to increase U.S. GDP by $13 billion in 1996, with long-run gains estimated at $40 billion a year. U.S. exports in textiles, transportation equipment, and electronics had benefited from Mexican tariff reductions. Despite the peso crisis of 1995, exports to Mexico rose. Likewise, U.S. exports to Canada increased during the three years following NAFTA's approval.

NAFTA made a "modest positive contribution to the U.S. economy in terms of net exports, GDP, employment and investment" ("Report to Congress" 1997; U.S. House Committee on Ways and Means 1997). Between 1993 and 1996, total trade among the North American three grew by 45 percent ("NAFTA Increases Trade" 1997: 27–28).

NAFTA's impact on U.S. employment and economic sectors is more mixed. One-fourth of the industrial sectors examined in an International Trade Commission study experienced changes as a result of NAFTA. Work hours increased, whereas hourly earnings generally went down (U.S. House Committee on Ways and Means 1997: 6). NAFTA had a positive, indirect impact on U.S. productivity in certain industries. Joblessness rose in four sectors, apparel, women's nonathletic footwear, sugar, and glassware (Orme 1996: 43). That meant, however, that unemployment did not go up in sixty-six other sectors. The U.S. Labor Department estimated 78,038 job losses (Weintraub 1997: 12). A presidential report claimed that NAFTA contributed $13 billion to U.S. real income and $5 billion to business investment in 1996, two years into the implementation of the agreement (U.S. House Committee on Ways and Means 1997: 7).

The downside was relatively minor, if viewed in broad terms. U.S. trade balances with Canada and Mexico were negative for the time immediately following the agreement's approval. U.S. job creation was also negligible as a result of NAFTA. There was no evidence that U.S. workers were helped substantially or that they were being paid more as a result of the job creation from the trade agreement. Jobs created by trade are harder to document.

NAFTA may have affected U.S. policy. The Uruguay Round was finalized not long after NAFTA was approved, launching the World Trade Organization as the successor to the GATT in 1995 (Sanger 1997: 1G). Political opposition to NAFTA or similar pacts in the future was well entrenched in the Congress during the late 1990s (Sanger 1997: 1G). Mexico's peso crisis in 1995 and the scandals over drug enforcement did little to help the case for NAFTA and further bolstered the resolve of those who had opposed it in the first place. The United States has also been on the losing side of several trade rulings from the trinational commissions set up for dispute resolution under NAFTA.

Mexico

Mexico's record during the 1990s was extremely mixed. During the mid-1990s, Mexico had a severe economic downturn. Shortly thereafter, it mounted a fairly robust recovery. Mexican exports to the United States went up 83 percent from 1993 to 1997. During the last half of the 1990s, Mexican exports to the United States increased more than threefold (Weiner and Gori 2000: Business section 1, 12). Exports to Canada went up 53 percent. Without this export expansion, the 1995 recession would have led to even larger net losses for the economy as a whole ("NAFTA Increases Trade" 1997: 26–27). From 1994 to 1997, Mexico became attractive for long-term foreign direct investment, second only to China among the developing countries. What is more, Mexico weathered its economic crisis in 1995 while following NAFTA rules. It did not revert to statism and protectionism. Another change was greater specialization within industry and across boundaries (Weintraub 1997: 34). The trade in autos is increasing between the United States and Mexico. NAFTA has diverted apparel exports to the United States, favoring Mexico over other countries. Exports, investment, and other international indicators of progress highlight a favorable impact. For those Mexicans working in the booming export sector, salaries are 30 percent higher than for those working in jobs related to the domestic market (Jordan 2000: 1J).

Still, the collapse of the peso and its economic fallout in 1995 were profoundly unfortunate. Between December 1994 and December 1995, capital outflow (mostly in portfolio investment) surged alarmingly as money managers lost confidence in Mexico's economic management. The economy contracted by 6 percent in 1995 ("NAFTA Increases Trade" 1997: 27). In the manufacturing sector, real wages dropped by 22 percent (Bosworth et al. 1997: 10). Unemployment went to 18 percent; investment fell by almost one-third. Interest rates doubled, and 30 percent of outstanding loans became delinquent (Weintraub 1997: 65).

Why did all this occur? Policy errors and political failures deserve much of the blame. NAFTA was no more than a secondary factor. Most of the capital coming into Mexico in anticipation of NAFTA's positive impact was highly mobile rather than long-term foreign direct investment. This made it relatively easy for institutional investors and mutual fund managers in the United States to withdraw funds at a moment's notice. During 1994 that is just what happened. Politics in an election year turned sour. The Zapatista rebellion in Chiapas was launched on the day that NAFTA took effect. The assassination of the dominant party's presidential candidate in March further roiled the waters in the first presidential election since the debacle of 1988. Edgy about Mexico, foreign investors who bought short-term government bonds cashed them in and took the money out of the country in search of safer and higher returns from rapidly rising interest rates in the United States (Dropsy 1995: 365; Weintraub 1997: 54).

Neoliberal Mexico on the verge of approving an RIA with the rest of North America was an attractive country for foreign capital during the early 1990s. In fact, this was a major reason for Mexico's decision for proposing NAFTA. The agreement would heighten investor confidence. Still, the task of persuading international creditors that Mexico could be a good-faith partner in NAFTA may have forced a delay in the peso devaluation until it was too late. An earlier devaluation could have shaken investor confidence and even besmirched Mexico's claim to financial stability as a member of the North American club. Currency stability had been a central pillar of Mexico's respectability. It needed this reputation if it was to finance further development.

A number of related factors put the whole strategy at risk. Government secrecy and miscalculations were business as usual in Mexico. Politics had much to do with the failing confidence in Mexico (Dropsy 1995: 365). The current account deficit ballooned beyond prudent levels. Structural problems with a developing economy also played a role. Large external debt, unequal income distribution, low job creation, low worker productivity, and low investment in infrastructure were at work to set the context for the crisis (Peach 1995: 375). NAFTA opened up the Mexican economy and made it more vulnerable to rapid financial transactions. Given Mexico's failures in economic policy, NAFTA served to remind one and all of the problems such economies will have in playing within the rules of neoliberal developed states. Other countries have also learned these lessons. A few years after Mexico's crisis, the liberalizing economies of Brazil, Indonesia, and Russia similarly suffered massive capital outflows.

The shock therapy that the government applied in 1995 did have the intended effect. A year later the economy bounced back, growing by 4.5 percent. The stock market (the *bolsa*) and the peso also recovered some lost ground. The U.S.-led rescue package of $13.4 billion helped Mexico stabilize its current account; the controversial loan was repaid in early 1997 through refinancing with private lenders.

The overall picture in Mexico is mixed. Mexico gained from NAFTA, but some have done better than others. Markets are more open and some economic units are more efficient. Growth in exports was strong, even during the 1995 recession. But none of this has led to high, sustained growth or to rising wages overall. This is due in part to the mix of neoliberal policies and the failure to coordinate macroeconomic stabilization with longer-term goals of market restructuring (Pastor and Wise 1997: 419). Employment in manufacturing fell, the poorly paid informal sector of the economy grew, and assets became more concentrated. Average wages for most of Mexico's industrial workers dropped 10 percent since the early 1990s, largely because of the financial crisis of 1994–1995 (Jordan 2000: 1J). Relative social spending has declined since the late 1980s. The North American Development Bank has yet to have a major impact on cleaning up the U.S.-Mexican border (Pfister 2000: lJ, 6J). Many Mexicans have not yet supped at the table of free trade prosperity. Meanwhile, Mexican democracy is inching forward, although it is hard to connect this directly to NAFTA itself.

A Bottom Line?

Promise and peril are linked. The first act of this regional drama is coming to a close—the RIAs are being implemented. But there are more acts to follow. Those who cheer and those who jeer have yet to see the curtain fall. Since the implementation of the RIAs, hopes and fears have held sway over an incomplete, mixed record.

NAFTA has helped to expand trade and investment. Exports among all three countries have gone up. First and foremost, NAFTA is a commercial pact. Those who have reaped the most were those who stood the most to gain in the first place. Others may have benefited, if not a great deal, whereas still others may have got little or nothing from the RIAs of North America. Some, especially the least competitive and the poor, may even have been hurt by the RIAs. At this point it is really very hard to tell for sure.

Discovering a bottom line may require a consensus, not quite achieved as yet, about who is to profit and how from the regional experiment. All of the players, including states, firms, workers, and others, may share some hopes for the RIAs. They may also share some fears. But as an experiment in regional political economy, NAFTA in particular galvanized a political debate among those who thought they would gain more than lose from it and among those who thought they would lose more than they would gain.

NAFTA is an imperfect crucible for free trade and markets. Liberal economic experiments like this one are filtered through political contestation. Hopes and fears, promise and peril, winners and losers are testimony to the politics as well as the economics of North American regionalism. The hope that all will win something, if not in equal proportions, is a powerful incentive for supporting the RIAs into the future. NAFTA and regional integration may in one way or another transform North America in the twenty-first century. Yet the bottom line for North American regionalism may always be a matter of controversy. To arrive at a fair and reasonable judgment about what has been wrought will require that we understand more fully what in fact will come out of the RIAs of the late twentieth century and what, if anything, is done to build upon them early in the twenty-first century.

8

NORTH AND SOUTH

The North American three share a region. But they also share a hemisphere. North American relations with the Americas as a whole may transform or be transformed by regionalism in the Americas.

Unlike North America, most states of the Americas are in the global South. Only Mexico is a global South country in North America. The global North and South now coexist in North America. NAFTA went beyond a traditional free trade agreement to accommodate countries with very different wage levels in the North and South (M. Smith 1993: 85). The question in the early twenty-first century, however, is whether and how North and South America can forge a regional integration agreement that accommodates the demands and needs of the global North and the global South throughout the entire hemisphere.

Bringing together the North and South in the Americas is part of an emerging enterprise. How North America fits within this broader task may shape inter-American relations well into the first part of the twenty-first century. To create a Free Trade Area of the Americas (FTAA) is something of a priority for virtually all countries in the Americas. A look at how and even if it will in fact unfold provides a fascinating glimpse into the new directions the Americas will be taking.

The goal of bridging North and South through an FTAA is indeed formidable. It recalls some of the issues surrounding North American regionalism in the early 1990s. The North American states may play a central role in devising a hemispheric RIA, yet finding common ground between the NAFTA three and the rest of the states in the Americas could ultimately transform hemispheric relations.

North America's role in the new regionalism of the hemisphere raises four intriguing questions. First, how did regionalism in the Americas evolve to this point? Second, what options did the NAFTA states consider for bridging North and South? Third, how have the NAFTA states, especially the United States, involved themselves in the issues and controversies embedded in the FTAA negotiating process? Fourth, how has the global South—in particular how have subregional RIAs like Mercosur (now made up of Brazil, Argentina, Paraguay, and Uruguay) and subregional leaders like Brazil—approached hemispheric regionalism?

Looking Backward

Regionalism of one sort or another has been a part of the Americas for more than a century. During the Cold War, the crosscurrents of inter-American relations put Latin America at odds with the United States. Communist influence, U.S. intervention, economic development strategies, political instability, and revolution in Cuba and Central America all became flash points for hemispheric rancor. But even as divergence sometimes seemed to pervade the hemisphere, convergence was also taking hold.

Security and development were particularly critical in the early Cold War years. The United States and Latin America held different perspectives on security and economic development. From the late 1940s to the early 1990s, the United States gave containment and strategic concerns priority over economic development in Latin America. Even the Alliance for Progress (1961–1971), a massive U.S. assistance program for its time and place, was really a geoeconomic strategy for containing communism within Cuba. Latin America, however, was as worried about economic development as it was about more Cubas. Still, its leaders were unable to convince the United States that economic development should be the principal national interest of the United States in the region. U.S. economic and trade policy was subordinate to security concerns in Latin America and elsewhere in the world during the last half of the twentieth century. Latin America was seen as a trouble spot more than a place of opportunity. Relative peace in Latin America brought benign neglect from the North. Instability and insurgency brought intervention and engagement.

Hemispheric divergence also went beyond these priorities. Well into the 1970s and even beyond, Latin American nationalism collided with U.S. interests in Latin America. Statism in Latin America clashed with U.S. fondness for markets. For much of the twentieth century, official policy in Latin America was prone to protectionism, subsidies, nationalization, export controls, and the like. U.S. policy preached the virtues of the market, private capital, and lenient rules for foreign direct investment. Latin American leaders argued for compensatory treatment and concessional aid from the United States. This did not go over very well in U.S. circles, except as a security policy for the Caribbean Basin in the 1980s. U.S. economic aid to Latin America and elsewhere was strategic more than developmental; it focused on a few hot spots rather than on the region as a whole. Moreover, the U.S. economic presence was keenly felt in some places (especially in the Caribbean Basin) but far less elsewhere (such as in the Southern Cone countries of Argentina, Brazil, Uruguay, and Paraguay).

Other asymmetries raised hackles in the Americas. The poor South needed the rich North far more than the other way around. For the United States, the blame for North-South difficulties rested with the mistakes and policies of poor, inward-looking states addicted to government intervention, inefficiency, and corruption. For Latin America, the North-South divide stemmed more from the use and abuse of U.S. economic power to extract unfair advantages from poor states. Seen from the South, the problem was located in the North. Seen from the North, the problem was due to Southern failures.

For many years, regionalism mirrored these divergences. Until well into the 1980s, the United States had its own take on inter-American cooperation. The United States wanted hemispheric regionalism as a Cold War weapon. U.S. leadership in inter-American organizations had been focused on security rather than economics. The Rio Pact and the Organization of American States served these goals. This inter-American system, as it was called, forced Cuba out of the OAS in the early 1960s, used military intervention from the 1950s to the 1980s, and offered Latin America benign neglect on most nonsecurity issues. Regionalism was about security.

To Latin America, regionalism meant something more. Borrowing from the ideas of South American liberator Simón Bolívar, Latin American regionalists sought unity while excluding the United States. These subregional economic blocs were not crafted in the U.S. mold. Rather, they were heavily protectionist and preferential, following import substitution strategies. By the 1960s and 1970s, the Central American Common Market (CACM), made up of Costa Rica, Nicaragua, El Salvador, Honduras, and Guatemala; the Andean Pact among Colombia,

Ecuador, Peru, Venezuela, and Bolivia; the fourteen members of the Caribbean Community (CARICOM); and other entities had become a presence, keeping the United States at bay. Regionalism for Latin America was economic, but it was not really Pan-American (Rocha Valencia 1997: 177). Neither was it really market-driven.

By end of the twentieth century, this had changed. Democratization, liberalization, regionalization, and globalization during the 1980s and 1990s set economic relations in the Americas on a somewhat different path. In the wake of the Cold War, the United States had also changed its tune: It adopted economic regionalism as its own. But so did Latin America. Latin America had gone from import substitution protectionism and its exclusive economic blocs to a more open and liberal approach. Convergence had opened the door to the "new regionalism."

Regional Rumblings

The year 1990 was crucial for regionalism in North America as well as South America. Two initiatives surfaced almost simultaneously. The first came from an improbable source. Five years earlier, Canada had been the "reluctant regionalist" (Weintraub 1994: 88); North America drew closer together. Not to be left out, Mexico became a demandeur of a free trade agreement with the United States in early summer 1990. This started a four-year process of creating the trilateral NAFTA.

The second initiative was perhaps more visionary. In June of that same year, the Bush administration announced the Enterprise for the Americas Initiative (EAI). As it turned out, the heart of the proposal was a Western Hemisphere free trade agreement. The U.S. preference for the Pan-American approach had once again reasserted itself. Bold, ambitious, and well-received, the EAI promised free trade and liberalized investment between the United States and Latin America. It also linked these promises to promoting democracy, human rights, and liberalization. The United States had shown a regionalist interest in North America and the Americas at the same time.

These two tracks—one for North America and one for the Americas as a whole—were not pursued with equal vigor. North America came first. By 1993 the United States had committed itself to NAFTA. The "three amigos" (as the Canadian prime minister dubbed the North American states in 1994) put each other as their number-one priority in regional trade negotiations during the early 1990s. It was not hard to discern the logic behind this. After all, the bond between the United States and Mexico was so unique that it resembled in some ways the economic relations between two developed countries (Gonzalez and Velez 1995). What is more, the developing country (Mexico) had to make more concessions than the developed ones in the agreement (Haggard 1995: 113). This may have led the rest of Latin America to have second thoughts about joining North America. Shared borders may have also tipped the scales toward North America. NAFTA promised freer cross-border trade, but it stopped short of going the extra mile by harmonizing domestic economic policy. This made it easier for the North American three to sign on the dotted line. Also, NAFTA foretold a diminished role for the state (Conroy and Glasmeier 1992–1993). At the time, the rest of the South in the Americas may have been less enthusiastic about this North American preference (see Table 8.1).

Although North America came first, the Americas were by no means left out. The argument was made that NAFTA could be the foundation to build a bridge between North and South in the Americas

Table 8.1 Share of U.S. Exports to the Western Hemisphere as a Percentage of U.S. Exports to the World, 1994

	U.S. Exports
North America	
Canada	22.29
Mexico	9.92
Mercosur	
Brazil	1.58
Argentina	0.87
Paraguay	—
Uruguay	—
Other Latin America	
Chile	0.54
Dominican Republic	0.54
Andean Pact	
Colombia	0.79
Ecuador	0.23
Peru	0.27
Venezuela	0.78
Bolivia	—
Central American Common Market	
Costa Rica	0.36
Guatemala	0.26

Source: Calculated from International Monetary Fund 1995: 436–438, 261–263.

rather than just in North America (Weintraub 1995: 77–84). Some were not so hopeful (Grunwald 1995: 71). Whatever the case, the second track was revived in the same year that NAFTA came into force. At their 1994 Miami summit, Western Hemispheric leaders adopted a "declaration of principles," which laid the foundation for a free trade agreement for the Americas. The declaration linked greater economic ties and free trade in the Americas to democracy, integration, prosperity, poverty reduction, and sustainable development. At the Santiago summit a few years later, the countries of the hemisphere renewed their vows to create an FTAA by 2005 and set in motion the negotiating structure to reach that goal.

The FTAA

North America's role in designing a new RIA for the Americas has shifted with time, revealing among other things that negotiating a free trade area for the Americas is not exactly the same as inventing NAFTA. Consequently, although U.S. influence in the invention of the new regionalism for the Americas is indeed impressive, it is not as overwhelming as it was in the creation of NAFTA.

First of all, as a U.S.-led RIA, NAFTA offered several possibilities for regionalism in the Americas. It served as a stimulant for other subregional efforts in the South in the Bolivaran tradition. During the early 1990s, Mercosur and the liberalized RIAs in the Andean and Central American areas clearly were influenced to some extent by what was happening in the developed North. For another thing, NAFTA might also be an anomaly. As a bridge for North-South relations, it was codifying a very unique relationship between the United States and Mexico. This "exceptional" bond does not exist throughout the Americas (Gonzalez and Velez 1995). In fact, in 1994, the year NAFTA came into force, most U.S. exports to Latin America did not even leave North America—they went only as far as Mexico (see Table 8.1). That is even more true now. What is more, there was some speculation that NAFTA could deepen into a genuine community leading to a more integrated region than envisioned under the original agreement (Doran and Drischler 1996; Inglehart et al. 1996; Earle and Wirth 1995; Bonser 1991). This would entail a transformation of the original NAFTA in which a European-style social contract in regionalism would use state policy to deal with disparities and gaps (Conroy and Glasmeier 1992–1993; Bulmer-Thomas et al.

1994: 212, 215). Deepening in North America would also increase economic benefits, especially with a currency union (Doran 1996: 68; Weintraub 1994: 12; Holle 1999: A11). Still, this would have been politically difficult to pull off, and it certainly would have sent to the south the message that North America was going it alone.

Two other options the North American states originally considered were more appropriate for the FTAA. First, NAFTA could be expanded or extended to the rest of the Americas through the accession clause. Among other things, this widening or broadening would allow for a more sweeping spread of benefits (Lawrence 1996: 77). Yet for a number of reasons, this option slipped away. For one thing, the political climate turned cool to regional free trade agreements in the United States after NAFTA. Next in line to join NAFTA, Chile instead opted for associate membership in Mercosur. For another, Brazil and Mercosur resisted joining a U.S.-led RIA like NAFTA. The second option is the use of the disciplines and the provisions of NAFTA as a model or guide for negotiating the FTAA. The United States, Canada, and Mexico agreed to stand alone rather than together as a bloc in the FTAA negotiations (Wrobel 1999: 297). Yet all three will no doubt engage in the FTAA process based on national preferences and the NAFTA precedent. The United States is particularly interested in seeing to it that NAFTA or NAFTA-friendly provisions on several critical points are included in the FTAA.

The North American states carved out for themselves their own positions on the FTAA. Canada was the only North American state to be very enthusiastic about the FTAA in the beginning (Morton 1999: 254). In the early negotiations, U.S. interest was lukewarm, perhaps fostered by the lack of fast-track authority to negotiate trade agreements in the U.S. Congress. Besides, the U.S.-China free trade agreement stirred the political cauldron in early 2000, although domestic opposition was not nearly so virulent toward the trade bill to extend freer trade to Central America, the Caribbean states, and sub-Saharan Africa (Schmitt 2000: A1, A12). Mexico is deeply ambivalent about the FTAA. Although it has no choice but to go along, its leaders believe that the FTAA will dilute Mexico's privileges under NAFTA.

The hemispheric summitry that put in motion the process toward the FTAA was clearly important for a North American role in designing the future architecture of inter-American economic relations. At its most basic, the Miami summit in 1994, as well as those summits that followed, confirmed the rise of the Pan-American approach to regionalism that the United States has long favored (Rocha Valencia 1997). Although subregionalism was allowed to coexist side by side with this hemispheric approach, the FTAA is an obvious vindication of U.S. preferences about broadening the liberal economic agenda and using regionalism to strengthen multilateralism. The United States was able to get the FTAA process to focus on some, but not all, NAFTA concerns, and it was able to broaden the negotiating process beyond existing hemispheric institutions (Feinberg 1997: 332).

But the United States made early concessions that may prove significant down the line. The United States gave up on the expansion of NAFTA; rather, a new complex negotiating process would be used to design a new RIA. This was a victory for Brazil, Mercosur, and others (Wrobel 1999: 297). The United States further agreed that negotiations should be based on an all-parties conference (Feinberg 1997: 139). Thirty-four states would theoretically be participants in negotiating the FTAA, compared to only three for NAFTA. The negotiating process would be a "single undertaking." The North American positions on this issue had been that this allowed for partial agreements leading to an overall deal at the very end, permitting small steps that could be implemented before a comprehensive FTAA package was adopted as early as 2005. But Canada and the United States did not prevail on this point. Brazil and Mercosur were able to argue successfully that "nothing is agreed until everything is agreed" (Morton 1999: 263). This, in effect, slows the process.

The difficulty of coming to terms on the FTAA revealed other differences within the Americas and within North America. The Americas are a far more diverse and unequal collection of states and economies than is North America. This makes an FTAA much harder to negotiate, but it also raises questions about the principles of reciprocity and equality enshrined in NAFTA. On this point North American states could not agree. The United States held to the classic NAFTA orthodoxy that even small, poor states in the Americas must play by the same rules as the larger ones. Canada disagreed, arguing rather that exceptions and concessions should be granted to the poor countries of the global South in the Americas (Morton 1999: 263). Other differences surfaced as well. Although the United States pressed hard for the protection of intellectual property rights in NAFTA, it was unable to get Canada to agree to a hard-and-fast IPR position without exemptions. Perhaps even more important, the United States virtually stood alone in the hemisphere about retaining domestic trade policy prerogatives such as countervailing duties and antidumping provisions.

Services, labor, and the environment also play up the possibility for discord in the FTAA process. The service sector, including finance and transportation, will likely be liberalized as it was under NAFTA and under the General Agreement on Trade in Services (GATS), a WTO-sponsored initiative. The United States, however, sought a "positive" approach that would liberalize these sectors more quickly, as opposed to the WTO approach favored by Brazil and others that would require a "listing" of sectors to be included. That is not all, of course. Labor and environment are NAFTA innovations that may be widely resisted in the negotiations. In fact, the technical working groups did not include either in their areas of competence. Yet it seems unlikely that, given the domestic climate in the United States, U.S. approval may be tied to these nontrade issues.

Labor and environment could eventually be the make-or-break issues for the FTAA if the United States insists on such provisions as it did during the NAFTA process. Although the early FTAA framework for negotiations does not include these issues directly, they could be critical for U.S. approval. It depends on two conditions. First, how hard the United States seeks to press for concessions on labor and the environment beyond the original negotiating framework could determine to a great extent whether they are in fact incorporated into the FTAA. NAFTA-like provisions on labor and environment are not very strict. If these were adopted in the FTAA, most countries in the Americas would find them rather easy to accommodate. But much depends upon whether trade sanctions are linked to the failure to meet national labor and environmental standards. In fact, this is a fundamental sticking point between many global South countries like India, on the one hand, and the United States, on the other, in any new round for multilateral negotiations sponsored by the WTO. Many global South members saw such a provision as "protectionism in the guise of idealism" (Dugger 1999: C4). Keeping labor and environment off the FTAA agenda would enhance the prospects of agreement on its final text.

The second condition involves the status of the free trade coalition in the United States and its influence in Congress. After NAFTA and the Uruguay Round in 1994, the free trade coalition in the United States ran into stern resistance. The politicization of free trade during the late 1990s meant that both opposition and advocates were locked into a competitive stalemate that slowed U.S. involvement in RIAs. For example, the bitter battle over NAFTA essentially precluded NAFTA's expansion and the inclusion of Chile during the late 1990s. The agreement on U.S.-China trade and the U.S. trade bill for the Caribbean and

Africa showed that free trade has not been removed from the agenda. It does, however, indicate that free trade prospects are by no means preordained. National elections, especially in the U.S. House of Representatives, may be key to renovating the free trade coalition and the prospects for free trade and for the FTAA in particular. But economic liberalization through regionalism and globalization has brought with it a strong backlash over equity, adjustment, and social programs in the United States and elsewhere (Rodrik 1997). If this continues to hold sway in domestic politics, then the free trade coalition in the United States may have a difficult time delivering the support needed to approve an FTAA without concessions on these issues.

The test of U.S. willingness to approve an FTAA may be fast-track authority. Fast-track authority allows a quicker and more certain passage of complex trade legislation by requiring both houses of Congress to vote the agreement either up or down, without making substantive changes. Opinions differ on how crucial this may be for the success of the FTAA. The slow progress in the negotiations early on suggested that without U.S. fast-track authority to approve the trade agreement, the eventual success of negotiating the FTAA in the Americas was up for grabs. The failure of the Clinton administration to secure fast-track authority in 1997 and again in 1998 certainly compromised U.S. credibility in the FTAA negotiation process. The U.S. Congress is severely cross-pressured on free trade legislation, and this made granting fast-track authority or even eventual approval of a trade bill harder to foresee (Destler 1998: 148). Still, this may not be the entire story. The Uruguay Round of negotiations, which lasted eight years, began without any guarantees about fast-track authority. In fact, withholding fast-track authority in the initial stages may be an inadvertently wise avenue for expanding negotiating advantages for the global North.

Perhaps more ominous for free trade agreements are the post-Seattle atmospherics surrounding complex trade negotiations at the multilateral or even regional levels. The protests and discord at the WTO meeting in Seattle in late 1999 provided a "wake-up call," according to President Clinton (Kahn 2000: A6). Free trade cannot be advanced in the U.S. political environment and perhaps elsewhere unless these "new voices" are taken into account and issues of equity, environment, and justice are put on the table. Essentially, the fallout from the "battle in Seattle" meant that a new round of multilateral negotiations under the auspices of the WTO would have to be postponed. This reflects the "globalization syndrome" associated with the global division of labor and power, the new regionalism, and resistance politics (see Mittelman 2000: 4). The syndrome has certainly made itself felt, and it is unclear to what extent it could affect the FTAA.

Mercosur

NAFTA members are important players in the FTAA process, but they are hardly the only ones. The future of hemispheric regionalism depends upon what happens in the South as well as what happens in the North. An FTAA without key members of the global South would be as crippling for hemispheric regionalism as an FTAA without the NAFTA members.

As we have seen, regionalism in Latin America has a distinguished pedigree. But since the 1980s, it has taken on a somewhat different task. The Central American Common Market, the Caribbean Community, and the Andean Pact were first-generation regional economic areas. As such, they used state policy to protect markets and to serve national interests. Created in the era of import substitution strategy, they preceded by many years the conversion of Latin American states to economic liberalization and market precepts. During the last part of the twentieth century, however, these first-generation arrangements went through a transition, adopting more liberal codes and rules.

The most formidable subregional economic zone in Latin America is second generation. In the early 1990s, and to some extent in response to NAFTA, four countries in Latin America created their own subregional grouping. The Common Market of the South, or Mercosur, is the world's third largest RIA. At the time of its founding, it was made up of Brazil, Argentina, Paraguay, and Uruguay, with some 200 million people and a combined GDP of $900 billion (1995), and it accounted for $100 billion in world trade. Since then, Chile and Bolivia have become associate members and others are thinking about joining.

What the United States is to NAFTA, Brazil is to Mercosur. Brazil's sheer economic presence allows it to hold sway over this southern experiment with regional economic integration. Argentina is the junior partner, attracted to but still leery of Brazil's regional hegemony. Paraguay and Uruguay are the small members, now hitching their economic fate to the other two.

Regionalism in the Southern Cone stands on its own. It does not imitate NAFTA or even the EU. Even so, Mercosur has not sealed itself off from the North or from the rest of the world for that matter. The South needs the North, and this interdependence must be managed or at least orchestrated through several strategies, including common policies on trade and investment (Hurrell 1992: 124). But Mercosur is also an exclusively southern RIA, with its own way of doing things.

The global South in the Americas and Mercosur in particular have incentives for reaching out to the North. For one thing, there is economic efficiency. Bringing North and South together in some fashion could maximize economies of scale, production efficiencies, and comparative advantages. Mercosur would therefore expect to reap some gains if it were to "multilateralize" its ties beyond the Southern Cone and to build connections between the two most robust versions of regionalism in the Americas. Mercosur countries would stand to gain from a merger with the North in an FTAA. Like Mexico, Latin America and especially the Southern Cone would stand to benefit from greater, guaranteed access to the U.S. market; to be excluded or put at a disadvantage by remaining outside the North American bloc would be unfortunate. Linking up with the United States would also allow Latin America to use North America as a gateway to the world economy. Bridging the North and South would strengthen the ethos of free trade and liberalization, build upon the multilateral trading system, improve regional security, and foster growth (Dornbusch 1995: 37–39).

The Common Market of the South has already achieved something. Under the Treaty of Asunción of 1991, it staked out an ambitious program of tariff reductions and other liberalization, coordination of macroeconomic policy, a common external tariff to increase member efficiency, a trade litigation framework, and institutional development with several subgroups (Manzetti 1993–1994: 105–106). In principle, it stood for free trade in goods and services with factor mobility among members (Nogues and Quintanilla 1993: 296). By the mid-1990s Mercosur had achieved some but not all of its goals. Free trade and subregional institutions are its relative strengths, but it is also burdened with important difficulties. The CET is only partially operational (on 85 percent of tariff items), full liberalization of nontrade activity has still not been attained, and the problem of relative gains continues to plague an association unbalanced by asymmetries of market size, divergent domestic policies, and unfair trade. The common market goal still awaits completion.

Whatever its accomplishments thus far, Mercosur is no NAFTA wannabe. Its approach as an RIA stands apart from that of NAFTA. Mercosur grapples with liberalization after its own fashion. In some ways it is open and nondiscriminatory, but as a customs union it is also inclined to protectionism. NAFTA insists on reciprocity among unequals. Reciprocity may be unappealing to more independent countries of the south like Brazil. Oddly enough, NAFTA is also more demanding in some areas than Mercosur, even though NAFTA is "only" a free trade agreement whereas Mercosur aspires to become a common market. North America under NAFTA is better prepared for economic integration than are Brazil, Argentina, Paraguay, and Uruguay (Hufbauer and Schott 1994: 6). Regionalization as a structural process is more advanced and movement of capital, labor, and goods is more intense in North America than in the Southern Cone.

Yet Mercosur has deeper aspirations than NAFTA. Its partial common external tariff might make it harder to merge with NAFTA, which does not have one. But it is perhaps best described as an imperfect customs union rather than a common market (Nofal 1995: 211). Even so, this is farther than the FTA-plus agreement of North America goes. There are other differences as well. Mercosur at first did not tackle NAFTA issues of liberalizing foreign direct investment, the service trade, finance, or the protection of intellectual property rights (Nofal 1995: 216). What is more, the side agreements in NAFTA, specifically on the environment and labor, could be another stumbling block to the merger of these two dynamic experiments in economic regionalism in the Americas. Environmental standards for a regionwide arrangement, even based on national criteria, may cool Latin American interest in an FTAA. These states remain sensitive about domestic prerogatives (Pearson 1995: 330).

There are other issues. NAFTA specifies dispute settlement processes more than does Mercosur. The United States has dealt forcefully with Brazilian steel exports, imposing import restrictions for alleged dumping (Sanger 1999: C1, C3). NAFTA has stricter rules of origin since it is a free trade rather than a customs union arrangement. The further evolution of Mercosur could arguably make it more likely that NAFTA and Mercosur could one day find common ground, but for now they are parallel paths to basically the same goals.

Mercosur wanted nothing to do with a NAFTA merger, although Argentina flirted with the idea. The reasons have to do with the evolution of Mercosur and the political as well as economic agendas of its founding members. The emergence of Mercosur testifies to the importance of domestic change and reform as well as the international political economy. Regional trade and a common external tariff were the main features of a process that Mercosur states bring to the table over FTAA negotiations.

Brazil, its dominant member, could affect whether Mercosur becomes a stepping-stone toward a North-South merger of some sort (Nofal 1995: 219). As the South's foremost example of economic regionalism, Mercosur may even be regarded as a counterweight to a NAFTA-led hemisphere. Reluctant to accept NAFTA officially, Mercosur may still have to deal with NAFTA-inspired propositions about national treatment, reciprocity, and dispute settlement in the FTAA process.

Brazil, Mercosur, and the FTAA

Brazil has a lot—perhaps the most—at stake in Mercosur. This RIA provides Brazil with a measure of prestige, even preeminence, that it might not have enjoyed if Mercosur had in fact been merged with NAFTA or even if it shares the hemisphere with an FTAA. Brazil dominates Mercosur. Early on, Brazil got more out of the RIA than did Argentina. Brazil's more-regulated economy has been able to take advantage of Argentina's less-regulated economy. Despite Brazil's dominance, this led to mini trade wars. Brazil's currency crisis in early 1999 cut Argentina's exports to its largest trade partner by 30 percent. Later that same year, Brazil canceled trade negotiations with Argentina, and Argentina threatened to impose tariffs on Brazilian exports (Romero 1999: B2). Such disputes may be part and parcel of Mercosur's evolution. Policy harmonization and coordination have not pressured Brazil into a "fairer" and more "liberal" economic position within Mercosur. By practicing some preferential protection for its own economy, Brazil has been able to take advantage of liberalization without conceding as much in return. This has been shown to occur in trade balances favorable to Brazil (Nofal 1995: 210). Brazil has come out ahead so far and may be reluctant to compromise its lead.

There is something to be said for Brazil's proprietary attitude about Mercosur because it allows Brazil to gain more in absolute and relative terms than it would otherwise. Argentina and Brazil do share an imperfect consensus over Mercosur's benefits (Soares de Lima 1996: 148). Yet Argentina has looked north toward the United States more than has Brazil. To move closer to the United States could be a difficult choice for Brazil. Brazil's easier access to the U.S. market, investment, and external support for stabilization policies could certainly make a North-South merger more attractive. North America accounts for 87 percent of the hemisphere's output. Mercosur's trade is only 8 percent of the hemisphere's trade. But with the FTAA Brazil might have to play by U.S. rules, and such an agreement might also force the pace of Brazilian domestic reform, including deregulation, liberalization, and the end of export subsidies. This would be hard for Brazil to accept, although it may eventually be pressured to do this anyway.

So Brazil has reasons of its own to resist or at least be very cautious about an FTAA. The FTAA could accord a less dominant role for Brazil in a hemispheric relationship. If Brazil can consolidate Mercosur under its own leadership, it could circumvent the United States in its own attempt to reach out to the global economy. From a Brazilian perspective, an independent Mercosur would provide greater national flexibility at the expense of benefits derived from being included in NAFTA. Brazil's global foreign policy may therefore be an important reason for the political motivation to be cautious about a regional integration of North and South in the hemisphere.

The South and especially Mercosur will no doubt have an impact on the FTAA process. Mercosur has approached the negotiations as a bloc, enhancing Brazil's influence even more and entrenching Mercosur's place as a subregional force to be reckoned with (Wrobel 1999: 297; Morton 1999: 271). The Bolivaran approach will not go quietly in the face of hemispheric cooperation.

Mercosur and Brazil have taken positions in the FTAA negotiations that show how the FTAA will not be NAFTA writ large. Led by Brazil, Mercosur's cautious and even suspicious stand on the FTAA implies that moving too quickly is unwise. It is also quite clear that early in the negotiations Brazil and Mercosur were skeptical about North American and especially U.S. positions on regulatory policy, liberalization of the service sector, and protection of intellectual property rights, to mention just a few. Brazil was also triumphant in the sense that an FTAA rather than an expansion of NAFTA would be the mechanism for creating a hemispheric RIA, and it was able to prevail with others on the issue of comprehensive final text.

Brazil confronts opportunities as well as risks in the FTAA process. The opportunities for taking advantage of the U.S. market are enormous. Trade is growing quickly between Brazil and the United States; Brazilian manufactured exports would receive a major boost from a more accessible North American market. But the risks are also serving as restraints on Brazilian enthusiasm for an FTAA. Brazil is playing a complex strategic game. On the one hand, it wishes to maximize its gains by jumping on the bandwagon with the United States and North America. On the other, it wishes to play off the power of the United States in South America. The most obvious way to do this is to emphasize multilateralism over regionalism and to emphasize tighter relations with the European Union, its largest trade partner. In this way Brazil would have a better chance of gaining more from the tighter North-South economic relationship because it would keep open options to go global or even European as a counterweight to the economic and political power from the north. Brazil's efforts to conclude a trade agreement with the EU should be seen in this light. In fact, the net economic effect of the EU agreement on Brazil would probably be greater than that of the FTAA (IRELA 1999: 13). Brazil's trade, credibility, and bargaining positions would be enhanced from such an agreement with the EU and, what is more, it might give Brazil a modicum of leverage with the United States on key sectors such as agriculture and textiles (IRELA 1999: 8).

The Others

The United States with the other NAFTA states and Brazil with the other Mercosur states are the major players in the FTAA process. Their engagement may hold the key to success or disappointment in creating a new regionalism for the entire hemisphere. But they are not the only states to have a voice or to be affected. The Andean Pact and the Central American Common Market are renovated first-generation regional blocs that have adapted to the shifting breezes of a more liberal economic climate. As such, they along with the twenty-nine members of the Association of Caribbean States and some other small states are also participants in the process. Small economies with some degree of shared interests, the Andean and Central American countries have their own experience with subregional integration to contribute to the FTAA process, but they cannot presume to be major players in designing the architecture of hemispheric regionalism in the way that NAFTA and Mercosur states will.

The Andean Pact set a course toward liberalization to which the FTAA would make a contribution. In 1990 at La Paz, the Andean Pact states renewed the Andean Treaty with the Act of Barahona. In so doing, they committed themselves to a more outward and more liberal approach to trade and investment that is generally in tune with the spirit of the FTAA. For example, they adopted national treatment of foreign investment and curbed nontariff barriers. They also created a free trade zone for Ecuador, Peru, Bolivia, Colombia, and Venezuela and adopted a common external tariff with exemptions for some sectors such as agriculture and autos. The commitment to this transformation does vary a bit, however. Bolivia and Peru are strong supporters of liberal economic integration, but the others are less enthusiastic (Nogues and Quintanilla 1993: 300). A former member of the pact, Chile, the most liberal economy in the global South, prefers to keep its options open and to affiliate with larger, more liberal movements.

The Central American Common Market has similarly followed a parallel evolution. It saw the light of day in the 1960s as a managed, inward-looking trade bloc. Yet it, too, modified if not totally transformed itself to become a more liberal experiment in subregionalism. Renewed in the Declaration of Antigua in 1990, after years of economic and political crisis in Central America, the CACM set forth ambitious goals toward a more liberal vision of economic integration, the most important of which were to expand free trade among the members, to fashion a partial CET, and to harmonize agricultural policies, rules of origin, and antidumping policies (Nogues and Quintanilla 1993: 301–302).

The Andean Pact and CACM are followers rather than leaders of hemispheric regionalism. If anything, they are trying to cover their bets. The CACM is disadvantaged in the U.S. market by Mexico's privileges under NAFTA. Along with the Caribbean states, the members of the CACM could reap some economic rewards from a relationship with NAFTA that goes beyond the Caribbean Basin Initiative. This could be partially accomplished through duty-free access to the U.S. market in the Caribbean and African trade bill. For their part, some of the Andean Pact members are also going beyond the pact as well. For example, Bolivia (as well as Chile, a former pact member) has an affiliated status with Mercosur. The smaller players are gravitating to one of the two regional poles in the Americas.

North, South, and the FTAA

The Pan-American vision of an integrated, free trade area from Prudhoe Bay in the far north to the Tierra del Fuego in the far south is inching toward an uncertain destiny. The Americas have undertaken a Herculean task of economic statecraft. Whether it succeeds or not, the process itself could crystallize within the region a new sense of engagement and cooperation from North and South. Inter-American relations will perhaps never be quite the same. The thirty-four states in the FTAA process, as different and unequal as they are, will come to a point that they are closer together for having engaged in this hemispheric experiment, however it may turn out.

Like the states that make up North America, the two Americas are not equal partners. The FTAA must be forged within a context of exchange, asymmetry, and bargaining. This creates opportunities and challenges to affect inter-American relations for decades to come.

The states of the existing RIAs and the domestic coalitions within those states could be decisive in bridging the North and South in the Americas. Devising an FTAA through a single negotiating process with all states may ultimately depend upon the ability of different states to marshal support, both domestic and regional. To arrive at a WTO-consistent FTAA will require building on the past while reconciling different interests and tendencies in the uncertain process of regionalism. This is a task worthy of Prometheus, but it is not impossible. What regionalism in the Americas and in North America has so far taught us is that the improbable can—and sometimes actually does—occur eventually. With or without an FTAA, the Americas cannot escape the very hemispheric realities that led the states of the region to venture forth on this ambitious quest in the first place.

9

Between East and West

As was discussed in Chapter 4, regionalism and regionalization elsewhere in the world helped to persuade North Americans that they, too, must draw closer together. Asia Pacific and the European Union clearly had something to do with the invention of North America in the 1990s.

So where does this leave the three main regions at the turn of the century? This question is vital for understanding North America's place in a world of regions, but it is also important for understanding how links among these three regions may affect globalization. North America is the only one of the three regions that has extensive relations with the other two. North America is truly situated between east and west. How North America fares in its relations with the Asia Pacific and the European Union could shape regionalism in a globalized world well into the twenty-first century.

Asia Pacific, the EU, and North America are different peas in the same pod. Take structure, for example. The EU is led by Germany and France. Even after years of recession, Japan still leads the Asia Pacific. Only in North America is the core state so dominant. Unity and diversity vary from region to region as well as within regions. Wealth and power are more unevenly distributed in Asia and North America. What is more, the EU and the Asia Pacific traditionally favor a more dominant role for the state in capitalism than does North America. The regions are different institutionally, too. The EU is the most sophisticated and ambitious, whereas the other two, especially the Asia Pacific, are not very institutionalized. Regionalism is strong in Europe, moderately vibrant in North America, but not as robust in Asia.

What all three regions share is important, however. The tripolar world forms a plutocracy. At the hub or core of each region is at least one great economic power. Size and economic power bestow on the United States and North America special status. Although relatively less important than it was at midcentury, the U.S. economy was (in 1996) more than twice as large as Japan's economy, with a GDP of $7.5 trillion compared to $2.5 trillion (OECD 1997a: 24). Recession and stagnation in Japan and Germany during the 1990s did nothing to dislodge either of them from their status as great economic powers in their own regions.

The other states in the three regions are likewise well-off in relative terms. All but two of the top twenty of the world's countries in terms of GDP per capita are located in one of the three regions. All three countries in North America make this list (World Bank 1995: 18, 19). In size alone, the United States is almost as big as all members of the EU combined. What makes all of these countries so privileged is no secret. Educated human capital, finance capital accumulation, technological innovation, and organizational and material resources are concentrated in the three regions. Many states in the three regions score high on measures of quality of life, such as life expectancy.

Not only do the tripolar regions cut a wide swath in the world economy, but their states are the world's leading trading states. The United States accounts for 14.2 percent of all trade in the world, leading all others. On a smaller scale, the rest of North America is made up of trading states as well. Canada accounted for about 3.4 percent of the world's trade in the mid-1990s and Mexico about 1.5 percent (Economist 1999: 30).

If anything, the other two regions are even more involved in trade. Asia Pacific is home to important trading states. Using its own brand of state-market collaboration, Japan decades ago launched an aggressive national strategy of export expansion and import control. Since 1945 it sought to prosper by increasing trade surpluses through aggressively exporting to the rest of Asia, North America, and to some extent even Europe. In the mid-1990s Japan made up 9.3 percent of the world's trade. Some of its regional trading partners have followed suit. The tigers of Hong Kong, Taiwan, Singapore, and South Korea have become almost legendary as second-generation trading states. China and other Asian states are or are becoming major trading states as well. Although Asia has exporting juggernauts, Europe is the world's leading trade region, accounting for more than two-fifths of all the world's trade (WTO 1995: 38). A good deal of it is conducted within the region. Germany is third behind the United States and Japan in world trade. Clearly, trade is the lifeblood of the tripolar regions.

West Meets West

North America and Europe are the two western poles of the tripolar world economy. Transatlantic relations have evolved dramatically since 1945. During the last half of the twentieth century, U.S.-European relations progressed through several stages. Emerging from a wartime alliance, the transatlantic bond was hegemonic. U.S. interests in Europe rested on Soviet containment and European recovery. But the pacification of Europe was another major concern. Bringing peace to Europe made regionalism more compelling. The opposite was also true: Regionalism enhanced peace within Europe.

By the end of the twentieth century, Europe's lofty aspirations were haltingly moving toward reality. European regionalism had been blessed by the United States, but it is largely beyond its control. Pursuing deeper and wider integration in the 1990s, the European Community (later the European Union) had in many ways reached economic parity with the United States. In the twilight of the Cold War, the United States was no longer the economic and security hegemon in Europe that it once was (Calleo 1987; Lepgold 1990).

Out of the Cold

The Cold War (1947–1989) set the context for transatlantic relations in the last half of the twentieth century. To rebuild Europe was an immediate goal after World War II. The United States sought a united, independent center of power in Europe. To defend Europe the North Atlantic Treaty Organization (NATO) was created. To rebuild a prosperous Europe, the United States funded the Marshall Plan. The United States also opened its market to European exports. By the 1950s, six states had taken steps toward European unity. The free trade agreement, followed by the Treaty of Rome in 1957 and subsequent acts, deepened Europe's regionalism with each passing decade. The United States was generally supportive.

A united Europe served U.S. security goals. European economic regionalism was seen as a tool for containing Soviet power in Europe. The creation of NATO under U.S. sponsorship in 1949 extended deterrence against a possible Soviet invasion to Western and Central Europe. Canada joined with the United States in making NATO a transatlantic pact to defend Europe. To recall Lord Ismay, NATO kept the United States in, the Soviets out, and the Germans down. By pacifying Europe, NATO sowed seeds for economic regionalism as well.

Cold War Years

For the most part, though, the Cold War encouraged European unity. The German question and the crises over Berlin in 1949 and 1961 tested the alliance. U.S. resources and military might were the pillars of the alliance, but a cooperative junior partnership made the asymmetry in relations palatable. A notable exception was the French decision in the mid-1960s to develop its own independent nuclear force. In the early 1980s, there was another dustup over defense issues. The deployment of intermediate nuclear forces in some NATO countries shook the alliance. Through all of this, European unity eventually began to take root.

Canada had a hand in transatlantic security as well. In fact, as North America's most loyal Anglophone country, Canada historically looked east more than it did to Latin America. Indeed, it is for this reason that the United States opposed Canadian membership in the Pan American Union after World War I (Thompson and Randall 1994: 7, 86). If Britain was Canada's historic parent, NATO was Canada's institutional link to the European continent.

U.S. and Canadian views on Europe usually converged on the fundamentals, if not always on the details. All the while, the United States often expected Canadian loyalty in dealings with Europe and the Cold War. For its part, Canada wanted to be heard, perhaps as a broker between the United States and Europe. It sought a role as a middle power committed to multilateralism and independent of U.S. grand strategy (Nossal 1989: 46).

What brought Canada and the United States even closer together was that they shared fundamentally the same view of international politics in the Cold War era. The Soviet Union, Canada, and the United States played a role in European security (Fox 1985: 8). Like the United States, Canada had a strong aversion to Soviet foreign policy. This uncompromising opposition to the Soviet Union rested primarily on the same premise that the United States adopted for its containment policy in Europe: the fear of Soviet expansionism (Thompson and Randall 1994: 189–190).

Mexico and Europe were less actively engaged with each other for much of the twentieth century. Historically leery of European colonialism and a victim of Hapsburg ambitions in the 1860s, Mexico kept its diplomatic distance. It stayed out of the Cold War as much as possible. And it sometimes took stands contrary to the United States on such issues when they flared up in its own region. Cuba was a classic case. On the whole, Mexico's stand in the world was defensive nationalism. In the 1970s it made a bid for Third World leadership. It walked a tightrope between U.S. domination and Soviet intentions. For Mexico, Europe was a potential ally as it tried to offset growing U.S. dominance in its neighborhood. But Mexico was of limited interest to Europe. During the 1980s Europe (except for Great Britain) was sympathetic to Mexico's official posture against U.S. intervention in Central America. Overall, though, Mexico stood on the sidelines.

The Ties That Bind

During the 1990s, North America and Europe had to build their relationship in the absence of the Soviet threat. Although security concerns in Eastern Europe and the Balkans tested the relationship, the most enduring interests were clearly elsewhere.

The EU is a formidable economic player. Its efforts to promote a single market with a monetary union in the 1990s were largely independent of North American initiatives but with its approval. The EU is both a counterweight and a partner of North America. Cordial relations generally prevail, but the United States and the EU do not see eye to eye on all issues.

One tie that clearly binds them both is trade. True, the states of each region tend to trade more among themselves than with anyone else. Just over one-third of all merchandise trade for North America was intraregional, and just over two-thirds of such trade was intraregional for the EU (WTO 1995: 38). Still, both regions rely heavily on each other for transatlantic trade. The EU ranks first or second for North America as an export market outside North America. Likewise, North America ranks first for the EU. Mexico exports more to the EU than it does to any other region outside North America. Canadian and U.S. exports to the EU are surpassed only by the value of their exports to the Asia Pacific. Neither Europe nor North America could easily do without the other.

Even more than trade, investment is what really reinforces the overarching importance of economic relations between the EU and the United States. Indeed, generally friendly trade relations in the absence of a specific bilateral agreement between North America and the EU can be attributed to the high levels of foreign direct investment (Schott

1996: 32). Since the mid-1980s, transpacific trade has outstripped transatlantic trade. But Europe leads the world as a source for foreign investment in the United States. In 1996, 65 percent of all foreign investment in the United States came from Europe (see Table 9.1). The Netherlands, Britain, and Germany were the European countries with the greatest investment in the United States.

Investment is a two-way street. Europe is the preferred destination for U.S. investment abroad. Half of all U.S. foreign direct investment went to Europe in 1996; the EU countries received 43.7 percent of all U.S. investment (see Table 9.2). Still, U.S. private investment in Europe is selective. Great Britain receives more U.S. foreign direct investment (17.8 percent) than does any other EU state. In contrast, Japan has a

Table 9.1 Foreign Direct Investment in the United States, 1992–1999

	1992	1993	1994	1995	1996	1997	1998	1999
Total ($ billions)	423.1	467.4	496.5	560.8	630.0	693.2	793.7	986.6
% from Canada	8.8	8.6	8.4	8.6	8.5	10.0	9.3	8.0
% from Europe	59.0	60.9	61.1	63.6	65.1	62.4	66.6	69.5
% from Asia Pacific	25.7	24.0	—	—	—	21.5	19.6	17.0
Of which % Japan	23.1	21.5	20.7	19.2	18.7	18.0	16.9	15.0
Others	6.5	6.5	9.6	8.4	7.5	6.1	4.5	9.5

Sources: Data calculated from *Survey of Current Business,* Vol. 77, No. 9 (September 1997): 80, table 4; 84, table 10.1; 79, table 3; *Survey of Current Business,* Vol. 79, No. 7 (July 1999): 58, table 4.1; *Survey of Current Business,* Vol. 80, No. 7 (July 2000): 68–69, tables 4.1, 4.2.

Table 9.2 U.S. Foreign Investment Position Abroad, 1993–1999

	1993	1994	1995	1996	1997	1998	1999
Total ($ billions)	564.7	621.0	711.6	776.4	865.5	1014.2	1132.6
% to Canada	12.3	12.0	11.4	11.4	11.1	10.0	9.8
% to Europe	50.5	49.8	51.0	50.1	48.5	52.0	51.3
% to Asia Pacific	16.4	17.4	17.7	17.6	16.9	15.3	16.4
Of which % Japan	5.5	5.9	5.5	—	5.3	3.5	4.2
Others	21.8	21.8	19.9	21.9	23.5	19.2	18.3

Sources: Data calculated from *Survey of Current Business,* Vol. 77, No. 9 (September 1997): D-62, table G.2; 120, table 3; 126–128, table II.1; *Survey of Current Business,* Vol. 79, No. 7 (July 1999): 56, table 3.1; *Survey of Current Business,* Vol. 80, No. 7 (July 2000): 66–67, tables 3.1, 3.2.

relatively low exposure to U.S. foreign direct investment. Even though Japan is the world's second largest economy, it absorbed only 5.5 percent of all U.S. foreign direct investment. In other words, Europe is more than a major trade partner for the United States. Unlike Asia, the EU has both very strong trading and investment relations with the United States.

Two Paths

Europe and North America pursue their own regionalist paths. The European Union diverges in significant ways from the North American Free Trade Agreement. The EU is a fairly self-absorbed, integrated, institutional, and ambitious venture in regionalism. Economic and even political union is its goal. The EU also aspires to supranationality. Its member states pool and perhaps even surrender sovereignty over important issues of economic policy in what has been called a "federal system minus" (Kahler 1995: 82–83). They aspire also to develop a common foreign and security policy for the future. Labor migration, taxation, monetary policy, fiscal policy, and a host of economic issues are susceptible to regional governance. The EU wants to do more than merely coordinate and harmonize policies; it wants to raise the level at which these policies are made.

The EU's commitment to deep integration will likely go at its own pace and in its own direction, but important challenges still lie ahead. Monetary union is an example. The euro as a regional currency is a bold effort, even with some holdouts. The problem of widening may also challenge EU aspirations for regionalism. As the EU expands to the east, others await membership. A deepened region with even more new members could be an arduous task.

NAFTA is a different RIA. As an FTA-plus agreement, it is a more modest approach to regional integration than is the EU. It rids North America of barriers (mostly at borders), but it does not intend to build strong supranational efforts on economic policy. Its goal is to regionalize markets but not to create a new community. It expects less of its members, and it insists that the RIA serve the three states rather than the other way around. In Europe the region is becoming larger than the sum of its parts. That is not yet the case in North America.

Although their paths diverge, North America and the EU are not that far apart in some ways. Both western poles of the tripolar world economy are deeply committed to global and interregional economic ties. Notwithstanding their different approaches to regionalism, both are part of the globalized economy and both remain committed to multilateralism. EU–North American relations can move ahead despite their regionalism. In fact, it is absolutely necessary that they do so. Regionalism and globalization as well as cooperation and conflict coexist in the world political economy.

This mostly peaceful coexistence is not always easy. U.S. trade officials must be prepared to deal directly with Eurocrats independently of the leaders from the member states. In fact, in the mid-1990s the United States and the EU tried but failed to come to terms on a trade agreement. Mexico and the EU, however, did arrive at such a pact. States can still do things that regions cannot. A Transatlantic Free Trade Area (TAFTA) could move the EU away from its "parochial concentration" on things European (Dobbins 1996: 18–19). But different regionalisms march to their own drummers. When that happens, bilateralism and multilateralism are still available for states.

Agreeing to Disagree

The EU and North America agree on a great deal, to be sure, but they also disagree. "Markets," "states," and "liberalism" are often the code words in such transatlantic disputes. But fundamental issues involve distribution of gains as well. In recent years the North American chorus has sung largely in unison. Free trade, markets, liberalism, and competition have become the North American rallying points for seeking EU concessions on trade and other issues. But the Washington consensus is not European. The drumbeat of liberal market capitalism emanating from North America has been heard in Europe, but some have not picked up the rhythm. Germany and France, the anchors of the EU, have their own preferences. Germany's "social market economy" commits the government to social and other programs to make up for the lack of conscience found in the imperfections of pure market economics (Garten 1992: ch. 4). State subsidies and higher unemployment were fixtures of such economies in the 1990s. France harbors its own doubts about American liberalism. In the Anglo-American view, the French dirigiste model allows for an "over-sheltered, welfare-cushioned, state-stifled, centralised, quaint, and archaic" role for the state in the economy ("France: The Grand Illusion" 1999: 5). The Gallic view is different. The French prime minister in 1997 condemned the "ultracapitalism" of the United States. Always sensitive to cultural slights, the French also are prone to regard U.S.-style market capitalism as distasteful Americanization. Free trade could even be seen as an English-speaking principle (Carlisle 1996: 118). Even so, French business is becoming more liberal as time goes by.

Naturally, such differences set the tone for specific transatlantic issues. Americans and Europeans have crossed swords on trade and subsidies time and again. When the United States squared off with the EU during the eight years of the Uruguay Round of GATT negotiations, the friction over agricultural free trade almost scuttled the whole process. The United States sought a total ban on agricultural subsidies and protection within ten years. The EU's rejection of this position, sustained by powerful agricultural interests in countries like France and other opponents in some southern EU countries, led to months of stalemate. Eventually, the United States backed off its position and the Uruguay Round was concluded in 1995.

In the late 1990s, sparring over trade and subsidies continued. Once again agricultural commodities were at ground zero. U.S. companies were unable to export bananas into the EU and suffered financially for it. The United States sought compensation for Chiquita Brands and Dole Food Company from the WTO. In April 1999 the WTO ruled in favor of the United States (Schwartz 1999: 1D, 2D). U.S. beef exports to the EU have also been restricted. Genetically engineered food and other products have likewise been the subject of controversy. The EU has its own list of complaints. It has argued that U.S. law allowing companies such as General Motors, Microsoft, and Boeing to avoid paying taxes on some overseas sales by channeling them through offshore subsidiaries is illegal under the WTO rules. The WTO agreed (Olson 2000: C4).

These tensions are important in the transatlantic relationship. But they have not fundamentally altered or degraded the generally harmonious relations between the two regions. When west meets west, one should, after all, expect a few bumps in the road.

Around the Rim

North America's relations with the Asia Pacific is the main East-West connection within the tripolar economy. Asia Pacific is a far-flung collectivity more than it is a coherent region. It is a broad expanse of many disparate countries on the western edge of the world's largest ocean. North Americans looking to the east tend to focus on the rising sun. Although Japan may have been uppermost in the North American mind when North America organized itself in the early 1990s, Asia Pacific is more than Japan. Indeed, China's rise as a regional power may be the defining feature of the area: It is projected to become the world's largest economy in the first part of the twenty-first century. Asia Pacific also includes the diverse states of the tigers (Hong Kong, Korea, Taiwan, and Singapore), Southeast Asia, the Philippines, and culturally anomalous Australia and New Zealand. Distracted by its post-Soviet problems, Russia has yet to become deeply committed to the Asia Pacific. From Japan in the northwest Pacific to Australia and New Zealand in the far southwest, the Asia Pacific is clearly something to be reckoned with.

Compared to the other two regions, the Asia Pacific leaves an imprint all its own. Unlike North America and perhaps the EU, security issues are far more pivotal in the western Pacific. The northwest Pacific remains an unsettled subregion. The Koreas are the fulcrum of security concerns. What is more, the role of Japan and China in the Asia Pacific is still problematic, as is the long-term U.S. military presence. The Taiwan issue remains a potential source of regional insecurity. Still, what makes Asia Pacific important is its economic weight in the world. Tied more to North America than to the EU, the Asia Pacific is an indisputably vital area for the future of the world economy and its prospects for regionalism.

Insecurity

The Asia Pacific was a U.S. security concern during the second half of the twentieth century. After the Korean conflict in the early 1950s, U.S. security interests came to a head in Vietnam. Thanks largely to the Vietnam War, the Asia Pacific became an overriding issue for U.S. leadership well into the 1970s. The United States justified its role in Vietnam by pointing to Chinese and even Russian interests. The United States also blurred the distinction between "vital areas" and "peripheral areas" in its containment of Soviet and Chinese power in the world (Gaddis 1982). This helped to engender discontent closer to home.

Neither Canada nor Mexico was enthusiastic about the Vietnam War. Most of the open skepticism came from the north. Canada advocated negotiations over conduct of the war and stood by its principle that force should be approved and used multilaterally, under the UN Charter, rather than used as a unilateral instrument of national power.

As ill conceived as Canada may have felt the policy was, Canada was in no position to push hard for its view. After all, "not being a bad neighbor is the characteristic Canadian contribution to making an unequal relationship tolerable" (Fox 1985: 92).

Although economic issues resonate more forcefully than they did in the Cold War era, the Asia Pacific still raises security specters for North America. Japan's domestic leadership and the residual fears in many parts of the Asia Pacific about an assertive military role for Japan remain important constraints (Akaha 1993: 109–110). And then of course there is Japan's powerful neighbor, China, an aspiring superpower with a heavily militarized political structure. China's bid for regional and perhaps global importance may make it the focal concern for North America on issues of security. China's control of Tibet, its nuclear espionage aimed at the United States, Taiwan's bid for statehood, and the export of missiles to the Middle East are specific irritants in U.S.-Chinese security relations. The United States may still seek to play the part of honest broker and guarantor of security (Christensen 1997: 94). Nevertheless, U.S. power in the region is in relative terms on the wane even as its stake is increasing (Manning and Stern 1994: 79).

Rising Suns

Five of the twenty largest national economies in the world are in the Asia Pacific: Japan (second), China (seventh), South Korea (thirteenth), Australia (fifteenth), and Taiwan (twentieth) (World Bank 1995: 18, 19). The rise of the Asia Pacific shifted world economic power eastward. It was also a large part of the reason that the Pacific Rim, including both the Asia Pacific and the Americas, makes up more than one half of the world's economic product.

Asia Pacific is dynamic, complex, and problematic. "Asian dynamism" was the catchphrase of the 1980s, and for good reason. In the 1990s, however, instability and crises overtook the region. Recession in Japan led to the possibility that, at least for a time, the sun in the east was actually setting rather than rising. Yet even deeper problems coupled with financial crises plagued much of the Asia Pacific as well. The "threat" to North America from the region came from crises rather than economic competition in the Asia Pacific.

The western Pacific Rim is hard to fathom. The Asia Pacific contains some of the largest and richest economies and some of the smallest and poorest ones. More than that, it always seems to be in flux: The shift from military to economic issues, the growing intricacy of international relations, the emergence of multiple agendas, layers of issues confronting the region, and the blurring of domestic and international political economy make the area a major challenge (Chan 1993: 132–133).

The Asia Pacific is also very diverse, making it sometimes difficult to see the forest for the trees. Many of its states have modified Japan's developmental capitalism to fit their own situations. This mostly means an emphasis on state intervention in the economy and aggressive export strategies with state subsidies in order to yield large trade surpluses. But cultural, historical, and political as well as economic diversity sorely tests the region's coherence. Beliefs and practices vary on key economic activity. For example, environmental, labor, and "fair" trade policies are different enough to provoke some mistrust. The global North meets the global South in the Asia Pacific as well. From Papua New Guinea in the south to Japan in the north, the region is an Asian variant of the North-South divide. Such contrasts in wealth favor trade based on comparative advantage. Even so, this can stand in the way of harmonizing and coordinating economic policies.

Robust economic growth, evident in the Asia Pacific well into the 1990s, led to shifts in world power. That in turn raised issues about global management. By the early 1990s, the idea of collaborative leadership between Japan and the United States was broached. Such a "bigemony" or duopoly on the global and regional level was proposed for a time as the basis of a useful partnership (Bergsten and Noland 1993: 234; Stallings and Székely 1993: 18; Johnson 1993: 48). Yet this did not happen, at least not formally. Trade disputes, Japan's recession, ambivalence on sharing power and responsibility, and the rise of other actors in the Asia Pacific made such a partnership improbable at best.

In the late 1990s, the area faltered economically. Several key economies shuddered but managed to avoid financial collapse. This further complicated North America's task of managing transpacific issues. While much of the Asia Pacific sank into recession, the eastern side of the Pacific Rim experienced solid growth. These polarities only made transpacific relations more important. The emergencies and crises in the western Pacific raised uncertainty levels even as the stakes in the Asia Pacific became higher during the last two decades of the twentieth century. In 1997 the financial turmoil became widespread. Monetary instability in Thailand highlighted the problem. Much as the United States did for Mexico in 1995, Japan put together its own financial package to head off the worst effects of the crisis in Thailand as the International Monetary Fund (IMF) came up with a total package of $17.2 billion. Later that same year, financial instability led to IMF emergency measures in Indonesia, with the United States providing a backup financing package. Southeast Asia raises worries about the future. Diversity, export weakness, and free markets could put it at a disadvantage with China and other Asia Pacific countries (Arnold 2000: C4).

Rim Trade

If nothing else, North America and the Asia Pacific are supercharged trading regions. They trade a great deal with each other (globalization), and they trade within their own areas (regionalization) (see Table 9.3).

Without the formal integration of the EU, the Asia Pacific is nevertheless a remarkably busy place. In the mid-1990s Asia as a whole made up 27 percent of world merchandise exports, compared to more than 40 percent for the EU, the world's foremost trading region. Of Asia's total exports, almost half were traded within Asia itself (WTO 1995: 38, 73). Like the EU and North America, its own region comes

Table 9.3 Merchandise Exports of Selected Trade Partners as a Percentage of Total Exports of Trade Partners, 1996, 1997

	To U.S.	To Canada	To Mexico	To Asia[a]	To Japan	To European Union
From United States						
1996	—	21.2	9.1	19.2	10.8	20.4
1997	—	21.8	10.3	18.5	9.5	20.4
From Canada						
1996	82.3	—	0.4	4.1	3.7	5.3
1997	67.5	—	2.5	7.7	4.6	9.8
From Mexico						
1996	84.0	1.2	—	1.3	1.4	4.7
1997	85.6	1.9	—	0.9	1.0	8.9
From Japan						
1996	27.5	1.2	0.8	44.1	—	15.3
1997	22.4	2.8	0.4	52.4	—	13.3
From EU						
1996	7.0	0.6	0.3	6.9	2.2	—
1997	8.3	1.0	0.5	7.7	2.3	—

Source: Data calculated from International Monetary Fund 1997 and 1998.
Note: a. Data in Asia column do not include Japan.

first in trade. After Asia, the region's exports—about one-fourth of the total—were more likely to go to North America (WTO 1995: 39).

As seen from the eastern side of the Pacific Rim, trade with Asia is also crucial. Intraregional trade in North America was 36.9 percent of its total merchandise trade, but Asia was second, with about one-fourth of all trade, and the EU accounted for 16.4 percent of North America's exports (WTO 1995: 42). Trade between the regions continues to grow, even though the largest shares of exports stay within the respective regions.

Of the three North American states, the United States is particularly attracted to the Asia Pacific. The United States is Japan's single largest buyer, although Asia as a whole is more important for Japanese exports. North American trade with Japan and Asia is mostly U.S. trade. Exports to Asia and Japan are just as important to the United States in relative terms as are its exports to North America. Exports to the EU are as important as they are to Asia (not including Japan) but less important if Japan is included.

U.S. dominance in North American trade has only strengthened with time. Neither Canada nor Mexico substantially increased its share of exports to Japan. Canada's export presence in Asia is low key. From 1987 to 1996, Canadian export shares to Japan declined, while its reliance on the U.S. market went up. In 1987 the share of Canadian merchandise exports going to Japan was 5.7 percent; a decade later it was 4 percent. During the same period, the United States became even more important as an export market. The same is true of the EU. Canada's trade with the EU was less important in relative terms by the mid-1990s than it was in the late 1980s.

Mexico is in the same boat. Regionalization is stronger than transpacific or transatlantic trade. As Mexico becomes more tied to the U.S. market, it cannot substantially increase its exports to either Asia or the EU. True, Japan was Mexico's second largest trader in the 1980s (Elton 1993: 235). Japan emphasizes exports to Asia Pacific rather than to Latin America. Japanese exports are even more dominant in the Asia Pacific than U.S. exports are in Latin America. The United States exports as much to the Asia Pacific as it does to Latin America.

Just How Pacific Is the Rim?

Japan and the United States sometimes give the impression that the Pacific Rim is really the site of a series of skirmishes in a durable trade war between the two largest economies in the world. There is some truth to this. Both subscribe to their own views of state and markets. They publicly blame each other for their own difficulties. Even though trade and cooperation permeate the rim, conflict does intrude, once again suggesting that politics and states share the stage with economics and markets. The blend of cooperation and conflict in this critical bilateral relationship also helps explain why North America resorted to its own brand of regionalism in the 1990s.

Rather than liberalism, individualism, free markets, and a hobbled state, Japan has preached a communitarian capitalism. Market share and value-added maximization count for more than short-term profits (Thurow 1992: 118–220). Japan's system has also been termed "developmental" capitalism. The state in Japan is called upon to "promote national goals through manipulation and development of the industrial structure" (Garten 1992: 109). This form of market-state relations takes a long view, favoring growth in productivity rather than the social welfare of the consumers (Bergsten and Noland 1993: 11–12). Japan has therefore stressed a neomercantilist trade policy. Exports are aggressively promoted, imports are restricted by nontariff barriers, and large trade surpluses enhance the national standing within the world economy.

The United States became more or less combative with Japan, depending on the times and domestic priorities. In the 1990s the United States objected time and again to long-standing Japanese ways of doing things in corporatist government, financial markets, labor-management relations, state–private-sector relations, and relations among business groups composed of many companies linked to a particular manufacturer, called *keiretsu* (Bergsten and Noland 1993: 3–5). These domestic practices subsidized Japanese exporters and harmed U.S. investors in Japan, according to the official U.S. view. U.S. exporters collided with nontariff barriers and found it very difficult to compete. Japan was not playing "fair." What is more, it was not playing by U.S. rules. U.S. trade imbalances have not disappeared.

When elephants fight, the grass gets trampled. Canada and Mexico did not want to get trampled. A more open Japanese economy would perhaps benefit Canada and Mexico, but they could not be major players in the reform of Japan even if it were brought about. Also, Canada and Mexico shared an interest in tranquil trade relations across the Pacific. Japan-U.S. friction raised concern, but both Mexico and Canada stayed diplomatically on the sidelines. Canada is a North American middle power rather than an Asia Pacific one (Canada, Senate 1997: 10). The same is true for Mexico. Both have too much at stake in their relationships with the United States to side openly with Japan. For Canada, Asia is important but not critical. The United States ranks first, the EU second, and the Pacific Rim third for foreign investment coming into Canada as well as Canadian investment abroad (Canada, Senate 1997: 19; Meyer and Green 1996).

In the short run, NAFTA could be seen as an anti-Japanese ploy of the United States. Mexico wanted a more liberal invitation to Japanese investment so that Japan would invest more in Mexico (Orme 1996: 265). As it was devised, the investment rules of NAFTA favored the United States over its regional partners. In the long run, NAFTA could affect Asia Pacific prospects, for good or ill. Trade and investment patterns and a deepening of the North American experiment could adversely exclude Asian or other outsiders (Tsunekawa 1994: 3).

Bridge over Troubled Waters?

The Pacific Rim embraces two poles of the world economy. Asia Pacific and North America, with some others, are building a bridge between the two poles. What North America and the Asia Pacific are doing is something that North America and the EU have yet to do: invent a transregional arrangement to develop a free trade area. Such a transregional integration agreement (TIA) is evolving slowly under the rubric of the Asia Pacific Economic Cooperation forum. Started in the late 1980s as an all-Asian affair, APEC has become a Pacific Rim venture involving Asian states and states from North and even South America.

Fourteen states of the western Pacific were among the first generation of APEC members: the two Asian giants (Japan and China), the tigers (Hong Kong, Korea, Taiwan, and Singapore), and a third contingent of diverse non-Asian (Australia and New Zealand) and Asian (Indonesia, Brunei, Philippines, Malaysia, Thailand, and Papua New Guinea) countries. Vietnam joined at the end of the 1990s. For a time, it seemed that APEC might become Asia Pacific's response to regionalism elsewhere in the world. That is not what happened. By the early 1990s, it had become something quite different. APEC is an inclusive, transpacific, and free-trade-oriented association of Pacific Rim states (Manning and Stern 1994: 88). On the eastern side of the Pacific Rim, APEC had five members by the end of the 1990s. The three members of NAFTA had come into the forum early in the decade, with two South American states, Chile and Peru, joining later in the decade.

Europe does not share such an economic enterprise with North America and caution over such an arrangement may make it unlikely (P. Wonnacott 1996: 102). The expansion of APEC to North America had more than one political rationale behind it. Without North America, Japan would be the sole developed power in the forum; the United States was too important to exclude. But it could also be seen as an Asian attempt to guard against an inward-turning North America under NAFTA. Just as North American regionalism was in part a response to Asian dynamism, a transpacific APEC was a strategy to keep North America from becoming more like Europe. Because Asia saw regionalism in Europe and the Americas as a threat to multilateralism, it would not devise discriminatory practices such as the rules of origin found in NAFTA (Bergsten 1994: 21–22). Asia feared these provisions and therefore wanted to embrace North America (Young 1993: 141).

APEC has lofty ambitions. The forum committed itself to free trade by 2010 for its developed member states and by 2020 for the developing ones. This is a declaration or resolution more than it is a treaty or policy, however. There are no intermediate deadlines or enforceable processes to bring this about. For another, APEC's lack of institutions leads one to conclude that it will be difficult to coordinate national policies. By comparison, NAFTA's institutions, even though weak, are more credible. Finally, APEC's aspiration to become a community of free trading states in the Pacific Rim must confront daunting diversity. Asia Pacific and North America are diverse enough each in their own ways, but trying to bring them together could severely test the limited coherence of the Pacific Rim.

Differences remain. Clashes over subsidies, labor rights, environmental practices, national treatment of investment, and intellectual property rights could stand in the way of a liberal economic enterprise like APEC. U.S. trade deficits with China have already led to disputes about how much China must liberalize its domestic economy as a condition of its membership in the WTO (Morici 1997). China perhaps even more than Japan presents a challenge for realizing the goals of a transpacific free trade area based upon U.S. preferences.

APEC procedures and the differences among its members raise some doubts. APEC may not be able to reach its goals by the two deadlines. What is more, the 1995 APEC summit sidestepped a crucial area of liberalization. No deadline was set for ending protectionism in agriculture and other sensitive industries as NAFTA mandated. The slower growth and monetary instability in the Asia Pacific in the late 1990s may also retard progress toward trade liberalization. Indonesia joined China and others in the region in their preference for "national autonomy" programs, mercantilism, and protectionism. Once again, an Asian-style capitalism may make it harder for APEC to realize its stated aspirations, at least in the way that North America may envision them. International trade imbalances could undermine the liberalism of APEC to lower external barriers throughout the Pacific Rim as well as to those outside the area (Carlisle 1996: 120–122).

Whatever its future, APEC is nothing if not open and dynamic. Perhaps more amorphous sentiment than a viable strategy, it stands somewhere between regionalism and multilateralism. As problematic as it now is, APEC does seek to soften regionalism of the other two poles of the Pacific Rim and, in the bargain, to bolster the multilateral liberalization. And as dynamic as Asia Pacific is, APEC is an intermediary between globalization and regional tendencies.

North America in the Tripolar World

North America as a region and North America as a leg of the tripolar world are compatible as long as the overall commitment to an open global economy is unwavering. Although Canada and Mexico are more regional than global, all three North American states find it imperative to balance the needs of cultivating ties among themselves with expanding economic ties to the other two poles of the tripolar world.

The United States is the dominant player in its own region and a leading player in the tripolar world of which it is a part. The United States supported European regionalism but remained only a guarantor of regional security rather than a prime mover in the economic integration of Western Europe. For its part, Canada agrees with the goals of European regionalism even, as time went on, as it was being drawn closer to its own region. Transatlantic ties rest on the EU's status as an exclusive club; both sides of the Atlantic are dependent upon the economic bounty of globalization.

North America's role with the Asia Pacific emerged differently. Despite the diversity of the Pacific Rim, the United States and North America have an opportunity in APEC to help shape the future of economic liberalism. The key to bridging the two regions in the late twentieth century was the U.S.-Japanese relationship. Although APEC has potential for designing the agenda for the Pacific Rim, it must become something more than it is at the present. The transpacific bridge linking the Asia Pacific and North America can be built only with other efforts as well. China and perhaps Russia will begin to affect the evolution of the Pacific Rim.

Collaboration and conflict will pervade relations within the tripolar network of regions. Competing power centers, different varieties of capitalism, divergent policies within and among the regions, and problems in adjustment will coexist even as the three centers of economic wealth pursue greater integration within the regions and greater interdependence among them. The central dilemma facing North America in the tripolar world is that it does not have the leverage to coordinate these centers from its own region, even if the United States has a special place within the global economy. Yet the three poles of the global political economy are unable to form a global partnership for sharing the leadership burdens of a more complex global economy. The critical issue for North America and for the other two legs of the triad is how the leaders manage global economic relations among themselves even as they find it tempting to focus on their own regional agendas. Regionalism may be critical to the global economy, but it has yet to show that it can be a substitute for it.

10

Conclusion: Predicaments and Possibilities

North America has a future rather than a destiny. Nothing is chiseled in stone; nothing is predetermined about North America as a region. Indeed, there may be more than one future in store for it. There may even be a future in which inventing North America becomes at times more compelling and at times less compelling for the states and other actors in North America.

The future can be an extension of the past, up to a point. But inventing North America means working toward the future as well. What has happened so far in North America is worth our consideration for many reasons. North America is a stage for playing out critical issues from the previous century into this one. Unity and diversity, centralization and fragmentation, states and markets, hegemony and interdependence, regionalization and globalization are the crosscurrents that affect North America and the world. They may be profoundly important for the future of North America just as they were important in the late twentieth century.

As North Americans grapple with these crosscurrents of change, they will frame responses in the future. What they decide to do about inventing North America or about pursuing alternative directions is not strictly up to them alone, of course. States, firms, workers, nations, private groups, region states, RIAs, and others from outside North America are entwined in complex networks within a constantly fluid world. From all of this may emerge a more coherent North America with a life of its own. Only time will tell.

Inventing North America is ultimately about the three states' using regionalism for their own purposes in an increasingly globalized world.

Regionalism requires the collaboration of states; regionalization is a long-term structural process of change that weds disparate parts of their economies and societies, much like globalization itself. If regionalism wanes, North America will take a different turn as it invents itself. If regionalization becomes what most defines North America's future, then inventing North America may be a matter of structural evolution rather than deliberate creation. Either way, it won't happen tomorrow, and it certainly won't be easy.

North America faces essentially six predicaments if inventing North America is to be a part of the region's future. These may make it hard to devise a region that is more integrated and coherent than it is now. For the time being, North America is no greater than the sum of its parts. The central question tying all these predicaments together is whether North America as a region will become more than a mere blip in a fast-changing and complex trajectory. If it does become something more than that, then North American regionalism could well make a real difference to the future of the states and to many others inside and outside the region.

The Six Predicaments

The first predicament facing North America is about North America itself, what it may become and if and how it will flourish. The second involves the issue of who rules, whose North America it really is; and the third revisits the whole matter of the state in regionalism, regionalization, and globalization. The fourth predicament is the resistance to regionalism and globalization; the fifth is about North and South in the Americas and the problems it may raise for North America. Finally, inventing North America must confront the challenge of inequality.

Will North America Flourish?

Born in the late twentieth century, will North American regionalism prosper in the twenty-first? North America's RIAs may be like yesterday's revolutions: It might be easier to make them than to make them work. CUFTA and NAFTA were remarkable departures for the region. This guarantees them a place in the history of international relations. Yet building upon them could be an even more arduous undertaking.

In the beginning North American regionalism was advanced by and aimed at a few, but with long-term promises for the many. Investors, importers, workers, environmentalists, trade officials, agribusiness, automakers, transportation companies, customs officials, labor unions, and others were prone to see the new North America as an emerging political economy. This is entirely understandable. After all, they live with this world. Interdependence is not merely a concept; it is more and more becoming a daily reality for many.

Still, for some, little is new, different, or better as a result of the RIAs. Some features of civil society, economic sectors, and geographic sections within all three states have yet to experience the regional and global impact of liberalization. Without a major and immediate stake for them, some actors may believe that it will take more than shared rules on trade, investment, intellectual property rights, and the like to make North America as a region come to mean something very vital for them.

North America is a regional experiment in commerce and investment. Inventing North America may go well beyond the world of business. For example, there is no such thing as a North American per se. Individuals are not North American, but companies and firms are more frequently than ever becoming North American. Regionalism or regionalization has only just begun to affect loyalties or identities for most people. It used to be that Mexicans referred to people from the United States as *norteamericanos*. Today North Americans could be Canadians and even Mexicans as well. For now, the term "North American" alludes to an amazingly complex set of activities, mostly but not entirely economic. Until it becomes something more, the region will have this incomplete, uneven quality.

To the extent that North America is being invented in some fashion, it remains mostly peripheral to the states that launched it. Unless it gains or even just sustains momentum, it may not leave behind large footprints on the continent. North American regionalism could be helpful to its member states, but it has yet to become indispensable to them. To invent North America would eventually mean giving it a life of its own, something that would be an overarching goal rather than just another handy tool for states to use in making their way in a globalized economy. At the dawn of the century, states in North America can do without regionalism. The reverse is not true and may never be true.

A region can do reasonably well without becoming a political or economic union of former states. At this point this may be what at most can be expected of North America. Although North America may prosper with regionalism as it now stands, it may also develop mutual vulnerabilities. This warning was delivered with full force from outside the region. In 1998 Brazil, Indonesia, and Russia experienced default, inflation, devaluation, and other economically disturbing trends. In Asia the free movement of capital, long championed by U.S. and other policymakers, fostered vulnerabilities with very severe, short-term consequences (Kristoff and Sanger 1999: A1). Allowing mutual vulnerabilities without fostering mutual coordination could be a fateful mistake. Mexico's crisis in 1995 and the North American response came at a price. It may have slowed the enthusiasm for more integration in the region. Regional crisis management may patch the system together, even as it raises doubts about the credibility of the whole enterprise of liberal regionalism and globalization. Although regionalism may be given too much credit for the good that it does bring, it may also get more blame than it should for the volatility of the liberal political economy.

Whose North America?

The second predicament is also formidable. It has to do with who rules North America. Perhaps no one does. That is certainly a possibility. The region does not have a structure of supranational governance. No such leap is immediately in the cards either. Still, things have a way of evolving, regardless of public statements and rhetoric. Dispute settlement panels could be a small step, but much more than that would have to be put in place to establish cross-national governance. Nor does one seriously expect that North America will have one official center for supranational consultation any time soon.

Another possibility is that everyone rules because everyone is, or will be, involved in the evolving region. Governments, peoples, firms, groups, and individuals all have a stake in the region. Producers, investors, policymakers, consumers, taxpayers, and workers consent by what they do. For them, elites matter less than the interconnectedness of gains.

There is a less sanguine answer as well. Who rules the region is the same as who rules the states and their economies. This does not merely mean public leaders; it also means private centers of power in important economic sectors with large capital and technology to apply to the integration of production and commerce throughout North America. These leaders may speak English, Spanish, or French, but they are the main proponents and benefactors of North American regionalism. For them, regionalism comes from above, even though growing interdependence will gradually engulf most people throughout North America.

States are not equal, and this is particularly true in North America. In the pyramidal view of North America, rules for the region are really rules of one state. Even beyond North America, the world still relies upon U.S. power far more than it should (Kupchan 1998: 40). At the regional level, this is even more the case. The United States is the core of a "natural unipolarity" in North America. The region is really a U.S. enterprise (Clarkson 1998: 14). North American regionalism becomes a hegemonic formality with Canada and Mexico at the periphery of this unipolar system.

If regionalism is to work in North America, a unipolar hegemony is ultimately not the answer. A consensual bargain between the core and periphery blends power asymmetry and consensus (Kupchan 1998: 42–43). Power is not exercised unilaterally or arbitrarily because the core and the periphery live in the same neighborhood. Mutual vulnerabilities weaken unipolar arrogance. Moderation, self-constraint, and self-binding actions dilute the harsher possibilities of a relentless, domineering core (Ikenberry 1998–1999: 45). Partnership can evolve even in a region of hegemonic unipolarity.

At the dawn of the twenty-first century, North America is situated somewhere between domination and partnership. But what of the future? If North America is to become a full-fledged region, it must gradually move away from the former and closer to the latter. In a regionalized North America, everyone is in the same boat. Interdependence and national problems cannot be contained; they are indivisible. If Canada breaks apart, its disunity may affect the other two states. If Mexico is unable to move out of poverty and underdevelopment, its plight may affect the others. If the United States is overbearing, it may make genuinely regional solutions all but impossible.

The State's Fate

In the early twenty-first century, the state is moving in directions different from what it was even in the mid-twentieth century. Global pressures and subnational trends are forcing the state to make adjustments in what it does and how it does it (Mittelman 2000: 26). This does not mean that the state as an important player in North America is facing oblivion. National governments will continue to surrender bits and pieces of their prerogatives in economic policy to markets and social forces.

Regionalism has kept the state in. Without the state, there would have been no RIAs in late-twentieth-century North America. States play a part in economic liberalization. They are the midwives of globalization, but they can also serve the same role in North America. The irony of North America is that the state is being used to create a region that makes less use of the state.

The state's role in regionalism is constrained but hardly superfluous. It permits domestic trade legislation to have a role within North America, and it keeps outsiders from being free riders. But if globalization becomes the more dominant influence, states may have to adjust again to shifting roles. North America is being regionalized. This means that actors other than states are powerful engines of North American regionalism. States may follow more than lead the regionalization of North American interdependence. For another thing, markets are making rules. When markets do not serve everyone's needs, the state may be called upon to strike a balance among different interests. Politics and states do not end with regionalism.

In a sense, the future is already here. Cautious about giving any regional authority much real power, the states of North America are grappling with challenges from below as well. All three states are lessening national governmental control over their own economies and polities.

Canada is already highly decentralized, and the individual Canadian provinces are shaping North American regionalism. Even more uncertain is Canada's ability to hold together. The ethnopolitical problem for Canadian unity may turn North America into a region of four rather than three states one day. Mexico seems headed in the same direction. Pressured by regionalization and globalization, the Mexican state also faces a future with fewer levers and fewer privileges. With increasing democratization, things could get tougher for the Mexican state. Mexico has adopted the cant and the practice of liberal regionalization and globalization as its own. Yet it remains to be seen if these pressures can be accommodated within an increasingly fragile and fragmented system of national governance. Although the central government is gradually dispersing the power to make decisions to the local and regional levels, regionalization and globalization may rob local entities of their ability to control their own destinies. States are more vulnerable to local, regional, and global factors.

The United States is somewhere in the middle. The consensus seems to be to keep the state on a short leash but allow it to tinker with the side effects of markets and problems. North America does not appear to be looking for active, aggressive states searching for answers to regional or national problems. The fate of the state may well be a supportive rather than formative role.

The state in North America is perhaps not what it once was, but neither is it rapidly sliding into an abyss. The state is there to implement the NAFTA transition, develop dispute resolution, and enforce protectionist policies such as rules of origin against nonmembers. And no doubt subsidies, tariffs, and nontariff barriers, investment codes, and other traditional types of state intervention in the economy will gradually erode. In the meanwhile NAFTA is a hybrid of state and private authority in economic governance (Morales 1999: 36). Regionalism, even with a clear market inclination, has a place for the state even as the RIAs tilt toward the market-friendly trends of efficiency, competition, and liberalization (Frankel 1997: 207).

The future is predictable, if only for its unpredictability. One thing does seem certain: The future of regionalization and globalization is unimaginable without the state. States can do some things that markets cannot. What has yet to become clear is just what role the state will play in a state-sponsored regionalism favoring markets and liberalism. The fate of the state is tightly intertwined with the future of regionalism.

Will Resistance Prevail?

Resistance to regionalism, regionalization, and globalization should not be minimized. Resistance comes from within each North American state. It pits nationalist-statist coalitions against liberal market ones. The opposition to free trade and free market policies lost the first round over the RIAs in the early 1990s. Later in the decade, however, they mobilized efforts in the United States against extending liberalization through expanding NAFTA, approving fast-track authority in the U.S. Congress, and pursuing other free trade agreements.

By the mid- and late 1990s, the momentum had slowed perceptibly. A nationalist-statist coalition in the U.S. Congress, based on Democratic opposition in the lower house, threw a wrench into trade policy. In a gradually more democratic Mexico, the enthusiasm for free market policies waned a bit, as many Mexicans suffered from a series of economic body blows. The liberal technocrats and ruling politicians also impaled themselves on economic downturns and political scandals. Still, the new leaders in Mexico are committed to the regional agenda. In Canada the Tory government took a leap of faith for free trade in the

1980s (Clarkson 1998: 19). Yet the successor Liberal government has built upon rather than reversed the earlier initiatives on trade. In fact, both Mexico and Canada have pursued bilateral free trade agreements with a number of countries as well as the European Union (in the case of Mexico). They have borrowed heavily if not entirely from NAFTA's precepts.

Changing circumstances and momentum had a lot to do with strengthening the resistance. First, international economic conditions were different. The "threat" of aggressively exporting economies in the Asia Pacific lessened considerably when several economies, including that of Japan, sank into a deep recession for most of the 1990s. Financial weakness in Asia did not awaken the same sense of urgency in North American regionalism as did Asian financial prowess. Second, the economic boom in North America relieved some of the political pressure to pursue a regionalist option quite so ardently. Fueled by the U.S. economic resurgence, North America gradually pulled out of its economic lethargy from the late 1980s and early 1990s. Prosperity for many and stagnation for some has not translated into stronger support for the regional agenda on free trade. Third, good and bad news elsewhere in North America had an impact as well. Canada's slow recovery from recession, which some blamed primarily on trade policy, made regionalism less compelling. As for Mexico, bad economic news turned domestic support into opposition or at least skepticism. The economic roller coaster of the mid-1990s unsettled the credibility of liberal market options for a time. Neoliberal leaders who had favored free trade were discredited for the general management of the national economy. Growing unemployment and poverty badly shook faith in Mexico's neoliberal project.

All in all, the regional balance of power over free trade had shifted somewhat. Domestic coalitions favoring free trade and liberal policies were weakened but not toppled. Less formidable than they were in the early 1990s, they still have strong supporters in financial, corporate, and government circles. The United States will be the main battleground. Nationalists, populists, unions, environmentalists, and cultural defenders had been able to deny further inroads for North American regionalism. The nationalist-statist coalitions remain skeptical of regional cooperation because it siphons off economic help for some groups and curbs redistributive policies (Solingen 1998: 40–41). There is probably no more important forum for the struggle over free trade than the U.S. Congress.

Without an overwhelming majority for the liberal market coalition, free trade initiatives are contentious in Congress. Protectionism has not really become stronger, but there is a lack of consensus about trade-related issues that blocked a free trade agenda from gaining momentum in Congress in the late 1990s (Destler 1998: 139). The stress and strains of neoliberal regionalism and globalization are also rippling more widely throughout the societies and politics of many countries (Rodrik 1997: 4). During the WTO meeting in Seattle, Mexican protesters marched on the U.S. embassy in Mexico City. McDonald's restaurants, a premier symbol of globalization, are a favorite target for the resistance movement in France and elsewhere. "Globaphobia," the fear and insecurity surrounding globalization, has spread to some places in North America and beyond.

Regionalism, regionalization, and globalization will face further tests in the United States. The Free Trade Area for the Americas and the WTO-inspired agreement between the United States and China will serve as two barometers of North America's commitment to free trade and economic liberalism. There is indeed some irony in that the resistance is strongest in the United States, whose support for free trade is most critical for the region and even for the world.

North America or the Americas?

Where does North America go from here? North America may be NAFTA and not much more for quite some time. Or it could reach out to the rest of the global South in the Americas by advocating the disruption of NAFTA as part of a design for a Free Trade Area of the Americas. By transcending its own area, North American regionalism could become something different and could even be a building block for hemispheric regionalism or multilateralism.

It used to be a safe bet to claim that the past is prologue for the future. If we had accepted that famous dictum, however, the RIAs of North America would never have been negotiated. Global and domestic factors make doing anything more than implementing the transition stage of NAFTA hard to envision. But shifting fortunes in trade politics within the United States could be decisive.

By the late 1990s, NAFTA's rules and ideas had acquired some resonance in the possible emergence of a hemispheric RIA. The summits of the 1990s laid the foundation for the Americas to come up with a comprehensive negotiating text for a hemispheric FTA. This is also a test for the United States. It could reveal how capable the United States is in promoting hemispheric cooperation through an FTAA. North American states will certainly have a great impact on the process, offering NAFTA as a model or template to create a hemisphere-wide integration movement such as the FTAA scheduled for 2005. After all, North American regionalism attempts to bridge the North and South. Any FTAA including the United States would have to consider U.S. positions on national treatment, intellectual property rights, rules of origin, and other NAFTA provisions. A convergence around these policies would make it possible for NAFTA to be reincarnated in some sense within the hemispheric agenda without actually widening NAFTA to include the South. NAFTA states may very well influence the FTAA, yet it is highly unlikely that the FTAA will be exactly like NAFTA.

Will a Bridge Be Built?

The last predicament is perhaps the most formidable of all. It implies quite strongly that North American states, especially the United States, must have some role in joining North and South. Mexico makes North America a crucible for North-South integration. Whatever Mexico's membership in the North American club may mean for bridging North and South, its belonging to North America is perhaps the toughest test for inventing North America as a region.

The easiest may have come first. Mexico agreed to the policies of the North. Mexico consented to a regionalist view based on liberal market precepts; it is willing to live with and play by North American rules of the game. In this sense, the South had a conversion to the North's prescriptions. In heading down the path toward North-South integration, Mexico gave up more than either of the other North American states. It also has the most to gain, in relative terms, if North-South integration succeeds. Mexico's convergence with the North is mostly about economic policy and rhetoric. It adjusted its policies on public debt, spending, and state intervention to put itself more in tune with U.S. views of the state. It is acting more like the North. But the hardest part may still lie ahead. Mexico alone cannot span the most important gap between North and South. It remains structurally in the South. The North-South bridge is under construction. It has a long way to go before it is completed.

To think that North and South can be connected through an RIA may be expecting too much too soon. Regionalism as state policy can only do so much in the short term. Regionalized interdependence must do a lot more in the longer term. Unless this happens, the gaps between the South and the North in North America may remain impressive, even if there is some narrowing over wages, incomes, and other economic indicators in the coming decades.

It is no surprise that NAFTA and liberalism in general have yet to bear fruit for everyone. There are winners and losers in regionalism, regionalization, and globalization, at least in the short term. Mexico did register absolute gains in trade volume, investment, and growth. Some have become well off and others have further padded their already substantial assets. But as in the rest of North America, the relative gains within Mexico are very uneven. Of course, not everything can be laid at the doorstep of North American regionalism. Each of the states is responsible for its own economic policies. Still, the benefits of liberalism and regionalism in Mexico are decidedly mixed. The promise of such initiatives in the late 1990s were unfulfilled for many Mexicans. For the time being, the gaps between North and South overall may indeed be widening.

Eventually, success for North America must be more than success for those sitting in corporate boardrooms or government conference rooms. To be sure, protecting property rights is a goal of regionalism, regionalization, and globalization. The state plays a courtesan role by servicing powerful clients who seek its help or even acquiescence (Mittelman 2000: 25–26). If North America is to become something more than this, if it is to spread the benefits more widely and deeply, then being a courtesan is far too narrow. For North America to have a future, for it to flourish and prosper, it will have to increase aggregate wealth and tackle the problems of gaps in the North-South relationship.

It may come down to outcomes. Inequality is an outcome that most challenges the whole idea of North American regionalism. The global South faces a dilemma. If it is excluded from globalization, it will lose out. If it is included, it may experience mounting poverty (Oman 1999: 37). In North America, to the extent that regionalization and globalization feed off each other, both may have had some impact on growing inequality. If North and South are to benefit, then a wide array of people and businesses north and south of the Rio Grande must enjoy relative gains as well. Aggregate gains or gains for large business are not enough to claim success for this daring experiment.

A fairly clear record of achievement for NAFTA, however difficult that may be to document, could bolster the optimism behind North

American regionalism. It might serve as a model or inspire different models for other regional integration arrangements involving the global North and South. If the record is far less rosy, North American states will reflect more than transcend the North-South divide.

North America in the Twenty-first Century

Like many states, the United States, Canada, and Mexico share a future as well as a region. But like most states, the North American three have their own reasons for coming closer together to face the present and the future. Huddling together in an RIA may afford each of them comfort and advantage. But regionalism cannot solve all their problems, and in some cases it may simply change the circumstances under which common problems must be confronted. Regionalism in North America is a matter of economic diplomacy. It is not a goal in itself, worth sacrificing traditions, distinctiveness, and prerogatives. Whether it ever rises to the highest levels of the agendas of all three states is for the future to tell.

North America must work out for itself an accommodation of markets and states. Bringing the North American states closer together is a limited responsibility of the nation-state in the region. Neither will the states of North America surrender what power they still have to a supraregional state. Nibbled at from below and resistant to pooling sovereignty from above, the North American states will have a constricted but still vital role in shaping the region in the twenty-first century.

This century may well be the North American century. Regionalism and cooperation in North America may affect the peoples, businesses, and states of the North American three more than anyone can now imagine. But the task of working together on common problems is as daunting as it is vital. The region faces issues so fundamental that they call into question the very nature of the region itself. Neighbors must become partners, but there is nothing to preordain just how helpful this may be in the long run.

When all is said and done, North America's predicaments ultimately come down to some familiar themes. They are really about power and interests, asymmetry and partnership, fragmentation and integration, states and markets, regionalization and globalization. The future of North America is therefore what still remains to be made of it. North America may one day have the unity, credibility, and coherence to affect the collective well-being of its members. If it does, it will also have the potential to influence the destinies of the region, its states, and its peoples.

References

Abele, Frances (1997). "Understanding What Happened Here: The Political Economy of Indigenous Peoples." In *Understanding Canada: Building on the New Canadian Political Economy*. Ed. Wallace Clement. Montreal-Kingston: McGill-Queen's University Press, pp. 118–140.

Aguilar Zinser, Adolfo (1995). "A Critical View of a NAFTA Including Mexico." In *NAFTA as a Model of Development: The Benefits and Costs of Merging High- and Low-Wage Areas*. Ed. Richard S. Belous and Jonathan Lemco. Albany: State University of New York Press, pp. 106–112.

Akaha, Tsuneo (1993). "Japan's Security Policy in the Posthegemonic World: Opportunities and Challenges." In *Japan in the Posthegemonic World*. Ed. Tsuneo Akaha and Frank Langdon. Boulder: Lynne Rienner, pp. 91–112.

Arnold, Wayne (2000). "Southeast Asia Losing Ground in New Economy, Report Says." *New York Times* (September 7): C4.

Arsen, David (1996). "The NAFTA Debate in Retrospect: U.S. Perspectives." In *Policy Choices: Free Trade Among NAFTA Nations*. Ed. Karen Roberts and Mark I. Wilson. East Lansing: Michigan State University Press, pp. 37–58.

Aubry, Jack (1997). "Cree Claim Hydro-Quebec Plan Is 'Ethnic Occupation.'" *Calgary Herald* (September 9): B9.

Banks, Arthur S., Alan J. Day, and Thomas C. Muller, eds. (1997). *The Political Handbook of the World 1997*. Binghamton, New York: CSA Publications.

Barber, Benjamin R. (1995). *Jihad vs. McWorld: How Globalism and Tribalism Are Reshaping the World*. New York: Ballantine Books.

Barry, Donald (1995). "The Road to NAFTA." In *Toward a North American Community? Canada, the United States, and Mexico*. Ed. Donald Barry, with Mark O. Dickerson and James D. Gaisford. Boulder: Westview Press, pp. 3–14.

Belanger, Louis (1998). "Redefining Cultural Diplomacy: Cultural Security and Foreign Policy in Canada." Paper presented at the International Studies Association meeting, Minneapolis, March 17–21.

Belausteguigoitia, Juan Carlos, and Luis F. Guadarrama (1997). "United States–Mexico Relations: Environmental Issues." In *Coming Together? Mexico–United States Relations*. Ed. Barry Bosworth, Susan M. Collins, and Nora Claudia Lustig. Washington, D.C.: Brookings Institution Press, pp. 91–124.

Bell, David V. J. (1992). *The Roots of Disunity: A Study of Canadian Political Culture*. Toronto: Oxford University Press.

Belous, Richard S., and Jonathan Lemco (1995). "The NAFTA Development Model of Combining High- and Low-Wage Areas: An Introduction." In *NAFTA as a Model of Development: The Benefits and Costs of Merging High- and Low-Wage Areas*. Ed. Richard S. Belous and Jonathan Lemco. Albany: State University of New York Press, pp. 1–20.

Bergsten, C. Fred (1994). "APEC and World Trade." *Foreign Affairs,* Vol. 73, No. 3 (May-June): 20–26.

Bergsten, C. Fred, and Marcus Noland (1993). *Reconcilable Differences? U.S.-Japan Economic Conflict*. Washington, D.C.: Institute for International Economics.

Bhagwati, Jagdish (1993). "Regionalism and Multilateralism: An Overview." In *New Dimensions in Regional Integration*. Ed. Jaime de Melo and Arvind Panagariya. Cambridge: Cambridge University Press, pp. 22–51.

——— (1995). "U.S. Trade Policy: The Infatuation with Free Trade Areas." In *The Dangerous Drift to Preferential Trade Areas*. Ed. Jagdish Bhagwati and Anne O. Krueger. Washington, D.C.: American Enterprise Institute for Public Policy Research, pp. 1–18.

Bhagwati, Jagdish, and Arvind Panagariya (1996). Preface to *The Economics of Preferential Trade Agreements*. Ed. Jagdish Bhagwaiti and Arvind Panagariya. Washington, D.C.: American Enterprise Institute Press, pp. xiii–xx.

Birdsall, Nancy (1998). "Life Is Unfair: Inequality in the World." *Foreign Policy,* No. 111 (summer): 76–93.

Blank, Stephen (1993). *The Emerging Architecture of North America*. Coral Gables, Florida: North-South Center, University of Miami.

Bluestone, Barry (1995). "The Inequality Express." *American Prospect,* No. 20 (winter): 81–93.

Bonser, Charles F., ed. (1991). *Toward a North American Common Market: Problems and Prospects for a New Economic Community.* Boulder: Westview Press.

Bosworth, Barry, Susan M. Collins, and Nora Claudia Lustig (1997). Introduction to *Coming Together? Mexico-U.S. Relations*. Ed. Barry Bosworth, Susan M. Collins, and Nora Claudia Lustig. Washington, D.C.: Brookings Institution Press, pp. 1–24.

Bothwell, Robert (1992). *Canada and the United States: The Politics of Partnership*. New York: Twayne.

Boyer, Robert, and Daniel Drache (1996). "State and Market: A New Engagement for the Twenty-First Century? In *States Against Markets: The Limits of Globalization*. Ed. Robert Boyer and Daniel Drache. London: Routledge, pp. 84–114.

Brinkley, Douglas (1997). "Democratic Enlargement: The Clinton Doctrine." *Foreign Policy,* No. 106 (spring): 111–127.

Britton, John N. H. (1996). "Conclusion: Canada's Emerging Economic Geography." In *Canada and the Global Economy: The Geography of Structural and Technological Change*. Ed. John N. H. Britton. Montreal and Kingston: McGill–Queen's University Press, pp. 445–451.

Brodie, Janine (1996). "New State Forms, New Political Spaces." In *States Against Markets: The Limits of Globalization*. Ed. Robert Boyer and Daniel Drache. London: Routledge, pp. 383–398.

Brooks, Stephen (1996). *Canadian Democracy: An Introduction*. Second Edition. Toronto: Oxford University Press.

Brunelle, Dorval, and Christian Deblock (1992). "Economic Blocs and the Challenge of the NAFTA." In *North America Without Borders?* Ed. Stephen J. Randall. Calgary: University of Calgary Press, pp. 119–131.

Bulmer-Thomas, Victor, Nikki Craske, and Monica Serrano (1994). "Who Will Benefit?" In *Mexico and the NAFTA: Who Will Benefit?* Ed. Victor Bulmer-Thomas, Nikki Craske, and Monica Serrano. New York: St. Martin's Press, pp. 203–232.

Burtless, Gary, Robert Z. Lawrence, Robert E. Litan, and Robert J. Shapiro (1998). *Globaphobia: Confronting Fears About Open Trade*. Washington, D.C.: Brookings Institution Press.

Caballero Urdiales, Emilio (1991). Introduction to *El Tratado de Libre Comercio: Mexico, Estados Unidos, Canada* (The Free Trade Agreement: Mexico, the United States, Canada). Ed. Emilio Caballero Urdiales. Mexico: Universidad Nacional Autónoma de México, pp. 3–12.

Calleo, David P. (1987). *Beyond American Hegemony: The Future of the Western Alliance*. New York: Basic Books.

Canada. Senate (1997). *The Importance of the Asia Pacific Region for Canada*. Ottawa: Standing Committee on Foreign Affairs.

Caporaso, James (1993). "International Relations Theory and Multilateralism: The Search for Foundations." In *Multilateralism Matters: The Theory and Praxis of an Institutional Form*. Ed. John Gerard Ruggie. New York: Columbia University Press, pp. 51–90.

Carlisle, Charles R. (1996). "Is the World Ready for Free Trade?" *Foreign Affairs,* Vol. 75, No. 6 (November-December): 113–126.

Castaneda, Jorge (1993). "Can NAFTA Change Mexico?" *Foreign Affairs,* Vol. 72, No. 4 (September-October): 66–80.

Chan, Steve (1993). *East Asian Dynamism: Growth, Order, and Security in the Pacific Region*. Boulder: Westview Press.

Chavez, Manuel, and Scott Whiteford (1996). "Beyond the Market: Politics and Socioeconomic Principles of NAFTA for Mexico." In *Policy Choices: Free Trade Among NAFTA Nations*. Ed. Karen Roberts and Mark I. Wilson. East Lansing: Michigan State University Press, pp. 15–35.

Cheney, Timothy D. (1998). *Who Makes the Law: The Supreme Court, Congress, the States, and Society.* Upper Saddle River, New Jersey: Prentice-Hall.

Christensen, Thomas J. (1997). "Perceptions and Alliances in Europe, 1865–1940." *International Organization,* Vol. 51, No. 1 (winter): 65–97.

Clarkson, Stephen (1998). *Fearful Asymmetries: The Challenge of Analyzing Continental Systems in a Globalizing World.* Canadian-American Public Policy Occasional Paper No. 35. Orono, Maine: University of Maine.

Clymer, Adam (1997). "House Votes to Punish Mexico over Drugs." *New York Times* (March 14): A7.

Conroy, Michael E., and Amy K. Glasmeier (1992–1993). "Unprecedented Disparities, Unparalleled Adjustment Needs: Winners and Losers on the NAFTA 'Fast Track.'" *Journal of Interamerican Studies and World Affairs,* Vol. 34, No. 4 (winter): 1–37.

Conybeare, John A. C., and Mark Zinkula (1996). "Who Voted Against the NAFTA? Trade Unions Versus Free Trade." *World Economy,* Vol. 19 (January): 1–12.

Covarrubias Velasco, Ana (1996). "Mexico: Crísis y Política Exterior" (Mexico: crisis and foreign policy). *Foro Internacional,* Vol. 36, No. 3 (July-September): 477–497.

Cremeans, John E., ed. (1998). *Handbook of North American Industry: NAFTA and the Economics of Its Member Nations.* Lanham, Maryland: Bernan Press.

Dealy, Glen Caudill (1992). *The Latin Americans: Spirit and Ethos.* Boulder: Westview Press.

Del Castillo, Gustavo (1995). "Convergent Paths Toward Integration: The Unequal Experience of Canada and Mexico." In *Toward a North American Community? Canada, the United States, and Mexico.* Ed. Donald Barry, with Mark O. Dickerson, and James D. Gaisford. Boulder: Westview Press, pp. 91–104.

Del Villar, Samuel I. (1988). "The Illicit U.S.-Mexico Drug Market: Failure of Policy and an Alternative." In *Mexico and the United States: Managing the Relationship.* Ed. Riordan Roett. Boulder: Westview Press, pp. 191–208.

De Mateo, Fernando (1988). "La Política Comercial de México y el GATT" (The trade policy of Mexico and GATT). *El Trimestre Económico,* Vol. 55 (January-March): 175–126.

De Palma, Anthony (1998). "Canada Pact Gives a Tribe Self-Rule for the First Time." *New York Times* (August 5): A1, A10.

Destler, I. M. (1998). "Congress and Free Trade." In *The Controversial Pivot: The U.S. Congress and North America.* Ed. Robert A. Pastor and Rafael Fernández de Castro. Washington, D.C.: Brookings Institution.

Deutsch, Karl W., Sidney A. Burrell, Robert A. Kann, Maurice Lee Jr., Martin Lichterman, Raymond E. Lindgren, Francis L. Lowenheim, and Richard W. Van Wagenen (1957). *Political Community and the North Atlantic Area.* Princeton: Princeton University Press.

Diebold, William (1988). "The History and the Issues." In *Bilateralism, Multilateralism and Canada in U.S. Trade Policy.* Ed. William Diebold Jr. Cambridge, Massachusetts: Ballinger, pp. 1–36.

Dillon, Sam (1998). "A 20 Year General Motors Parts Migration to Mexico." *New York Times* (June 24): C1, C4.

Dobbins, James F. (1996). "TAFTA: An Idea Whose Time Has Come?" In *Open for Business: Creating a Transatlantic Marketplace.* Ed. Bruce Stokes. New York: Council on Foreign Relations, pp. 10–19.

Dodd, Lawrence C., and Bruce I. Oppenheimer (1997). "Congress and the Emerging Order: Conditional Party Government or Constructive Partnership?" In *Congress Reconsidered.* Ed. Lawrence C. Dodd and Bruce I. Oppenheimer. Sixth Edition. Washington, D.C.: CQ Press, pp. 390–413.

Doern, G. Bruce, and Brian W. Tomlin (1991). *Faith and Fear: The Free Trade Story.* Toronto: Stoddart.

Doerr, Audrey D. (1997). "Building New Orders of Government: The Future of Aboriginal Self Government." *Canadian Public Administration,* Vol. 40, No. 2 (summer): 274–289.

Doran, Charles F. (1984). *Forgotten Partnership: United States–Canada Relations Today.* Baltimore: Johns Hopkins University Press.

——— (1996). "When Building North America, Deepen Before Widening." In *A New North America.* Ed. Charles F. Doran and Alvin Paul Drischler. Westport, Connecticut: Praeger, pp. 65–89.

Doran, Charles F., and Alvin Paul Drischler, eds. (1996). *A New North America.* Westport, Connecticut: Praeger.

Dornbusch, Rudiger (1995). "North-South Trade Relations in the Americas: The Case of Free Trade." In *Trade Liberalization in the Western Hemisphere.* Ed. Inter-American Development Bank (IDB) and Economic Commission for Latin America and the Caribbean (ECLAC). Washington, D.C.: IDB and ECLAC, pp. 33–51.

Dropsy, Vincent (1995). "NAFTA and the Mexican Economic Crisis: Causality or Coincidence?" *Social Science Quarterly,* Vol. 32, No. 4: 361–373.

Dugger, Celia W. (1999). "Why India and Others See U.S. as Villain on Trade." *New York Times* (December 17): C4.

Earle, Robert, and John D. Wirth (1995). "Conclusion: The Search for Community." In *Identities in North America: The Search for Community.* Ed. Robert L. Earle and John D. Wirth. Stanford: Stanford University Press, pp. 191–228.

Economist (1999). *World in Figures 1999.* Pocket Edition. New York: John Wiley and Sons.

Eden, Lorraine, and Maureen Appel Molot (1992). "The View from the Spokes: Canada and Mexico Face the United States." In *North America Without Borders?* Ed. Stephen J. Randall. Calgary: University of Calgary Press, pp. 67–80.

Elton, Charlotte (1993). "New Dimensions of Japanese Foreign Policy: A Latin American View of the Japanese Presence." In *Japan in the Posthegemonic*

World. Ed. Tsuneo Akaha and Frank Langdon. Boulder: Lynne Rienner, pp. 233–250.

The Europe World Yearbook (1997). London: Europa Publications Ltd., 1997.

Feinberg, Richard (1997). *Summitry in the Americas: A Progress Report*. Washington, D.C.: Institute for International Economics.

Fishlow, Albert, and Stephan Haggard (1992). *The United States and the Regionalisation of the World Economy*. Paris: OECD.

Fox, William T. R. (1985). *A Continent Apart: The United States and Canada in World Politics*. Toronto: University of Toronto Press.

"France: The Grand Illusion" (1999). *Economist*, Vol. 351, No. 8122 (June 5):1–18.

Francis, R. Douglas (1993). "Regionalism and Regions." In *Canada*. Ed. Mel Watkins. New York: Facts on File, pp. 229–243.

Frankel, Jeffrey A. (1997). *Regional Trading Blocs in the World Economic System*. Washington, D.C.: Institute for International Economics.

Gaddis, John Lewis (1982). *Strategies of Containment: A Critical Appraisal of Postwar American National Security Policy*. New York: Oxford University Press.

Garreau, Joel (1981). *The Nine Nations of North America*. New York: Avon.

Garten, Jeffrey (1992). *A Cold Peace: America, Japan, Germany, and the Struggle for Supremacy*. New York: Times Books.

Gilpin, Robert (1987). *The Political Economy of International Relations*. Princeton: Princeton University Press.

Globerman, Steven (1993). "The Environmental Impacts of Trade Liberalization." In *NAFTA and the Environment*. Ed. Terry L. Anderson. San Francisco: Pacific Research Institute for Public Policy, pp. 27–44.

Goldsmith, James (1996). "The Winners and Losers." In *The Case Against the Global Economy and for a Turn Toward the Local*. Ed. Jerry Mander and Edward Goldsmith. San Francisco: Sierra Club Books, pp. 171–182.

Goldstein, Judith (1988). "Ideas, Institutions, and American Trade Policy." *International Organization*, Vol. 42, No. 1 (winter): 179–217.

——— (1993). "Creating the GATT Rules: Politics, Institutions and American Policy." In *Multilateralism Matters: The Theory and Praxis of an Institutional Form*. Ed. John Gerard Ruggie. New York: Columbia University Press, pp. 201–232.

Gonzalez, Jorge, and Alejandro Velez (1995). "Intra-Industry Trade Between the United States and the Major Latin American Countries: Measurement and Implications for Free Trade in the Americas." *International Trade Journal*, Vol. 9, No. 4 (winter): 519–536.

Granatstein, J. L., and Norman Hillmer (1991). *For Better or for Worse: Canada and the United States to the 1990s*. Toronto: Copp Clark Pitman.

Grayson, George (1995). *The North American Free Trade Agreement: Regional Community and the New World Order*. Lanham, Maryland: University Press of America.

Greenhouse, Steven (1998). "Mexicans Were Denied Rights, Suit Says." *New York Times* (May 28): A14.

Grilli, Enzo (1997). "Multilateralism and Regionalism: A Still Difficult Coexistence." In *Multilateralism and Regionalism After the Uruguay Round*. Ed. Riccardo Faini and Enzo Grilli. New York: St. Martin's Press, pp. 194–233.

Grunwald, Joseph (1995). "Expanding the NAFTA? From Early Pan-Americanism to Hemispheric Regional Integration." In *NAFTA as a Model of Development: The Benefits and Costs of Merging High- and Low-Wage Areas*. Ed. Richard S. Belous and Jonathan Lemco. Albany: State University of New York Press, pp. 59–76.

Gurr, Ted Robert, and Barbara Harff (1994). *Ethnic Conflict in World Politics*. Boulder: Westview Press.

Haggard, Stephan (1995). *Developing Nations and the Politics of Global Integration*. Washington, D.C.: Brookings Institution.

Haglund, David G. (1990–1991). "Being There: North America and the Variable Geometry of European Security." *International Journal*, Vol. 46 (winter): 81–112.

Handelman, Howard (1997). *Mexican Politics: The Dynamics of Change*. New York: St. Martin's Press.

Hansen, Roger D. (1971). *The Politics of Mexican Development*. Baltimore: Johns Hopkins Press.

Hanson, Gordon H. (1997). "Increasing Returns, Trade and the Regional Structure of Wages." *Economic Journal: The Quarterly Journal of the Royal Economic Society*, Vol. 107, No. 440 (January): 113–133.

Harrison, Lawrence E. (1997). *The Pan American Dream: Do Latin America's Cultural Values Discourage True Partnership with the United States and Canada?* New York: Basic Books.

Herzenberg, Stephen (1993). "Continental Integration and the Future of the North American Auto Sector." In *Driving Continentally: National Policies and the North American Auto Industry*. Ed. Maureen Appel Molot. Ottawa: Carleton University Press, pp. 303–327.

Hirst, Paul, and Grahame Thompson (1996). *Globalization in Question*. Cambridge: Polity Press.

Hoekman, Bernard, and Michel Kostecki (1995). *The Political Economy of the World Trading System: From GATT to WTO*. New York: Oxford University Press.

Holle, Peter (1999). "Canadians Wonder Whether the Loonie Is for the Birds." *Wall Street Journal* (August 6): A11.

Hufbauer, Gary Clyde, and Jeffrey J. Schott (1991). "The Realities of a North American Economic Alliance." In *Toward a North American Common Market: Problems and Prospects for a New Economic Community*. Ed. Charles F. Bonser. Boulder: Westview Press, pp. 89–104.

——— (1992). *North American Free Trade: Issues and Recommendations*. Washington, D.C.: Institute for International Economics.

——— (1993). "Regionalism in North America." *In Regional Integration and Its Impact on Developing Countries*. Ed. Koichi Ohno. Tokyo: Institute of Developing Countries, pp. 257–302.

——— (1994). *Western Hemisphere Economic Integration.* Washington, D.C.: Institute for International Economics.

Huntington, Samuel P. (1996). *The Clash of Civilizations: Remaking of World Order.* New York: Touchstone.

Hurrell, Andrew (1992). "Latin America in the New World Order: A Regional Bloc of the Americas?" *International Affairs,* Vol. 68, No. 1: 121–139.

Ikenberry, G. John (1998–1999). "Institutions, Strategic Restraint, and the Persistence of the American Postwar Order." *International Security,* Vol. 23, No. 3: 43–78.

Inglehart, Ronald, and Marita Carballo (1997). "Does Latin America Exist? (And Is There a Confucian Culture?)." *P.S.: Political Science and Politics,* Vol. 41, No. 7 (March): 34–46.

Inglehart, Ronald, Neil Nevitte, and Miguel Basanez (1996). *The North American Trajectory: Cultural, Economic, and Political Ties Among the United States, Canada, and Mexico.* New York: Aldine de Gruyter.

International Monetary Fund (1995). *Direction of Trade Statistics 1995.* Washington, D.C.: IMF.

——— (1997). *Direction of Trade Statistics Yearbook.* Washington, D.C.: IMF.

——— (1998). *Direction of Trade Statistics, 1998.* Washington, D.C.: IMF.

——— (1999a). *Direction of Trade Statistics Quarterly* (September). Washington, D.C.: IMF.

——— (1999b). *Direction of Trade Statistics Yearbook.* Washington, D.C.: IMF.

——— (2000). *Direction of Trade Statistics Quarterly* (June). Washington, D.C.: IMF.

IRELA (1999). *Prospects for an EU-Mercosur Free Trade Agreement and U.S. Policy Options.* Madrid: Institute for European–Latin American Relations.

Isaacs, Harold R. (1989). *Idols of the Tribe: Group Identity and Political Change.* Cambridge: Harvard University Press.

Johnson, Chalmers (1993). "History Restarted: Japan-American Relations at the End of the Century." In *Pacific Economic Relations in the 1990s: Cooperation or Conflict?* Ed. Richard Higgott, Richard Leaver, and John Ravenhill. Boulder: Lynne Rienner, pp. 39–61.

Johnston, Hazel T. (1991). *Dispelling the Myth of Globalization: The Case for Regionalization.* New York: Praeger.

Jordan, Mary (2000). "NAFTA Is Paying Dividends for Mexican Workers." *San Antonio Express News* (October 1): 1J, 6J.

Kahler, Miles (1995). *International Institutions and the Political Economy of Integration.* Washington, D.C.: Brookings Institution.

Kahn, Joseph (2000). "Clinton Shift on Trade: 'Wake-Up Call.'" *New York Times* (January 31): A6.

Keating, Tom (1993). *Canada and the World: The Multilateral Tradition in Canadian Foreign Policy.* Toronto: McClelland and Stewart.

Kegley, Charles, and Eugene Wittkopf (1999). *World Politics: Trends and Transformations.* Seventh Edition. New York: St. Martin's Press.

Kennedy, Paul (1987). *The Rise and Fall of the Great Powers: Economic Change and Military Conflict from 1500 to 2000*. New York: Random House.

Kirton, John (1993). *A New Global Partnership: Canada-U.S. Relations in the Clinton Era*. Orono, Maine: Canadian-American Center.

——— (1997). "NAFTA's Trade-Environment Institutions: Regional Impact, Hemispheric Potential." Paper presented at the joint meeting of the Mexican Association of International Relations and the International Studies Association, Manzanillo, Mexico, December 11–14.

Kristoff, Nicholas D., with David E. Sanger (1999). "How U.S. Wooed Asia to Let Cash Flow In." *New York Times* (February 16): A1, A10.

Krooth, Richard (1995). *Mexico, NAFTA, and the Hardships of Progress: Historical Patterns and Shifting Methods of Oppression*. Jefferson, North Carolina: McFarland.

Krueger, Anne O. (1992). "Political Economy, International Trade, and Economic Integration." *American Economic Review,* Vol. 82, No. 2 (May): 109–114.

Kupchan, Charles A. (1998). "After Pax Americana: Benign Power, Regional Integration, and the Sources of a Stable Multipolarity." *International Security,* Vol. 23, No. 2 (fall): 40–79.

Kurian, George Thomas (1992). *The New Book of World Rankings*. Third Edition. New York: Facts on File.

Lake, David A., and Patrick M. Morgan (1997). "The New Regionalism in Security Affairs." In *Regional Orders: Building Security in a New World*. Ed. David A. Lake and Patrick M. Morgan. University Park: Pennsylvania State University Press, pp. 3–19.

Lamont, Lansing (1994). *Breakup: The Coming End of Canada and the Stakes for America*. New York: W. W. Norton.

Langdon, Frank (1993). "The Posthegemonic Japanese–United States Relationship." In *Japan in the Posthegemonic World*. Ed. Tsuneo Akaha and Frank Langdon. Boulder: Lynne Rienner, pp. 69–90.

Lawrence, Robert Z. (1996). *Regionalism, Multilateralism, and Deeper Integration*. Washington, D.C.: Brookings Institution.

Lawrence, Robert Z., Albert Bressard, and Takatoshi Ito (1996). *A Vision for the World Economy: Openness, Diversity, and Cohesion*. Washington, D.C.: Brookings Institution.

Lemco, Jonathan (1996). "Canada, Quebec, and the United States: A Post-Referendum Assessment." *North American Outlook,* Vol. 6, No. 2 (July): 11–42.

Lepgold, Joseph (1990). *The Declining Hegemon: The United States and European Defense, 1960–1990*. New York: Praeger.

Lipset, Seymour Martin (1990). *Continental Divide: The Values and Institutions of the United States and Canada*. New York: Routledge.

——— (1993). "Canada and the United States Compared." In *Canada*. Ed. Mel Watkins. New York: Facts on File, pp. 651–663.

——— (1996). *American Exceptionalism: A Double Edged Sword.* New York: W. W. Norton.

Lott, Anthony (1997). "The U.S.-Mexico Border Environment and NAFTA: An Historical Analysis of the Creation and Maintenance of the New International Legal Regime to Protect and Improve the Border Environment." Paper presented at the joint meeting of the Mexican Association of International Relations and the International Studies Association, Manzanillo, Mexico, December 11–14.

Lusztig, Michael (1996). *Risking Free Trade: The Politics of Trade in Britain, Canada, Mexico and the United States.* Pittsburgh: University of Pittsburgh Press.

Maisel, L. Sandy (1998). "Political Parties on the Eve of the Millennium." In *The Parties Respond: Change in American Parties and Campaigns.* Third Edition. Ed. L. Sandy Maisel. Boulder: Westview Press, pp. 356–371.

Manning, Robert A., and Paula Stern (1994). "The Myth of the Pacific Community." *Foreign Affairs,* Vol. 73, No. 6 (November-December): 79–93.

Manzetti, Luigi (1993–1994). "The Political Economy of Mercosur." *Journal of Interamerican Studies and World Affairs,* Vol. 35, No. 4 (winter): 101–141.

McNaught, Kenneth (1993). "Canada: A Historical Overview." In *Canada.* Ed. Mel Watkins. New York: Facts on File, pp. 199–228.

Meyer, Stephen P., and Milford B. Green (1996). "Foreign Direct Investment from Canada: An Overview." *Canadian Geographer,* Vol. 40, No. 3: 219–237.

Milkis, Sidney M. (1993). *The President and the Parties: The Transformation of the American Party System Since the New Deal.* New York: Oxford University Press.

Miller, Judith (1999). "Globalization Widens Rich-Poor Gap, UN Report Says." *New York Times* (July 13): A8.

Mittelman, James H. (2000). *The Globalization Syndrome: Transformation and Resistance.* Princeton: Princeton University Press.

Morales, Isidro (1999). "NAFTA: The Governance of Economic Openness." *Annals,* Vol. 565 (September): 35–65.

Morici, Peter (1992). "Free Trade with Mexico." *Foreign Policy,* No. 87 (summer): 88–104.

——— (1997). "Barring Entry? China and the WTO." *Current History,* Vol. 96, No. 611 (September): 274–277.

Morton, Colleen S. (1999). "Progress Toward Free Trade in the Western Hemisphere Since 1994." In *Civil Society and the Summit of the Americas: The 1998 Santiago Summit.* Ed. Richard E. Feinberg and Robin L. Rosenberg. Miami: North-South Center Press, University of Miami, pp. 249–311.

Muirhead, B. W. (1992). *The Development of Post War Canadian Trade Policy: The Failure of the Anglo-European Option.* Montreal and Kingston: McGill-Queen's University Press.

Mumme, Stephen, and Pamela Duncan (1997–1998). "The Commission for Environmental Cooperation and Environmental Management in the Americas."

Journal of Interamerican Studies and World Affairs, Vol. 39, No. 4 (winter): 41–42.

"NAFTA Increases Trade and Competitiveness" (1997). *El Mercado de Valores* (September-October): 26–28.

Nevitte, Neil (1995). "Bringing Values 'Back In': Value Change and North American Integration." In *Toward a North American Community? Canada, the United States, and Mexico.* Ed. Donald Barry, with Mark O. Dickerson and James D. Gaisford. Boulder: Westview Press, pp. 185–209.

Nietschmann, Bernard (1994). "The Fourth World: Nations vs. States." In *Reordering the World: Geopolitical Perspectives on the 21st Century.* Ed. George J. Demko and William B. Wood. Boulder: Westview Press, pp. 225–242.

Nofal, Maria Beatriz (1995). "The Economic Integration of Argentina and Brazil, Mercosur, and the Regionalization of the Southern Cone Market." In *NAFTA and Trade Liberalization in the Americas.* Ed. Elsie L. Echeverri-Carroll. Austin: Bureau of Business Research, University of Texas at Austin, pp. 203–230.

Nogues, Julio J., and Rosalinda Quintanilla (1993). "Latin America's Integration and the Multilateral Trading System." In *New Dimensions in Regional Integration.* Ed. Jaime de Melo and Arvind Panagariya. Cambridge: Cambridge University Press, pp. 278–313.

Nossal, Kim Richard (1989). *The Politics of Canadian Foreign Policy.* Scarborough, Ontario: Prentice-Hall Canada.

Nye, Joseph S. (1990). *Bound to Lead: The Changing Nature of American Power.* New York: Basic Books.

Nymark, Alan, and Emmy Verdun (1994). "Canadian Investment and NAFTA." In *Foreign Investment and NAFTA.* Ed. Alan M. Rugman. Columbia: University of South Carolina Press, pp. 124–154.

Ohmae, Kenichi (1993). "The Rise of the Region State." *Foreign Affairs,* Vol. 72, No. 2 (spring): 78–87.

Olson, Elizabeth (2000). "U.S. and Europeans Raising the Stakes in Trade Impasse." *New York Times* (September 7): C4.

Oman, Charles (1999). "Globalization, Regionalization, and Inequality." In *Inequality, Globalization, and World Politics.* Ed. Andrew Hurrell and Ngaire Woods. New York: Oxford University Press, pp. 36–65.

OECD (1997a). *OECD Economic Outlook,* Vol. 61 (June).

——— (1997b). "Basic Statistics: International Comparisons." *OECD Economic Survey 1997: Canada.* Paris: OECD.

Orme, William A. (1996). *Understanding NAFTA: Mexico, Free Trade and the New North America.* Austin: University of Texas Press.

Pastor, Manuel, and Carol Wise (1997). "State Policy, Distribution, and Neoliberal Reform in Mexico." *Journal of Latin American Studies,* Vol. 29, No. 2 (May): 419–456.

Pastor, Robert (1993). *Integration with Mexico: Options for U.S. Policy.* New York: Twentieth Century Fund Press.

Peach, James (1995). "NAFTA and Mexico's Current Economic Crisis: Short-Run and Long-Run Perspectives." *Social Science Quarterly,* Vol. 32, No. 4: 375–388.

Pearson, Charles S. (1995). "Regional Free Trade and the Environment." In *Trade Liberalization in the Western Hemisphere.* Washington, D.C.: Inter-American Development Bank and Economic Commission for Latin America and the Caribbean, pp. 303–331.

Petrella, Riccardo (1996). "Globalization and Internationalization: The Dynamics of the Emerging World Order." In *States Against Markets: The Limits of Globalization.* Ed. Robert Boyer and Daniel Drache. London: Routledge, pp. 62–83.

Pfister, Bonnie (2000). "NADBank Challenges." *San Antonio Express News* (October 29): 1J, 6J.

Philips, George (1991). "Mexican Politics and NAFTA." *The World Today,* Vol. 47 (December): 204–206.

Poitras, Guy (1990). *The Ordeal of Hegemony: The United States and Latin America.* Boulder: Westview Press.

——— (1998). "Mexico's Problematic Transition to Democracy." In *Assessing Democracy in Latin America: A Tribute to Russell H. Fitzgibbon.* Ed. Philip Kelly. Boulder: Westview Press, pp. 63–75.

Poitras, Guy, and Raymond Robertson (1994). "The Politics of NAFTA in Mexico." *Journal of Interamerican Studies and World Affairs,* Vol. 36, No. 1 (spring): 1–36.

Posen, Barry R., and Andrew L. Ross (1996–1997). "Competing Visions for U.S. Grand Strategies." *International Security,* Vol. 31, No. 3 (winter): 5–53.

Prestowitz, Clyde V., Jr., Robert B. Cohen, Peter Morici, and Alan Tonelson (1991). *The New North American Order: A Win-Win Strategy for U.S.-Mexico Trade.* Lanham, Maryland: University Press of America.

Ramirez de la O, Rogelio (1991). "A Mexican Vision of North American Economic Integration." In *Continental Accord: North American Economic Integration.* Ed. Steven Globerman. Vancouver: Fraser Institute, pp. 1–30.

Randall, Stephen J. (1995). "Managing Trilateralism: The United States, Mexico, and Canada in the Post-NAFTA Era." In *NAFTA in Transition.* Ed. Stephen J. Randall and Herman W. Konrad. Calgary: University of Calgary Press, pp. 37–46.

Reich, Simon (1993). "NAFTA, Foreign Direct Investment, and the Auto Industry: A Comparative Perspective." In *Driving Continentally: National Policies and the North American Auto Industry.* Ed. Maureen Appel Molot. Ottawa: Carleton University Press, pp. 63–95.

"Report to Congress Says NAFTA Benefits Are Modest" (1997). *San Antonio Express News* (July 11): 8E.

Reynolds, Clark W. (1995). "The NAFTA and Wage Convergence." In *NAFTA as a Model of Development: The Benefits and Costs of Merging High- and Low-Wage Areas.* Ed. Richard S. Belous and Jonathan Lemco. Albany: State University of New York Press, pp. 21–26.

Reynolds, Clark W., Leonard Waverman, and Gerardo Bueno (1991). Introduction to *The Dynamics of North American Trade and Investment: Canada, Mexico and the United States*. Ed. Clark W. Reynolds, Leonard Waverman, and Gerardo Bueno. Stanford: Stanford University Press, pp. 1–14.

Riding, Alan (1984). *Distant Neighbors: A Portrait of the Mexicans*. New York: Vintage Books.

Rielly, John W. (1999). "Americans and the World: A Survey at Century's End." *Foreign Policy,* No. 114 (spring): 97–114.

Rocha Valencia, Alberto (1997). "América Latina en Su Labertino: Integración Subregional, Regional y Continental" (Latin America in its labyrinth: Subregional, regional, and continental integration). In *América Latina: Realidad, Virtualidad, y Utopia de la Integración* (Latin America: reality, virtuality, and utopia of integration). Ed. Jaime Preciado Coronado and Alberto Rocha Valencia. Guadalajara: Universidad de Guadalajara, pp. 170–196.

Rodrik, Dani (1997). *Has Globalization Gone Too Far?* Washington, D.C.: Institute for International Economics.

Romero, Simon (1999). "Argentines Lift a Threat of Sanctions." *New York Times* (July 31): B2.

Rosecrance, Richard (1986). *The Rise of the Trading State*. New York: Basic Books.

Ruggie, John Gerard (1996). *Winning the Peace: America and World Order in the New Era*. New York: Columbia University Press.

Rugman, Alan M. (1994). "North American Integration and Canadian Sovereignty." In *The NAFTA Debate*. Ed. M. Delal Baer and Sidney Weintraub. Boulder: Lynne Rienner, pp. 97–116.

Rugman, Alan M., and Alain Verbecke (1994). "Foreign Direct Investment and NAFTA: A Conceptual Framework." In *Foreign Investment and NAFTA*. Ed. Alan Rugman. Columbia: University of South Carolina Press, pp. 80–101.

Russell, Peter (1993). *Constitutional Odyssey: Can Canadians Become a Sovereign People?* Second Edition. Toronto: University of Toronto Press.

Saborio, Sylvia (1992). "The Long and Winding Road from Anchorage to Patagonia." In *The Premise and the Promise: Free Trade in the Americas*. Ed. Sylvia Saborio. New Brunswick, New Jersey: Transaction Publishers, pp. 3–31.

Safarian, A. Edward (1996). "The Free Trade Agreement and NAFTA: One Canadian's Perspective." In *A New North America*. Ed. Charles F. Doran and Alvin Paul Drischler. Westport, Connecticut: Praeger, pp. 29–47.

Sanger, David E. (1997). "Prosperity vs. Fear: Fast Track Rings False with American Workers." *San Antonio Express News* (November 23): 1G, 5G.

——— (1999). "Clinton Restricts Imports of Brazilian Steel and Australian Lamb." *New York Times* (July 8): C1, C3.

Schmitt, Eric (2000). "House Trade Bill for the Caribbean and Africa Passes." *New York Times* (May 5): A1, A12.

Schott, Jeffrey J. (1991). "Global Implications of the Canada–United States Free Trade Agreement." In *The Dynamics of North American Trade and*

Investments: Canada, Mexico, and the United States. Ed. Clark W. Reynolds, Leonard Waverman, and Gerardo Bueno. Stanford: Stanford University Press, pp. 73–90.

——— (1996). "Reflections on TAFTA." In *Open for Business: Creating a Transatlantic Marketplace.* Ed. Bruce Stokes. New York: Council on Foreign Relations, pp. 32–42.

Schram, Sanford F., and Carol S. Weissert (1997). "The State of American Federalism, 1996–1997." *Publius: The Journal of Federalism,* Vol. 27, No. 2 (spring): 1–31.

Schultz, Donald (1997). "Between a Rock and a Hard Place: The United States, Mexico and the Challenge of National Security." *Low Intensity Conflict and Law Enforcement,* Vol. 6, No. 3 (winter): 1–40.

Schwartz, Emily (1999). "U.S. Slaps Duties on EU Goods." *San Antonio Express News* (April 10): 1D, 2D.

Sheridan, Mary Beth (1998). "Still Angry over Sting, Mexico Rethinking Cooperation with the United States." *San Antonio Express News* (May 30): 7A.

Shifrin, Leonard (1993). "Welfare State Policies and Taxation." In *Canada.* Ed. Mel Watkins. New York: Facts on File, pp. 610–622.

Smiley, Donald V. (1993). "Federalism." In *Canada.* Ed. Mel Watkins. New York: Facts on File, pp. 247–258.

Smith, Murray (1993). "The NAFTA: Global Impacts." In *Regional Integration and the Global Trading System.* Ed. Kym Anderson and Richard Blackhurst. New York: St. Martin's Press, pp. 83–103.

——— (1996). "Canada and Economic Sovereignty." In *NAFTA and Sovereignty: Tradeoffs for Canada, Mexico, and the United States.* Ed. Joyce Hoebing, Sidney Weintraub, and M. Delal Baer. Washington, D.C.: Center for Strategic International Studies, pp. 39–68.

Smith, Peter H. (1992). "The Political Impact of Free Trade on Mexico." *Journal of Interamerican Studies and World Affairs,* Vol. 34, No. 1 (spring): 1–26.

Soares de Lima, Maria Regina (1996). "Brazil's Response to the 'New Regionalism.'" In *Foreign Policy and Regionalism in the Americas.* Ed. Gordon Mace and Jean-Philippe Therien. Boulder: Lynne Rienner, pp. 137–158.

Solingen, Etel (1998). *Regional Orders at Century's Dawn: Global and Domestic Influences on Grand Strategy.* Princeton: Princeton University Press.

Spicer, Keith (1995). "Canada: Core Values in Search of a Vision." In *Identities in North America: The Search for Community.* Ed. Robert L. Earle and John D. Wirth. Stanford: Stanford University Press, pp. 13–28.

Stairs, Dennis (1996). "The Canadian Dilemma in North America." In *NAFTA and Sovereignty: Tradeoffs for Canada, Mexico, and the United States.* Ed. Joyce Hoebing, Sidney Weintraub, and M. Delal Baer. Washington, D.C.: Center for Strategic International Studies, pp. 1–38.

Stallings, Barbara, and Wolfgang Streeck (1995). "Capitalism in Conflict? The United States, Europe and Japan in the Post Cold War World." In *Global Change, Regional Response: The New International Context of Development*. Ed. Barbara Stallings. New York: Cambridge University Press, pp. 67–99.

Stallings, Barbara, and Gabriel Székely (1993). "The New Trilateralism: The United States, Japan, and Latin America." In *Japan, the United States and Latin America: Toward a Trilateral Relationship in the Western Hemisphere*. Ed. Barbara Stallings and Gabriel Székeley. Baltimore: Johns Hopkins University Press, pp. 3–48.

Statistics Canada (1993). *Trade Patterns: Canada–United States: The Manufacturing Industries, 1981–1991*. Ottawa: International Trade Division.

Stevis, Dimitris, and Terry Boswell (1998). "International Labor Politics Under the North American Agreement for Labor Cooperation: Comparisons to the European Union." Paper presented at the International Studies Association meeting, Minneapolis, March 17–21.

Stewart, David K., and Ian Stewart (1997). "Fission and Federalism: The Disaggregation of Canadian Party Activists." *Publius: The Journal of Federalism,* Vol. 27, No. 3 (summer): 97–112.

Stewart, Gordon T. (1992). *The American Response to Canada Since 1776*. East Lansing: Michigan State University Press.

Strange, Susan (1996). *Retreat from the State: The Diffusion of Power in the World Economy.* Cambridge: Cambridge University Press.

Survey of Current Business (1997). Vol. 77, No. 9.

Teichman, Judith (1997). "Neoliberalism and the Transformation of Mexican Authoritarianism." *Mexican Studies/Estudios Mexicanos,* Vol. 13, No. 1 (winter): 121–148.

Thompson, John Herd, and Stephen J. Randall (1994). *Canada and the United States: Ambivalent Allies*. Athens: University of Georgia Press.

Thorup, Cathryn L. (1995). "Diplomacia Ciudadana, Redes, y Coaliciones Trasfronterizas en América del Norte: Nuevos Diseños Organizativos" (Citizen diplomacy, networks, and transborder coalitions in North America: new organizational designs). *Foro Internacional,* Vol. 35, No. 2 (April-June): 155–218.

Thurow, Lester (1992). *Head to Head: The Coming Economic Battle Among Japan, Europe, and America*. New York: William Morrow.

True, Philip (1998). "Drug Sting Pact Fails to Heal Rifts." *San Antonio Express News* (July 4): 1A, 18A.

Tsunekawa, Keiichi (1994). *NAFTA's Impact on Japan.* Washington, D.C.: Woodrow Wilson International Center for Scholars.

United Nations (1997). *World Statistics Pocketbook.* New York: United Nations.

U.S. House Committee on Ways and Means, Subcommittee on Trade (1997). *North American Free Trade Agreement: Impacts and Implementation*. Washington, D.C.: General Accounting Office.

Vernon, Raymond, Debora L. Spar, and Glenn Tobin (1991). *Iron Triangles and Revolving Doors: Cases in U.S. Foreign Economic Policymaking*. New York: Praeger.

Weiner, Tim, and Graham Gori (2000). "Can Mexico's New Leader Really Work Wonders?" *New York Times* (October 29): Business section 1, 12.

Weintraub, Sidney (1990). *A Marriage of Convenience: Relations Between Mexico and the United States*. New York: Oxford University Press.

——— (1992). "The Promise of United States–Mexican Free Trade." *Texas International Law Journal*, Vol. 27, No. 3 (summer): 551–575.

——— (1993). "The NAFTA Agreement: A U.S. Perspective." In *Assessing NAFTA: A Trinational Analysis*. Ed. Steven Globerman and Michael Walker. Vancouver: Fraser Institute, pp. 1–31.

——— (1994). *NAFTA: What Comes Next?* Westport, Connecticut: Praeger.

——— (1995). "The North American Free Trade Agreement and Developing Countries." In *NAFTA as a Model of Development: The Benefits and Costs of Merging High- and Low-Wage Areas*. Ed. Richard S. Belous and Jonathan Lemco. Albany: State University of New York Press, pp. 77–84.

——— (1997). *NAFTA at Three: A Progress Report*. Washington, D.C.: Center for Strategic and International Studies.

Whalley, John (1993). "Regional Trade Arrangements in North America: CUSTA and NAFTA." In *New Dimensions in Regional Integration*. Ed. Jaime de Melo and Arvind Panagariya. Cambridge: Cambridge University Press, pp. 352–382.

Wiarda, Howard J. (1995). *Latin American Politics*. Belmont, Massachusetts: Wadsworth.

Wilford, John Noble (1999). "New Answers to an Old Question: Who Got Here First?" *New York Times* (November 9): D1, D4.

Wilkie, James W. (1970). *The Mexican Revolution: Federal Expenditure and Social Change Since 1910*. Berkeley: University of California Press.

Windham, Gilbert, and Heather A. Grant (1995). "NAFTA: An Overview." In *Toward a North American Community? Canada, the United States, and Mexico*. Ed. Donald Barry, with Mark O. Dickerson and James D. Gaisford. Boulder: Westview Press, pp. 15–31.

Wonnacott, Paul (1996). "Beyond NAFTA: The Design of a Free Trade Agreement of the Americas." In *The Economics of Preferential Trade Agreements*. Ed. Jagdish Bhagwati and Arvind Panagariya. Washington, D.C.: American Enterprise Institute Press, pp. 79–107.

Wonnacott, Ronald (1995). "Canada's Institutions and the NAFTA." In *NAFTA as a Model of Development: The Benefits and Costs of Merging High- and Low-Wage Areas*. Ed. Richard S. Belous and Jonathan Lemco. Albany: State University of New York Press, pp. 140–144.

World Bank (1995). *World Bank Atlas 1996*. Washington, D.C.: World Bank.

World Trade Organization (1995). *International Trade: Trends and Statistics 1995*. Geneva: WTO.

——— (1996). "Canada's Domestic and External Reforms Help Create Stronger Base for Economic Expansion." TPRB/48 (November 11). Available at: http://www.who.org/Trade__Reviews/tprb48.htm.

Wrobel, Paulo S. (1999). "A Free Trade Area of the Americas in 2005?" In *Trade Politics: International, Domestic, and Regional Perspectives*. Ed. Brian Hocking and Steven McGuire. London: Routledge, pp. 290–303.

Young, Soogil (1993). "East Asia as a Regional Force for Globalism." In *Regional Integration and the Global Trading System*. Ed. Kym Anderson and Richard Blackhurst. New York: St. Martin's Press, pp. 126–143.

INDEX

About the Book

In the face of potent domestic and global forces, the United States, Canada, and Mexico—the North American three—have devised an enterprise that promises to draw them closer together in the twenty-first century. *Inventing North America* is an attempt to understand the three states' unique brand of regionalism within an increasingly globalized world.

Poitras dissects the commonalities and differences among the North American three that have created the foundation for—and set limits to—the integration of the region. He also explores how states use regionalism for their own purposes and how the North American enterprise must deal with predicaments about unity and diversity, gains and losses, and gaps between North and South. Testing the proposition that the North and South can play by the same rules within a regional regime, he portrays North America as essentially a two-level alliance between the dominant center and each of the smaller periphery states. Its fate, he argues, depends on whether and how this alignment changes and whether the three states of North America can embrace a comprehensive vision of the region as a community.

Guy Poitras is professor of political science at Trinity University in San Antonio.